SECURITY CONTROL:

Internal
Theft

SECURITY CONTROL:

Internal Theft

Bob Curtis

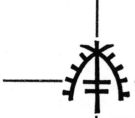

CHAIN STORE AGE BOOKS
an affiliate of
LEBHAR-FRIEDMAN, INC.
New York

SECURITY CONTROL: INTERNAL THEFT

Library of Congress Catalog Number: 72-90623
International Standard Book Number: 0-912016-14-0

To Harriet and Norman Felder,
with love.
They made it all possible.

CONTENTS

PART FOUR: Interrogating the Suspect

PART FIVE: Creating a Controlled Working Environment

PART SIX: Encouraging Honesty Among Employees

FOREWORD

A friend of mine was arrested for theft recently—not a close friend, but close enough so that the newspaper headlines were sufficient to give me that sinking, sick-at-the-stomach feeling that comes when tragedy pulls down someone we know. So writing this foreword, which last week I regarded purely as another professional exercise, has become an occasion for me to contemplate the pain experienced by those who find themselves in trouble with the law.

Most treatments of the subject of internal theft emphasize the economic costs, both direct and indirect, which are real enough. [Each of us pays a hidden tax to cover these costs every time we go into a retail store.] Without minimizing the importance of the economic costs, however, let us give some attention to the human costs represented by situations such as that confronting my friend.

Without forgetting for a moment the presumption of innocence to which he is entitled, the headlines nevertheless set one to thinking about the various dimensions of this tragedy: a promising career blighted, if not destroyed; probable indebtedness and possible financial ruin brought on by the drawn-out legal processes before he can square accounts and get back on a payroll; the setback and embarrassment to his associates; and the trauma for his wife and children which, even under the most optimistic assumption of full acquittal, must leave lasting scars. I will make a telephone call to his attorney and ask if there is anything I can do to help in picking up the pieces. There probably isn't.

If we were to stop here or to turn immediately to more pragmatic considerations, the preceding paragraphs would sound like a crime-does-not-pay lecture. It is not intended as such, however, because a moment's reflection concerning the other side of the coin reminds us that, for those people who take the gamble and manage to avoid getting caught, theft pays off well enough and often enough to encourage their continued activities. Since many thefts are never solved or even discovered, we must conjecture that, in the population around us, there are many successful (i.e., clever and/or lucky) thieves who have used the proceeds of their crimes for a variety of purposes, some of them positive in nature, such as starting a small business; paying for a college education; or financing expensive medical treatment for a family member.

I bring up these factors to make the point that in dealing with various forms of theft, and particularly with internal theft (which usually involves people leading otherwise respectable lives), we are dealing not only with a tangle of emotions and dilemmas characteristic of the human condition anywhere, but also with behaviors and complex relationships which run throughout the very warp and woof of the social structure. Perhaps we would understand them better if a Tolstoy or Henry James would bring to them the understanding of the human heart revealed by the insights of the psychologically oriented novelist rather than if we leave them to the writers of case reports and compilers of statistics.

Thus, in any company, useful approaches to the problem of prevention and control of internal theft must be broadly conceived with an awareness of the complicated skein of individual, organizational, and societal relationships involved. Simplistic "let's-catch-'em" campaigns or "handy-dandy" sets of systems and procedures just will not do. While such techniques may have an appropriate place in a systematic and comprehensive approach, some other ingredients are also necessary. Specifying these ingredients and their appropriate mix calls for a book written from a broad managerial viewpoint. One does not have to agree with all of his interpretations or emphases in order to say that Bob Curtis has given us such a book.

The author obviously writes out of long and responsible experience in the security field, both as a former security director of large retail organizations and as a consultant. This book, however, represents not merely a mining of his own considerable experience; it also represents a lifetime of study and a synthesis of other people's experiences.

As one who teaches security management to college students, I am particularly appreciative of an authoritative and sophisticated book such as this on which to base my instruction. This book, however, is also an important resource for security administrators as well as (and perhaps more so) for the store or warehouse manager.

Realistic approaches to the problem of internal theft require system-wide measures and top managerial support that are beyond the scope of the security manager. This suggestion may disappoint those managements that would prefer to deal with their theft problems without appraising their practices along a wide front. But those who are willing to adopt the broadly conceived measures advocated in this book will usually find that by the time they have succeeded in controlling their theft problems, they have also begun to gain some measure of control over such other problems as absenteeism, personnel turnover, poor workmanship, and poor customer relations. I submit that this would represent a good bargain.

Leon Weaver
Professor, School of Criminal Justice
College of Social Science
Michigan State University

ACKNOWLEDGMENTS

No book is written in a vacuum. It is the result of the efforts of many people, too many, unfortunately, for space to allow due recognition.

But first, and above all, I want to thank my beautiful, understanding, and patient wife who not only counseled me during the writing of this book but helped me over the rough spots as well. She gave me direct and honest appraisals of the material, which were at times painful for her to give and for me to receive. But her help was constructive, professional, and unfailingly correct.

In addition, she gave me moral support, reassurance, and the push writers invariably need at times but so seldom receive. She also gave me the time and privacy I needed to write the book, along with the understanding and the empathy which made it possible.

To a man who founded the field of modern retail security, George A. Callahan, I owe a great debt. He is the man who first hired and trained me in security at Lord & Taylor's in New York City. His fresh concepts captured my imagination. He was a great teacher and a kindly, patient man.

He was always ahead of his time. In the early 1940's, his concept of retail security was a full pendulum swing away from the derby-hat, high-button shoes, cigar-smoking security "chief" of that day. Today, he is security director of The Copps Company in Stevens Point, Wisconsin, where he continues to think and plan in terms that are years ahead of his time. He is, in my opinion, the most qualified retail security director in the nation today.

I am also deeply indebted to Dr. Fabian L. Rouke who, until his untimely death, was the nation's leading criminal psychologist. Although Dr. Rouke taught at Fordham University and was head of psychology at Manhattan College, he also found time to work closely with the Payne Whitney Clinic and with the Nassau County Police.

We met by chance, but he took a personal interest in my work and my development. Under his kindly and persuasive guidance, he encouraged me to major in psychology and to take an additional two year post-graduate course in abnormal psychology. But the most important training in criminal psychology came from working beside him day after day on actual cases with known and suspected larcenists—a close relationship and friendship that existed for nearly 15 years. We studied the motivations, needs, and drives of the business criminal, and our findings allowed us to develop new techniques to improve the control of business crimes. Many of the counter-measures found in this book are the direct result of the concepts we developed in our work together.

In addition, I am also indebted to Dr. Ralph Benay who, for 28 years, was chief psychiatrist at Sing Sing Prison, Ossining, N. Y. Dr. Benay worked together with Dr. Rouke and myself, and between us we stimulated much thought and insight.

I am further indebted to two other top men in this field: Dr. Karl Menninger and Dr. Carl Rogers. The ideas and experience, as well as the results of fundamental research done by these four men—Rouke, Benay, Menninger and Rogers—are reflected in many of the concepts advanced in this book, approaches to the control of business crimes that have proven highly successful in reducing theft losses and in recovering many millions of dollars in stolen merchandise and money for retail organizations around the country.

A total program of security must include detection of theft, but the reader will discover that the emphasis of this book will be primarily on effective techniques for preventing dishonesty among employees, and these techniques are proven and practical and are a direct result of the psychological teamwork, training, research, and experiments done by these four professionals and myself over the past 25 years.

Many outstanding professionals in the security field have also contributed a great deal to my education and their knowledge, experience, and help is woven into the tapestry of this book. Men like Edward Tubman, security director of Altman's in New York City; Dave Karstens, vice-president of Kaufmann's in Pittsburgh; Richard McLaughlin of Oak Security in Madison, Wisconsin; and men like Rudy Webber, security director of Von's, Los Angeles; Paul Lorenzo, Kenneth Honeycutt, Donald Hagler, Larry Glass, Glen Dornfeld, Russell Page, Louis Conroy, and many, many others.

I also owe a debt to the numerous individuals who have supported my security training efforts and have provided forums for the ideas you will find distilled into this book—men like Raymond Farber, Michael J. O'Connor, Edward Ricker, Gary Entwistle, Arnold Rands, Kenneth Galston, Van D. Spurgeon, William Maxwell, Frank Register, Edward Matthews, and more.

Thanks should also be extended to both Richard W. Funk, legislative counsel for the N.A.M.A., and Dave Cole, president of Security Devices, Chicago, for personal counseling which has been of great help in preparing this manuscript.

Much of the background material for this book grew out of my work as consultant to the President's Crime Commission, and I owe a sincere debt of gratitude to Professor Robert Chapman of the University of Oklahoma for inviting me to serve as consultant to President Johnson's Commission on Law Enforcement and the Administration of Justice.

I am grateful for the efforts on my behalf by the staff of the publisher and want to thank Emile LaFrenais for his many personal efforts on my behalf.

A special word of thanks needs to be said for the editor, Malorie Edelson. Had I never seen the original conglomerate of wild paper and only read her final polished copy, I would have been tricked by her magic editing into believing that the final edited form contained the exact words I had in mind when I wrote the original draft. My deepest thanks, especially, for her ability to subordinate her own style to allow my "voice" to come through the edited material.

Finally, I have saved the most important acknowledgment until last. Words simply cannot properly convey my gratitude for the tremendous contribution made toward this book by Marilyn Greenbaum, publishing director of Chain Store Age Books. Here is one of the most delightful and talented persons I have ever known. She has fantastic rapport and communication with an author, as well as energy, drive, creativity, and understanding. She inspires everyone with whom she comes into contact. There is simply no way of explaining the tremendous contribution Marilyn Greenbaum has made to this book. Thanks for everything, Marilyn!

Bob Curtis
Dayton, Ohio

P.S. I have almost overlooked one other important acknowledgment, and that is the contribution made to this book by the 32,000 business criminals I have dealt with during my security career, yes, and the many other thousands that got away. In the end, perhaps the thieves themselves taught me the most about how to establish effective controls over internal theft.

B.C.

INTRODUCTION

In my years of association with security problems and security professionals, I have become convinced that no field is as victimized by dishonesty—within and without—as the retail sector. Other industries may experience more spectacular single thefts, but the total annual losses of the retail industry dwarf the losses of any other category of business. This conclusion is confirmed by the Department of Commerce report of February 1972. While statistics in the field of security are debatable at best, the Department of Commerce is certainly "in the ballpark" when it estimates annual retail losses due to theft at more than the *combined* annual theft losses of manufacturing, transportation, and wholesaling—$4.8 billion.

The reasons why retailing leads other industries in theft losses are not hard to understand: attractive and accessible consumer goods, heavy traffic, a relatively large number of employees, little training, only modest-to-moderate pay scales, little or no screening of applicants, and—above all—the conviction that the name of the game is sales, rather than profit. Certainly no retailer can have profit without sales, but—as some have learned to their sorrow—it is possible to have sales without profit.

While it is rare to pinpoint any single cause for business failure, at least one Eastern chain is widely believed to have failed almost solely due to unchecked internal and external theft. It *can* happen. But more often the cost of theft is fed into overhead, and profitability is maintained by increasing prices, hopefully without pricing the store out of competition.

However, this "solution" is far less attractive when you consider that, at a 3 percent profit margin, a weekly theft loss of a modest $1,500 translates, in a year, to a total of $2.6 million in sales which must be transacted without profit, just to compensate for theft. This is just not good business.

Oddly enough, though, this is not the most important consideration for management. In my opinion, it is basically a matter of bad citizenship. We complain bitterly and justly about the rise in crime, but few of us stop to consider whether we ourselves are part of the problem.

It is axiomatic in the security profession that every confessed employee thief says two things in the same order: "Will this cost me my job?" and "It was the company's fault." The thief will volunteer to the interrogator exactly which controls are nonexistent or unenforced, precisely which management practices enabled the thefts to occur, and where others can occur—and I know no reason why employees should be smarter than management. That management knew, or management could have known, is what both the thief and the security profession have been trying to say for many years.

That's what this book is about, in my opinion: *the moral responsibility of management.*

Today's managers are responsible for the final net profit in both dollars *and* people. Employee turnover, theft, shortage due to error—management has the primary responsibility here and management is, or should be, the greatest beneficiary of constructive prevention policies. But employees benefit as well when their working environment actively encourages honesty and accuracy. It is an indissoluble bond: what benefits one must certainly benefit the other.

This book, then, takes up "how to do it"—what management can do to create a climate of honesty, to eliminate the "bad apples" who corrupt the working force, and to close the loopholes in procedures which tempt employees beyond their individual limits.

A wise security professional once said: "Ten percent of the people you hire will never steal; 10 percent will steal regardless of what you do; and 80 percent will stay honest if you create an environment which discourages and detects theft. Our job," he concluded, "is to keep the first 10 percent, to identify and get rid of the second 10 percent, and to protect the other 80 percent against themselves."

Bob Curtis's book on internal theft offers more concrete, tested suggestions for accomplishing this "climate of honesty" than any text I know. You may differ with him on some points—I do myself—but the heart of this book is what loss prevention ought to be—and must be—in the years ahead.

Raymond C. Farber
Publisher, *Security World* and
Security Distributing & *Marketing*
General Chairman, International
Security Conference

PART ONE

Security Control: Internal Theft

1

THE NATURE OF THE PROBLEM

Internal theft in retail operations has reached a crisis stage. The price tag on theft losses for American retailers will be nearly $5 billion dollars this year, and at least $3.3 billion of that loss will be in the form of cash and merchandise stolen by employees. In terms of dollar amounts and the number of people involved, thefts by employees of American companies far exceed the problems of crime in the streets. In fact, security expert Neal Holmes estimates that "dishonest employees annually cost business and industry twice as much in cash and merchandise as do all the nation's burglaries, car thefts, and bank holdups combined." What is worse, the problem is growing.

A New York retail shopping service with clients across the nation recently compared 1,000 current shopping tests with 1,000 tests made 10 years ago. The results showed that the incidence of cash register theft by employees and the amount of money stolen had increased by 86 percent, a dramatic rise in only 10 years.

3

Companies that have tested their employees on the lie detector confirm these results. One large drug store chain tested a cross-section of its employees. The study revealed that money or merchandise had been stolen by 76 percent of the employees in this group. The company discovered that each dishonest employee had taken more than $100 in merchandise or cash in the six months prior to the test.

The number of collusive thefts among employees has also increased significantly. In one typical case involving a supermarket company, the staff became so corrupt that, before management was aware of the situation, 90 percent of the company's employees were involved in collusive theft activities, including the very guards hired to prevent such thefts. In another instance, six receiving managers worked in collusion with 12 truck drivers and systematically looted a large warehouse of an estimated $2 million in merchandise before being detected.

Store inventory shortages are mainly caused by a combination of three factors: 1) paper work errors, 2) shoplifting losses, and 3) employee thefts. Of the three, employee theft is the most critical element. It accounts for an estimated 60 to 75 percent of a store's inventory shortages. Insurance companies presently estimate that nearly a third of all business failures each year are brought about by employee theft.

Thefts need not be large to have great impact upon a store. Because they are paid for out of a company's net profits, even the smallest employee thefts are costly. For example, a supermarket with yearly sales of $2 million may suffer theft losses of $16,000 or approximately .8 percent of sales. If the store makes a net profit of 1.8 percent, this means that $880,000 worth of merchandise must be sold without one cent of profit in order to replace the $16,000 that has been lost through internal theft. It also means that the manager and his staff must work more than five months without a penny of profit from their efforts just to pay for their employees' annual contribution to crime.

Unless action is taken by supermarkets and other merchants to stem this rising tide of thefts, the situation will continue to accelerate in the months ahead. The prognosis is disturbing. Many stores lose more money and merchandise to internal theft than they earn in net profits. Today's shortage statistics are so grim that even experienced store managers often reject them as impossible.

When thinking about the problem of dishonest employees, it is wise to keep in mind that internal thefts are costly in more ways than one. The actual loss of profits is serious enough, but there are additional costs, some of which are hidden and are therefore difficult to measure accurately. For example:

—the loss of one or more trained employees

—the possible contamination of other employees leading to new losses

—the cost involved in training replacement employees

—the loss of destroyed or stolen records

—the unfavorable publicity and damage to the store's prestige

—the lowered morale when suspicion is directed at honest and valued employees.

Our shortage problems today are more deep-seated than most retailers wish to believe. But it is not unrealistic to envision a future free of such problems. We need not be victimized by dishonesty. We need not suffer huge losses. But to accomplish this, we must first change management's attitude toward shortages.

To be sure, we can point with honest pride to our industry's many achievements as proof of our management ability. During the early years of growth, retailing leaders tackled problems whose demands on will and strength equaled or surpassed those we face today. These men gained a foothold on a new field of American enterprise, forged a new industry, and created new jobs and new markets. Such challenges demanded of us everything we could give. But in spite of our many achievements, we still have not learned how to manage our businesses. Today's shortages are naked proof of that fact. Carelessness, errors, and thefts are siphoning over 50 percent of industry profits.

The only hope we have of reversing the present situation is to awaken to the need for a changed attitude toward protecting our assets. We have to learn that the word "manage" means "control," and then we must learn the techniques needed to improve the control of our enterprises. Of course, there are individual management people and individual companies that are doing a top-notch job. But these control-oriented individuals and companies are rare. More typically, management has set up procedures that leave serious loopholes which it either fails to recognize or prefers to ignore. In other words, many stores have control systems that do not *control*.

Some stores do an indifferent job of personnel selection. The head of one company said: "We don't screen the background of anyone we hire. Experienced help is too hard to come by these days." He is typical of the many management members who do not realize that there is no easier way to corrupt honest employees than to employ dishonest people.

Department supervisors are also too often selected on the basis of seniority rather than on the skills needed to be effective managers. In addition, they are rarely trained for their complex responsibilities. In fact, in many stores the term supervisor is a misnomer, since the man so designated doesn't really supervise at all. As one manager said: "Our supervisors don't have time to supervise; they have too much stock work to do, or they have to replace people who are out on vacation." Too many firms look upon the department supervisor as a member of the working group—not as a member of management.

Control systems and procedures, even when they are sound and well designed, are often not strictly carried out. Management discipline is an empty space in many firms' operating policies. As one controller put it: "We have a major problem in getting procedures enforced. There are many obstacles put in the way of proper enforcement by people in key positions, the very people who should implement the enforcement. There are constant gripes about too much paper work, and we have great difficulty in getting cooperation or even accurate records." Yet, studies by experts have shown that employees *need* the emotional security provided by a *disciplined environment*.

Management decisions are often made without regard for shortage control or protection of company assets. Throughout the retail industry, there is nearly a total lack of understanding of the need for the value of using the security specialist. Only a few large firms have a security man on their payroll, and even then his job is often a thankless task with no real understanding on the part of management of what adequate security entails. Management shows little interest in and gives little support to the security department. The result is that the security man's scope of activity is often limited to providing physical security for store merchandise, trucks, and premises. His real potential for developing a total security program is ignored.

Besides these basic weaknesses in the management control concept, there are many instances of poor management judgment—decisions that encourage shortages, unrealistic policies, and a lack of under-standing of the entire control program, particularly as it relates to human psychology and motivation. Some stores even subscribe to an attitude of complete defeat with regard to controlling losses. As one manager stated: "Sure all my people steal. I know it. I did the same thing myself years ago when I was a salesman starting out. You can't do anything about it, so you might as well forget it."

Don't you believe it! Every retail firm can do something about its internal thefts. All that is really required is a change in attitude by company management. We must not be fooled by appearances. A retail firm does not run on growth and sales volume alone. It runs on motiva-tion, management skills, aspiration, on a vision of what it might become—and these are dependent upon management's ability to control its operations. A company *needs* a challenge. The people who work in it have to *want* something. What do we want now? If the highest goal we can come up with is to add another layer of sales volume or to operate a few cents cheaper, our days as a prospering enterprise are numbered.

But suppose we, as retailers, commit ourselves to an all-out effort to build effective store operations—not just emergency measures to put out yesterday's fires—but to the long-term task of transforming our industry? That would be a challenge to test our mettle. The job in your company may take five years or even ten—but the activity of restructur-ing a business, redirecting our management, routing out the dishonest employee, and investing in capable people could give purpose and focus to our energies. And it is the kind of task that builds new profit margins. Our efforts as an industry would generate economic benefits and expan-sion, create new jobs, and spur the dynamic thrust that we have had in the past and that we are in some danger of losing today.

But the thought of creating more profits is not the primary reason for tackling the job. The overriding motivation is that all of the accom-plishments you, as a retail operator, care about and have worked so hard for, all of the accomplishments that generations of Americans have brought about, are threatened today by crime, immorality, alienation, hatred, anger, apathy, and cynicism. Aside from sharpening our control systems and procedures, our management and supervisory techniques, and our preventive machinery to control internal theft, retailers should become more involved in the community in ways that will help eliminate these social problems and integrate alienated individuals into the mainstream of American life.

Each decade, business has had its great task to perform—founding the company, solving marketing problems, educating the public, generating sales, moving into new fields of endeavor. Isn't the great task of this decade to learn how to manage our business? To learn how to operate so we can protect our assets—money, merchandise, and, most of all, our people?

As management, it should be our task to build a business in which no person's growth will be stunted and no person's ability will be impaired by circumstances that can be prevented: a company in which the disease of dishonesty no longer tyrannizes; a company that assumes the responsibility to protect its people from undue temptation to steal.

The purpose of this book is to explore the nature, problems, and solutions to internal theft. If you are prepared to confront the situation and to apply the recommendations and procedures set forth, you can, without a doubt, substantially reduce internal theft losses in your operation.

PART TWO

Knowing the Basic Safeguards

2

PERSONNEL SCREENING

There is an old saying: "Future events cast their shadows before." This adage may be applied to dishonesty. Patterns of theft simply do not appear overnight. Often the clues are obvious in the past actions of the employee, but the store is too casual about screening its applicants to uncover these warning signals. Oddly enough, the same person who would never think of placing a bet on a horse without carefully checking its past performance record, thinks nothing of hiring a person without doing any investigation whatever of his background or character.

Far too many people rely on externals alone to evaluate the honesty of a person. No matter how unscientific or biased their judgment may be, they believe that if a person looks presentable and speaks well, he is undoubtedly honest. But we must keep in mind that every dishonest person who is discovered on our staff was selected and hired by our company. In too many cases, we should have known better.

Few people become dishonest all of a sudden. Usually they have left clues around for months or even for years which, if recognized, would have tipped us off that something was wrong. How often is a dishonest employee interrogated, only to discover that facts were revealed in his employment interview or on his employment card that should have indicated that he was a poor risk in the first place? His character is as apparent as if he had written "I AM A THIEF" in large letters across the face of the application. Many times, we also notice warning signs during the employment interview, but we may ignore them or rationalize them by saying to ourselves: "He did that a long time ago. It is none of our business. I am only concerned about the type of person he is today and tomorrow; I am not really interested in his past." How unwise!

Another problem is that we don't know what to look for. We may overlook valuable clues that should be checked because of weaknesses in our selection process, carelessness, or lack of knowledge. We simply don't check out certain provable statements or claims made by the person seeking employment.

Naturally, everyone who screens personnel wants to do a good job, but occasionally time limitations or the demands of people who need extra help force us to put the applicant's integrity and honesty at the bottom of our list of priorities. Yet, the backbone of every business is its people. If we fail to put character and integrity among the first requirements for any position in the company, we are making a basic mistake in concept which can be costly to the store and to every person who works there.

Upgrading the screening of new employees is probably the single most important safeguard for preventing internal theft. It is understandable, of course, that the person doing the screening is often primarily concerned with finding an individual capable of doing the job. What is difficult to comprehend is that so many retail stores appear to be completely *unaware* that honesty is even a factor for consideration at the point of employment. This is an attitude that does considerable disservice to the company. Such negligence of a fundamental security control can be extremely costly.

But how do you screen a person applying for a job? What factors do you look for? What are the sources of your information? How should you go about doing it? Over the years, professional security men have developed several methods that have proven successful in screening out high-risk candidates at the point of employment. Hundreds of firms across the country have upgraded their personnel and have substantially reduced internal theft by using these simple screening measures. Your store can do the same. The techniques require a bit of knowledge and effort; but taken one step at a time, none of them is arduous or difficult to master. Further, they pay off handsomely in providing your company with a mature and capable staff.

Look for Evidence of Past Dishonesty

Recent Supreme Court rulings have suggested that we can no longer ask "Have you ever been arrested?" on the employment application form. This question was first challenged when one large industrial organization turned down a black job applicant who had recently graduated from college. On the employment application the question was asked, "Have you ever been arrested?" The applicant told the interviewer that the form didn't have enough space to list all his arrests. He went on to explain that white people don't understand ghetto life; whenever there's trouble, the police arrest everyone in sight. He stated that he was never even tried, just detained a few hours or a day and then released. He admitted he had been arrested 13 or 14 times for "suspicion of theft," "suspicion of housebreaking," and so on.

The interviewer rejected the applicant. As a result, the man appealed to a civil rights group, charging the company with racial discrimination. The argument presented was that it is common knowledge that blacks are arrested without justification more frequently than whites. He claimed that the question about arrests is designed to screen out minority-group applicants. The company replied that it felt it had the right not to hire anyone with an arrest record, whether he was black or white.

The case went to the U.S. District Court, and the court held that the question concerning arrest is unfair and must be dropped from employment applications. "Excluding from jobs persons who have suffered a number of arrests without any conviction is unlawful. It has the effect of denying black applicants equal opportunity for employment." (39 L W 2049) The point to keep in mind here is that an arrest is not proof of guilt. The interviewer should concern himself only with convictions.

But even rejection on the basis of criminal conviction may soon be made unlawful. Courts and agencies appear to be heading toward a ruling that minority-group members cannot be denied jobs even if convicted, assuming the convictions are merely for youthful offenses or other "minor" crimes. What they will define as "minor" crimes will be an important guide in the screening process of job applicants. Thus, the present situation allows you to reject an applicant on the basis of a conviction for a crime against property, but not for an arrest on a "suspicion" of larceny.

Although this arrest question appears to be illegal at present, there is still no reason why the person in charge of employment should not make a reasonable effort to check out a candidate's past record of behavior. This is probably one of the most important screening controls we have. A person who has been involved in larceny is a poor risk in a retail store where merchandise and money are easy to take. Larcenists will generally repeat their theft patterns on and off for the rest of their lives unless they receive some type of psychological help or are placed in a working environment where there is little opportunity for theft.

No one should be hired unless you have checked to see if he has a previous criminal conviction for larceny. Look particularly for any convictions for crimes against property, such as shoplifting, automobile theft, burglary, and robbery. Employing a person with this type of background must be weighed carefully, because it is often unfair to the company and unfair to the applicant to place him in a position of temptation.

Is it possible for a person with a police record to be a good risk? Couldn't he have learned his lesson and gone straight? Unfortunately the evidence in support of this view in not encouraging. Studies by criminal psychologists, security specialists, and the federal government have shown that people who are arrested for various larceny offenses often repeat their crimes. The Federal Bureau of Investigation, for example, began studying the problem of repeating offenders back in 1963. In one of its first studies, it followed the careers of 17,837 individuals who were released by the court and penal institutions in 1963. The record of rearrest for these offenders in the 30 months from the date of their release was as follows:

—Of those released after serving a prison term, 67 percent had been rearrested.

—Of those released on parole, 75 percent had been rearrested.

—Of those acquitted or dismissed by the courts, 83 percent had been rearrested.

These figures are startling. The evidence is clear that most applicants with a police conviction for theft are a poor employment risk in a retail environment.

What if the man or woman got in trouble several years ago and hasn't been in trouble since? If the person was very young at the time of the theft incident, this should be considered. Many teenagers go through a stage in which they steal; but since no criminal pathology is involved, they don't become adult criminals. But do not be misled by the fact that a person of 39, arrested at the age of 24 and not again, is necessarily a good risk. The chances of apprehending a thief a second time are extremely low. Police, at the present time, are apprehending only 18 percent of the individuals involved in reported larcenies. This means that the chances of a reported larcenist escaping arrest favor the criminal by 82 percent.

If an applicant admits that he has stolen previously and even admits he has served time in prison, isn't that a good sign? Do not assume that such a person automatically becomes a good risk because he seems to be truthful about his police record. He may have confessed his past thefts because he feels you already know about them or that your investigation before hiring him will uncover the truth anyway. He is therefore putting his best foot forward by appearing to admit his past "mistakes." Surprisingly enough, many people who hire personnel are misled into believing that frankness about a previous criminal record is proof positive that the person is basically an "honest" person.

Check with the Local Police Department

In some cities, retailers check job applicants for a previous criminal record through the local police department. To do this, they provide the police with the full name of the person, his address, and his day of birth. If the applicant is female, then both her maiden name and married name should also be included. In other cities, local legal ordinances forbid the police to check out applicants. As a way around this situation, some stores provide the applicant with an "inquiry form" to take to the police station. After the police sign the form, stating that the individual does not have a record of criminal conviction, he returns it to the employment office. Although local law may forbid the store to check on a person's criminal record, it usually allows the person to do so himself.

It is also wise to check with the police in those cities in which the applicant lived during the past 10 years. There are three ways in which you can do this: 1) Ask a member of your police department to check out this information through his police contacts in the other cities. 2) Hire a local detective agency to make this check. Select one that belongs to a national association to insure that it has contacts in those cities from which the information must be obtained. The fee is nominal. 3) Use a letter of inquiry to the out-of-town police department giving the subject's name, address, the dates when he lived in the city, and his date of birth. Be sure to include a self-addressed, stamped envelope for the reply. While police in some areas will not be cooperative, this is not universally true and every attempt should be made to obtain such information on criminal convictions.

Contact the Local Stores Protective Association

If you are in a city which has a stores protective association and your company is a member, it is an excellent idea to check all applicants through the association's records. These records usually include the names of individuals who have been prosecuted or discharged because of theft or other crimes. The cost of checking employee names through the stores protective association is nominal, and the results can be valuable. If a stores protective association does not exist in your area or your company is not a member, it is a good idea to develop an informal working agreement with other stores for the exchange of information regarding prospective employees.

A person who has aleady been involved in a crime against a store would make an unhappy addition to any staff. The tendency is for such criminals to be drawn back to retailing for work. This is where criminal experience was obtained and where they feel confident they can steal with safety.

Speak with Past Employers

Most employment specialists raise considerable question as to the value of personal references listed on an employment application.

"What purpose do they serve?" they ask. "The reply will be watered down by kindness, forgetfulness, negligence, or a fear of committing oneself to some type of situation which may later prove embarrassing."

As real as these problems are, the case for checking references remains impressive. A systematic reference check and a skillful analysis of the information returned are good sources for evaluating the applicant's character, dependability, cooperativeness, level of production, and particularly his integrity and honesty. Further, the word gets around that your store checks references, and job applicants will be less inclined to give you false information.

To help you avoid the pitfalls of doing a personal reference check with the applicant's previous employers, conduct the reference by telephone or in person, rather than by mail. Conversation allows you to ask additional questions, and it yields more specific details than does a written reply. People are reluctant to put certain information into writing, particularly anything that is derogatory. If the former employer feels that the applicant is an honesty risk, he is more likely to say so or to hint at his suspicions on the phone. If he turns out to be reasonably frank, however, and states quite directly that he believes the employee is dishonest, then you can try to pin him down to specifics. What particular evidence does he have that led to his conclusion? Obviously, the most useful information will be obtained when you are personally known to the individual you are calling.

Sometimes when you do a reference check of previous employers, you find that the applicant has lied about his past job experience. He may never have worked for the firm, or you may find that the company he listed doesn't even exist. Uncovering these facts is important. Such lies are of sufficient magnitude to indicate that the applicant should be rejected.

Whether you check a person by telephone, by mail, or by talking to his former employer in person, try to contact all the companies the applicant has worked for during the past 10 years. Keep in mind that a sufficient length of time must be covered to make certain that the many facets of his personality have been properly considered. Clinical psychologists have observed that flaws in personality structure may appear infrequently, and by limiting the reference check to a brief period of time, say the last few months, you may fail to disclose important information that occurred periodically in past years.

It is also important to keep your investigation broad in scope. Obtain information from people who have seen the candidate in a variety of situations. It's a good idea, for example, to seek information not only from the personnel manager of the other store or from the employee's former superiors, but from someone he worked with, such as a colleague or a subordinate.

Evaluate Your Reference Sources

Because the sources you contact will evaluate the candidate in general or subjective terms, such references have limited value. They do, of course, give you some insight into how the person sees the applicant, but it's more productive if you can pin down these evaluations by asking for specifics. In other words, ask the reference how he arrived at his evaluation. If he gives you a negative report, you must determine if his attitude is biased. Perhaps there had been a personality clash or some other incident which resulted in his negative conclusions. His views may not be proven valid by the evidence at hand.

Don't forget you are not only rating the man applying for the job, but you are evaluating the person supplying the reference. As you talk with him, determine how objective he is. Does he seem to be biased in his viewpoint about this person? What standards does he use for making this type of evaluation? Does he seem to know the applicant well? Is he familiar with his outside life? Does he know his family or his hobbies, for example? Did the applicant work directly under the man with whom you are talking, or does he know him only through hearsay?

It sometimes helps if you prepare a list of questions in advance. In that way, you can get the information you want without later finding out that you have omitted something important from your telephone or in-person inquiry. Naturally, you should feel free to depart from your checklist whenever answers open up new leads. The checklist is only to give you some guidelines to follow so that you are certain to touch upon all of the important questions.

Here are a few points to be considered:

1) What were the dates of his employment?

2) What was his salary?

3) What were his duties on the previous job?

4) Was he a person of integrity and honesty?

5) What sort of record did he have for illness? Tardiness? Did he have any compensation claims against the company?

6) How cooperative and dependable was he?

7) Did he show initiative and ambition on the job? Was he hard working? Productive? A self-starter?

8) What were his relations with his associates? With his boss? How did they feel about him? Was he a loner? Did he drink a lot alone or with the gang after work? What sort of person was he exactly?

9) Would you rehire him? If not, why not?

If you are the manager of a store or if you are a top management executive in a chain of stores, don't hesitate to delegate this reference-checking job to the man in charge of the department where this particular worker will be assigned. After all, the department head should have a strong personal interest in hiring the right person for the job, so place some responsibility on him for selecting the employee. He is going to be careful in screening the applicant and in making his evaluation.

Wherever possible, try to check references *before* you put a person on the job. In order to speed up the hiring process, some companies postpone such screenings until after a person is employed. This is a risky procedure. In many cases, major thefts and the corruption of other honest employees have occurred in the two or three weeks between the time the person is assigned to work and the time the employment person discovers his criminal record. So try to screen the applicant *before* you put him to work.

Determine the Person's Financial Situation

Is the applicant under any unusual financial pressure? Does he owe payment on a lot of bills? Has he ever been brought into court for nonpayment of debts? Has his salary ever been garnisheed? Make it a routine practice to get a credit bureau report on each person before hiring him. Credit bureaus today have considerable information. The Associated Credit Bureaus of America, for example, has records on 120 million people.

Today's credit bureau files contain a lot more than a list of the cars and cameras purchased on credit. They tell you if a person owns his own home, what kind of furniture he has, whether he has passed bad checks, and so on. They also include newspaper clippings, records of lawsuits, data on police actions against him, and items of this nature. These reports, therefore, can often provide valuable background material to help you evaluate the applicant's past performance in terms of his record of personal integrity and honesty.

Conduct a Neighborhood Investigation

When the person being hired is going to be put into a critical job, such as head of the cash room, some companies make it a point to have a trained investigator talk to some of the people in the applicant's neighborhood. If such an investigation seems warranted, the investigator should talk to the neighbors either in person or by telephone to find out if there is any indication that the applicant is a poor risk. For example, is he known to be living beyond his means? Does he have undesirable associates? Does he have a reputation as a "heavy drinker?" Is he known to be a chronic gambler? Does he have a reputation for immoral conduct? Is he heavily in debt? An unfavorable report on any of these six factors should cause the person doing the screening to think twice before hiring this person for a job in a store where the supervision is minimal and the opportunity to steal is maximum.

Use a Bonding Company Application Form

Many companies have the job applicant make out a bonding company form as well as an employment application blank. The person with a previous criminal record is frequently more concerned about the bonding application than he is about the employment card. He is aware that bonding companies usually make an investigation into the background of individuals before they approve them. If the applicant has a previous criminal record, he may feel that the bonding company will surely uncover it and report it to the company. As a result, when the bonding company form is used, the dishonest applicant frequently does not return for his second interview. He thus screens himself out of the job.

For the same reason, a few firms today also fingerprint and photograph applicants. This is largely used as a psychological device to scare off the person who has a criminal record. Of course, this tactic may provoke an undesirable reaction on the part of an honest applicant. Such procedures have too many overtones of a "police state." Therefore, the company has to judge the advisability of this approach on the basis of the location of the store, the type of image it projects to the community, and the quality or type of individual it seeks to employ.

Most people, however, even those who are sensitive to any action that reflects on their integrity, do not resent a bonding company form; and for the most part the bonding company form is just as effective a psychological device as are the techniques of fingerprinting and photographing the applicant. It is certainly less traumatic for the honest person.

Review the Employment Application

Frequently the man doing the hiring looks over the application form without really knowing exactly what he is looking for. Most employment applications provide for a listing of previous jobs in order of dates of employment. This listing is extremely important to the interviewer. He should look carefully down the dates of employment to see if there are any gaps in the person's employment record. When he discovers such a gap, he should ask for an explanation. The answer given by the applicant may sound extremely logical. He may say: "I was in business for myself for a year selling storm windows. But I found that I couldn't make a go of it and had to go back to my former line of work." Or he may say he visited relatives in Europe that year, and so on. But no matter what the story is or how logical it sounds, it is extremely important for the interviewer to postpone any decision on hiring this person until he can do a factual check on the applicant's story.

More often than not, he will find that he has discovered a clue to trouble in the person's employment background. It may be that he worked for another company and was discharged for dishonesty, so he has omitted that period on his employment listing, hoping the interviewer won't notice it. In some cases, it has been found that the applicant was actually serving time in jail during the period when his application shows a gap in employment. So check out his story and get the facts.

It is also common sense to check out any claims that can be investigated. If a story contains specific details, then these can be verified by talking to the people involved. Particularly important are the simple factual checks that can be made during the interview itself. For instance, if the applicant says he was recently discharged from the army, ask him to show you his discharge papers; ask him also for a copy of his school graduation records, and so on. It is a good habit not to accept the applicant's word alone when the factual material can be easily requested and examined during the interview.

Watch for the Psychotic Person

The most dangerous type of thief in retailing is the "psychotic" or the "criminally minded" person. He is the most dangerous because once he becomes a member of the staff, little can be done to prevent him from stealing. His thefts are invariably large, but, what is worse, he often coerces normally honest employees to steal in order to protect himself. It also does little good to try to screen out this type of individual by using a lie detector test. A psychopath's personality is characterized by an abnormal lack of fear, so he can often pass a polygraph screening test with a clean record. Because the lie detector works on fear reactions, the test indicates he is a good employee risk. Only later does management realize the extent of its error, and usually it is too late to undo the damage.

Fortunately, however, researchers have developed tests to screen out such abnormally delinquent applicants. One which has proven effective is called a "Personnel Reaction" test. It was developed by Dr. Harrison Gough, Jr., Head of the Psychology Department at the University of California, Berkeley Division. The test consists of 64 questions which sound harmless to the applicant and give no indication that they are meant to reveal delinquency. Some typical questions are:

"Have you ever wanted to run away and join a circus?"
"Are you afraid of deep water?"
"Does a rainstorm frighten you?"
"Have you ever been afraid of being in a car wreck?"
"Does the thought of certain animals make you nervous?"

In a field study of this test, a few years ago, 830 part-time Christmas employees hired in November by a large department store in New York City were given Dr. Gough's "Personnel Reaction" test. The unrated tests were placed in a locked desk until February when all the temporary employees had left the company. At that time the tests were rated, and the results showed that 72 of the employees in that group were "delinquent." Although the store had a small security staff of only nine detectives who devoted the major part of their work to apprehending shoplifters, they had, nevertheless, apprehended 36 of the 72 employees rated delinquent by Dr. Gough's test. Through the use of such tests, this insidious criminal type can be identified before he unleashes his aggression on your store.*

Whether or not you use formal tests of this kind, by including questions in the interview that relate to the applicant's fears, you can often learn whether the person exhibits a normal range of fear reactions, or whether he appears to have psychotic tendencies. If there is any indication that the latter may be the case, and you are interested in hiring the person, then it would be wise to have him tested by a competent psychologist.

Be Alert to Giveaway Gestures

There is considerable interest today in how people reveal themselves through gestures. Although we may say one thing verbally, sometimes we are saying something quite different with our gestures. Interviewers should be sensitive to giveaway gestures during the job interview, and should try to uncover with further questions why a particular topic elicited such a reaction. The matter may not be significant, but

* (The reader may also want to investigate The Reid Report, the Stanton Reemployment test, and others.)

it should be looked into. Here are a few gestures the skilled interviewer should watch for:

—When a man passes his hand over his face while talking, usually when answering a question, this may mean that he wants to evade the issue under discussion. If you ask him, for example, "How did you get along with your previous boss?" and he rubs his face or passes his hands over his eyes before he says "Just great!" you can suspect that he would rather not tell you the real truth about the relationship.

—If he crushes his cigarette violently or draws a doodle with unusual force, perhaps breaking the point of his pencil, this may mean that underneath an apparently calm exterior lies a very hostile and angry person.

—During the discussion, if the subject becomes excited and bangs on the desk or shouts for emphasis, this often reveals an inward awareness that he is not telling the truth or that he believes his pretenses are being found out by the interviewer. The loudness of the argument and the violence of the pounding indicate a defensive attitude which has serious implications in the interview situation.

—If he rubs his nose while answering a question or during the discussion, this may reflect a personal dissatisfaction with what is being said in the conversation. Watch for this sign particularly when salary is being discussed.

—Itching and scratching may mean embarrassment or excitement and can indicate a person with an extremely low threshold of nervous control.

—A sudden loss of color from the face is frequently a sign that the person has been asked something that frightens him. Usually signs of fear will appear in clusters. The applicant's mouth will suddenly go dry, and you will notice that his tongue touches his lips to moisten them before he speaks.

In fact, the corners of his mouth may even firm up as though he were eating a lemon, a reflex reaction caused by fear.

—Excessive sweating by the applicant may indicate extreme anxiety.

Ask Probing Questions

To be effective, the interview with the applicant should range across several areas of his life. Questions should cover such topics as his education, his previous type of work, and his financial situation. Does he own his own home? What part of the city does he live in? What sort of hobbies does he have? How is his general health? You will also want to discuss his military service, what he did in the armed forces, and so on. Dig into any other matters that are directly related to the points you are concerned about. Why did he leave his last job? What is his family background? What are his hobbies and personal interests, his marital status, his personal aspirations and ambitions, and his previous income? Has he ever received workmen's compensation for an injury?

Ask other questions which will determine how stable his employment pattern has been in the past. Does he appear to be a man who hops from job to job or does he stay on one job for a considerable length of time? What has motivated him in the past to move from one position to another? Is he an overly dependent person? Is he a person with strong ambitions and drive? What sort of home life did he have as a child? What is his home life like today? Is he a stable person? Does he seem to be a drifter? Is he a man who agrees with whatever you say or is he a person with individual opinions? Are his opinions logical or emotional?

One characteristic that you must probe for, in particular, is the maturity of the person. Can he stand up under frustration? How does he handle his problems? Does he find that small incidents upset him? Is he mature enough to have developed techniques for avoiding frustrations, going around them, or working his way through them?

Because his ability to handle frustration is directly related to his risk level in the retail store, be sure to learn what his earning aspirations are. If they are too high in terms of the job for which you are considering him, then watch out! Chances are that he will soon become extremely frustrated in this job, and these feelings may lead to theft.

Another very important aspect of the interview is to find out what he thinks about the relative honesty of people in general. Most of us tend to believe that other people are like ourselves. For example, if we take a group of executives at random and say to them, "What percentage of the employees in the store do you think steal?" one executive will say 1 percent, another will say 10 percent, and another will say 20 percent. These estimates usually indicate that the person is himself relatively honest and therefore finds it difficult to believe that many people steal. On the other hand, if the executive says 75 percent or 85 percent steal, or if he says that 98 percent steal, then the interviewer should be careful. Chances are that this person is dishonest—we usually see ourselves in others.

The interviewer should also be alert to any indication of cheating or dishonesty on the part of the person being questioned, particularly any contradictions or discrepancies in the applicant's answers. He must take nothing for granted and must closely question those people who show any subtle indication of deceit. For example, these would be people who:

—cough, stammer, or hesitate before answering a question

—have ready-made alibis for rationalizing unfavorable reports, have glib explanations for gaps in their employment records, or who talk too easily, too rapidly, and too smoothly

—go into long and detailed descriptions about previous work experience and earnings

—give evidence of living or dressing beyond their income.

Evaluate the Applicant's Intelligence

Studies over the years have proven repeatedly that there is a relationship between intelligence and honesty. These studies show that a person with better-than-average intelligence is generally more likely to be honest than a person of lower intelligence.

There is usually an optimum intelligence level for most jobs. The retailer embarking on the use of intelligence tests is wise to test people who have worked for him successfully for several years in order to determine what the optimum level is for their particular jobs. By identifying the intelligence levels of present employees, you will establish useful guidelines for selecting individuals to fill the same or similar positions. Applicants scoring in the quarter of ratings below that level are probably going to be slow to learn the work, and they are going to be inaccurate. On the other hand, those who are in the top quarter may become restless, bored, and frustrated.

From the point of view of honesty, it is sound business to try to hire only those applicants who achieve at least the average level in the optimum intelligence standard set for each particular type of job. Those with lower-than-average scores are greater security risks, depending, of course, on how far down the intelligence scale they are and on the temptations to steal offered by the position.

Although the use of an intelligence test is highly recommended, it is not always convenient to use this approach. However, the interviewer can soon determine the relative range of an applicant's intelligence by such means as listening to how well the person speaks, reviewing his schooling, or finding out what he reads.

For example, if the applicant expresses himself clearly and is able to use words with abstract meanings, this is a sign of intelligence. The applicant who has finished high school should possess at least a low-average intelligence level. If he graduated high in his class, he will be either at the high average or superior intelligence level. The person who graduated from college is probably at the superior level, depending upon the standards of the college.

By discussing the candidate's preferences in reading matter, you can also often judge his intelligence level. Ascertain what newspapers or books the employee reads. Is he a comic book fan? Does he read sophisticated literary journals? His reading tastes can reveal much about his intellectual capacity.

When forming your personal estimate of an applicant's intelligence, be careful to avoid the pitfalls that can mislead you in making an accurate assessment. We are constantly taking the measure of people around us by their appearance. The intelligence of a good-looking and well-dressed person is usually overrated, while that of a less attractive person is generally underrated. These outward qualities tell us nothing about their brain power. To quote an old cliché: "You can't judge a book by its cover."

Also, be careful of misjudging people who have a singular talent or one major accomplishment. Outstanding athletes, musicians, or artists may be highly skilled in their particular area, but this does not mean that they are highly intelligent. We frequently overestimate the talented person's general intelligence, while, in fact, his specialty often limits his experience and knowledge about other fields of endeavor. Unusual accomplishments are generally due to some special capacity the person has, such as a color sense, physical coordination, and so on, which may be unrelated to intelligence.

Screen Teenage Applicants Carefully

Statistically, teenagers are an extremely high-risk employee group. How does a person 16 to 22 years of age compare with an older person as a security risk? To find out the answer to this question, a study was made of 370,508 larceny arrests of people between the ages of 16 and 34 in 1971. The findings indicate that the incidence of larceny arrests for persons between the ages of 16 and 22 was five times greater than for those aged 23 to 26. These facts are illustrated in Figure 1.

While the F.B.I. Report does not break down the number of larceny arrests by the nature of the thefts, the experience of most retailers is that teenagers commit more thefts than more mature employees. This may be attributed to the fact that many teenagers, being employed only part-time, do not have the opportunity to develop company loyalty. Combined with the lack of personal challenge provided by their job assignments, these factors contribute to the kind of frustration that promotes internal theft.

Faced with this reality, many stores have successfully cut their number of internal theft cases by the simple expedient of reducing the number of teenage employees to no more than 10 percent of their total staff. Even then, they are carefully screened and assigned to work only during the daylight hours when the store has maximum supervisory coverage. One of the most serious mistakes made by food stores is to

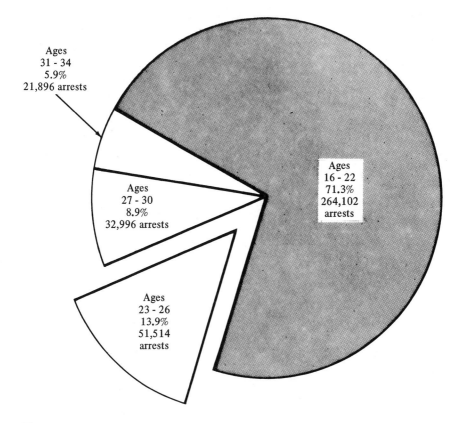

Figure 1. Distribution of 370,508 larceny arrests made in 1971, ages 16 to 34. Based on statistics appearing in the Uniform Crime Report published by the Federal Bureau of Investigation, Washington, D.C., on August 29, 1972.

hire teenagers to work the night hours when the store has a skeleton supervisory staff and controls are at a minimum.

This does not by any means suggest that you should not hire teenagers. Many teenagers are undoubtedly a good honesty risk. The problem is the maturity level of the teenager. Inability to handle frustration triggers thefts, and teenagers often do not have the experience or the emotional maturity to overcome their frustrations. The result may be a hostile reaction toward the store, their supervisor, or the "establishment," and the end result is often serious theft losses and an unfortunate situation for the apprehended teenager.

Therefore, before hiring any teenager, do a careful screening job. Contact his associates, learn about his hobbies, his interests, his emotional stability, his health, and his general attitude toward life and toward business. Be extremely careful not to take on an excessive number of teenagers under any circumstances, and assure yourself that those you hire are reasonably mature for their age and are well adjusted. Then see that they are placed in jobs which do not offer undue temptation to steal, which are well supervised, and where there is good discipline and enforcement of control systems and procedures.

Use the Polygraph When Advisable

Many store managers say: "Why spend all this time and effort checking into people's backgrounds. We can give them a polygraph test and learn the whole story in a matter of an hour or two with much less trouble." In theory, the lie detector used at the point of employment might seem to be a logical answer to screening job applicants. Certainly many companies use it today, and many feel it is effective. But three states have banned the polygraph at the point of employment and twelve states have statutes restricting its use in personnel work. The polygraph has extremely useful applications in business, particularly as a tool for investigating crime and for probing the details of employee dishonesty after a crime has been uncovered. But used at the point of employment, it raises some serious questions.

Through the efforts of the American Polygraph Association to establish a code of ethics and to police its members, the standards of professionalism in this field have risen steadily. Members of the A.P.A. must be college graduates, have matriculated in a polygraph school, and have served a six-month internship, among other requirements. While there are many extremely talented, well-trained, knowledgeable polygraph operators of the highest personal integrity, despite the men of achievement in the field, there are still other operators who are poorly trained, inexperienced, and lacking in psychological understanding. They are incapable of running reliable tests. The problem here is in locating the true professional and in avoiding the incompetent practitioner. While the legal status of the polygraph is currently in a state of flux, as of this writing, only 16 states have enacted laws requiring polygraph operators to be licensed. In the remaining 34 states, you do not need to have a license to operate a polygraph; there are no educational requirements. All you need is the money to buy a machine and a good sales pitch. Therefore, as one precaution, any company that is considering using polygraph tests should assure itself that the practitioner has been accepted for membership in the A.P.A.

In addition to the question of a lack of professional standards, many factors can cause a wrong diagnosis, and only the qualified operator has the training and experience to make an expert decision. Any really qualified polygraph operator will tell you that an inaccurate polygraph test can be caused by illness, pain, coughing spells, mental or physical fatigue, heart conditions, hay fever, asthma, tranquilizing drugs, and so on. Even how the examiner acts toward the subject before the test can have an effect on the results. These are only a few of the many problems encountered.

The really qualified examiner can spot these problems, and he will tell you that he cannot get a reliable reading of the subject. Also, a certain percentage of people who take the test neither pass nor fail it; they simply cannot be tested. Unfortunately, the less responsible operators tend to mislead the retailer and often claim specific results of innocence or guilt when, in actual fact, they are unable to make a professional determination based on the polygraph evidence. The genuine expert in polygraph work can spot variables and work around them or reschedule his test for another day, but the untrained operator may be ignorant of these factors and may therefore end up with a false reading.

Another drawback is that there is considerable evidence that using a polygraph for pre-employment testing can result in relationship problems between job applicants and the company that is considering them for employment. In fact, in many cases it adversely affects management's ability to build a really strong relationship of confidence with its employees.

If, however, the company does choose to use the polygraph at the point of employment, then tests of employees should be made every six months or so, just as you would require semi-annual health tests. This insures that the employees are continuing to maintain a high standard of honesty. For example, one retail store in Chicago had used the polygraph only at the time of employment. After the employees had passed the test and were hired, they were never given another polygraph examination. Recently, it was discovered that most of the employees who had passed the test when first employed were now stealing from the store on a large scale. The tested staff members apparently felt free to steal because they believed the test had proven them honest in the eyes of management.

Granted that the polygraph could be effective in screening if periodic tests were given to employees, but this is costly, time-consuming, and tends to set up a threatening work environment between management and staff. A nonthreatening work relationship is vital to reducing internal theft losses. Only in this atmosphere can employees grow, develop, and mature. The use of the polygraph may tend to destroy such a relationship. While it should be used in criminal investigations, it is a questionable substitute for the usual interviewing and screening methods used at the point of employment.

Another device that attempts to measure involuntary physiological changes that are caused by psychological stress is called the "psychological stress evaluator." This machine differs from the polygraph in that it measures variations in infrasonic voice frequencies rather than changes in blood pressure, respiration, pulse rate, and so on. The primary advantage to this voice-stress analysis technique is that sensors do not have to be attached to the body as is the case in normal polygraph testing. Moreover, the technique does not require the subject and the operator to be in the same room as tests can be made of voice frequencies that are transmitted through the telephone or a radio receiver.

As of this writing, the psychological stress evaluator is being tested by a variety of companies. While initial reports have been most favorable, it should be kept in mind that, like the standard polygraph, this new technique can be useful only if placed in the hands of a professional operator who is capable of making proper judgments.

Apply These Steps Systematically

Understanding these fundamentals of personnel screening is only the first step. You have to make them work. A sound approach to personnel selection requires self-discipline. You must force yourself to study each person you consider hiring even more closely than before. At first, it will be difficult, tiresome, and tedious. Then one day it will all come together, and the next thing you know you will have developed an intuitive professional technique of personnel selection. For now, you may have to do it one step at a time, thinking out the process as you go along; but soon it will become automatic.

Remember that screening employees is one of the most important jobs in the entire company. Of course, you will have some failures, even if you follow all of the suggestions outlined in this section. But don't let the failures discourage you. Everyone has failures, at times, whenever judgment is involved. Your goal should be to make a better-than-average percentage of right decisions. So when you do make an error and one of your carefully screened people turns out to be dishonest, don't let this discourage you. Your objective is to do a professional hiring job, and you improve your average by applying a scientific and systematic approach to screening personnel applicants.

In this chapter you have all the tools you need to do an effective professional selection job. But like any tools, they require some actual practice and experience before you become skilled at using them. However, keep in mind that they have been proven remarkably effective in many stores. Remember the personnel decision is the ultimate method of controlling internal thefts.

3

SPOTTING THE HIGH-RISK EMPLOYEE

In spite of the strictest screening measures, dishonest individuals may find their way into your retail operation. But even if every employee you hire has an unblemished record for personal honesty, circumstances may arise within their private lives which compel them to steal as a way of coping with their problems. At times the store itself is inadvertently responsible for triggering such thefts because of elements in the working environment which bring undue pressure or undue temptation upon the employee. Such elements should be guarded against and eliminated wherever possible. But regardless of circumstance, store management must safeguard its company's assets, and one way to do so is knowing how to spot the high-risk employee.

There are many clues that should act as warning flags to the alert manager. Such clues do not *prove* a person is dishonest, but they do indicate an employee who should be given special supervisory attention. The following are some of the basic signals to watch for in identifying potential problem people among your staff.

The Employee Living Beyond His Means

One of the most likely suspects is the employee living beyond his means. The manager who is close to his staff will recognize a worker who suddenly acquires an expensive wardrobe or who brags about a costly new car, clothes, or stereo he has purchased. Often, it is obvious that he could not buy the items on his salary. The main problem with this individual is that once he becomes accustomed to living beyond his means, it is difficult for him to stop. He is constantly trying to keep up his payments on a color TV set, a car, or his charge accounts.

If you suspect that an employee is living far beyond his income, what should you do about it? The position the employee holds is important. Is he an assistant manager or a checker? What is his theft potential? Does he have access to cash and merchandise or only to merchandise? Is he in a position of authority where he could embezzle from the firm?

Your answers to these questions will determine whether an inquiry into the employee's financial situation is warranted. But, keep in mind that such investigations, while vital to the control of internal theft, if they become known, can have a negative effect on staff morale especially with regard to honest employees. Therefore, any investigation should be undertaken in strict secrecy and only when there is good reason to believe that the individual is a high security risk.

If his position is strategic, then a most extensive investigation should be made. If his position is a minor one, and he has little access to large sums of money or little opportunity to manipulate documents by signing phony invoices, by altering the amounts on checks, and so on, then only a reasonable amount of time and effort should be spent to uncover the true source of his income.

Should you decide to investigate, and if you haven't already done so in your screening procedures, begin by checking for a police record, both locally and in other cities where he has lived. Next, ask the local credit bureau to run a detailed credit investigation on the suspect. If you have contacts in your local banks, find out how often he is depositing money and how much. Does there seem to be any pattern to these deposits? Are they excessive? Next, have someone drive over to his house and take a picture of it. Submit this picture to a real estate appraiser for an estimate on its value, and, of course, have your bank contact check out the payments being made on the house.

Try to get all the details you can on his expenditures—his car payments, appliance payments, rent or house payments, and so on. Then compare his expenditures with his known income. Be sure to check on whether other members of his family are employed and what they are earning. If the suspect's expenditures are obviously greater than the combined income from these sources, ask a local detective agency to do a discreet investigation to discover any additional means of income that the family might have.

Don't ever accept the subject's "explanation" of how he happens to have extra money. Investigate his story to get the facts. Too often, managers readily believe the tale of an unexpected inheritance when the culprit is actually stealing from the company. If, after a thorough investigation, you find no reasonable explanation for the employee's affluence, keep a watchful eye on his activities and spot-check his work for irregularities.

The Maladjusted Employee

A person who has shown himself to be emotionally unstable, erratic in behavior, and unpredictable in his emotional reactions to various job situations is one worthy of careful scrutiny. You should be concerned about any employee who formerly appeared well adjusted and then suddenly seems to undergo a change in personality. From a normally happy disposition, he may become sullen, withdrawn, and obviously depressed. Or his personality may change from that of a pleasant worker to one who is hostile and sarcastic. Both types of personality fluctuations may indicate that a person is under serious psychological stress and needs special management attention. Granted the average manager is not a psychologist and is in no position to diagnose such illnesses, but most managers are astute enough to be able to recognize a person undergoing a serious emotional upset. If an employee does appear to have such emotional problems, he can be a serious security risk to the store.

Studies have repeatedly shown that stealing is a common reaction by people in the depths of a neurotic crisis. Some steal when they become very depressed; others steal to "get even" with their bosses or with the company for some imagined wrong. Some neurotics steal because they have serious guilt feelings and want to be caught and punished. Still others steal in order to gain attention and to acquire status with their peer group.

When an employee with any problem of this type is discovered, the department head should immediately bring this to the attention of his manager, and consideration should be given to referring the worker to a counselor or a psychologist. Where no such corrective action is possible, the department manager has an obligation to protect company assets, and this means keeping an eye on the disturbed person, having him shopped, checking his packages periodically, and so on. A large number of maladjusted workers steal, and the department manager is a key to locating such suspects and placing them under observation.

The Heavy Drinker

Any employee who is a heavy drinker, particularly if he drinks on the job, is an honesty risk. Even when under the influence of only a few ounces of liquor, many people become "tranquilized." In fact, some psychologists say that liquor is perhaps the most frequently used tranquilizer in the nation. While in this state of temporary sedation, the employee's moral judgment becomes blurred, and many a man who is honest when sober becomes a thief when drunk.

Most managers recognize that the heavy drinker has his problems, but they seldom see the actual threat he represents to the store. Heavy drinking is costly. The alcoholic often feels he must preserve the appearance of being a "social" drinker (a more desirable label than that of an "alcoholic") and to do so he treats his friends and acquaintances to drinks. Before he knows what's happening, he is in financial distress. He is also cursed with an addiction that cannot be satisfied. Who will buy the next round of drinks? The store will! Any employee who drinks on the job, or who takes a few "healthy belts" during his lunch hour or relief period, is worth keeping an eye on.

The Drug User

Naturally, you should also be concerned about an employee who shows signs of drug usage. Although marijuana is not habit forming, it does create a euphoria, like alcohol, which can impair an employee's moral sense as well as affect his judgment. Like the heavy drinker, the drug user is not entirely responsible for his actions; and if he has any latent tendency toward dishonesty, the drug will enable him to steal without the usual barriers of fear or guilt.

The Chronic Gambler

Another likely suspect is the chronic gambler. Managers often know which employees place daily bets on the horses or numbers, and yet they fail to realize that chronic gambling is as much a disease as drug addiction or alcoholism. Recent studies show that there are an estimated six million chronic gamblers in the United States. Such people are a big problem for retail establishments. Gambling, if unchecked, may open the door to organized crime. Once gambling gets a foothold in your operation, it can spread like a brush fire through the store. It destroys employee morale, causes attitude changes that result in reduced employee productivity, and is the single most important cause of employee theft. According to a study of one thousand embezzlers made by the United States Fidelity and Guaranty Company, gambling was the cause of 23 percent of all the stealing incidents and was the most frequently cited motive for theft.

What happens when one of your employees becomes a chronic gambler? Gradually, his personal philosophy begins to change. He becomes "luck" oriented and develops a strong desire to "get something for nothing." Because he no longer believes in gaining the things he wants for himself and his family through honest work, his productivity drops. He becomes lazy, indifferent, and difficult to motivate. Furthermore, like all gamblers, he will inevitably lose and may resort to stealing from the store to secure the needed cash. The person who gambles is likely to take a chance on stealing. Such employees not only have poor judgment, but they are psychologically unable to control their own impulses. In the end, the store pays the gambler's bills.

To help stamp out gambling in your store, you can take the following four steps:

1) Make a clear statement to your employees of your own attitude against gambling and your company's policy against this practice, if such exists.

2) Refuse to allow gambling on company property.

3) Encourage strict enforcement of gambling laws in your community.

4) Teach employees why gambling is harmful.

Overly Attentive Employees

One type of employee who should arouse your suspicions is the overly attentive person. Some of the greatest thieves in retailing have been consummate actors. These "actors" play up to their boss. They get on his good side by doing him personal favors. Many times they even cultivate him socially and invite him into their homes or meet with him at a bar or restaurant outside the job. They offer to take care of menial little jobs, to run personal errands, or to do any number of small favors to ingratiate themselves with him. This strategy works. It provides a smoke screen behind which the manager cannot see. He is just unable to believe that a person he likes so much, and who seems to like him so much, would ever stoop to stealing from the store.

Only the "trusted" person can get away with large-scale thefts. The people we *don't* trust can't steal much because we keep an eye on them. But in the trusted person, we see only his good qualities and often pass him over as a possible suspect.

Long-Term Employees

While new employees, and especially teenagers, are a high security risk in terms of the number of thefts committed, insurance company statistics on fidelity claims reveal that long-term employees are a more serious security problem because their thefts involve larger sums of money. According to one study, employees involved in major thefts are not caught until they have been employed an average of nine years and three months by the company.

In contrast to the older employee whose honesty is too often taken for granted, the new worker is not yet trusted by his manager, so any furtive acts are immediately noticed and dealt with by the boss. Since we are more apt to be suspicious of new personnel, we also tend to catch more of them stealing. But their thefts are rarely sizable, as they have only recently begun their activities. By contrast, the dishonest long-term employee has usually built up a substantial theft figure by the time he is finally caught. The more serious and the more costly employee theft cases invariably involve long-term workers.

Another factor is the experience of a long-termer. He has worked several years in the store and during this time has learned the store's systems and operations. He has also learned a great deal about what the store checks and does not check, and what his manager checks and does not check. If a store has systems loopholes, he knows about them. If other dishonest workers are stealing, he knows their methods. This basic knowledge, plus the fact that most of his activities no longer arouse curiosity, combine to make him a greater theft threat in terms of dollar losses, than the new employee.

The Rule Violator

The employee who rebels against widely accepted store rules is also a poor risk. You may notice him sneaking out of the store before closing time without letting his supervisor know he is leaving early. He may have another employee stamp his time card so that he can arrive late in the morning or leave early in the evening. Although regulations require him to use a specific exit, he may use an unauthorized exit. Any person who shows a repeated record of violating store regulations should be closely scrutinized. This same failure to live by the rules of the store may show up in a lack of responsibility when handling store money or merchandise.

The Spendthrift

Credit bureau checks will often reveal that an employee is under serious financial pressure because of excessive debts. Some people can't handle their liquor; some can't handle their money. They aren't able to budget; they don't plan ahead; they are victims of impulse buying and overspending. In addition, they are easily seduced by advertising and, before they know it, are boxed in and heavily in debt. Demands by creditors for payments on bills soon lead to tremendous anxiety, and the need for money compels them to dip into the till where funds are instantly available.

The Employee with a Family Problem

Probably one of the greatest tragedies found among the dishonest employee group is the person facing an unexpected home emergency. For example, his spouse may be suddenly injured or taken ill and can no longer work. As the bills roll in, the problem becomes overwhelming. In this situation, the pressing need for money may cause the employee to steal as a last resort.

Marital difficulties may also lead to theft as a result of the financial burdens they impose. If a woman has been deserted by her husband or a man by his wife, this may mean sudden new expenses. This will also be true of the newly divorced individual. The divorced man who is still legally obligated to support his former wife and children can find himself in a tight financial squeeze if he remarries. The financial adjustment of the recently divorced woman may also be difficult. Caught in these situations, such individuals may feel compelled to extricate themselves by stealing store money or merchandise.

The natural sympathy that supervisors have for people with serious personal problems sometimes blinds them to obvious indications of theft. We somehow feel it would be unkind of us to suspect a person who has already been overburdened with problems. We reject the very thought of dishonesty when we see the hard-working cashier with an alcoholic husband, the salesman supporting an invalid wife, or the physically handicapped worker. These are people we admire for their self-sacrifice and courage. But while we cannot help feeling sorry for them, we don't have to feel guilty because we notice some action on their part that is questionable and suggests possible dishonesty.

The Chronic Liar

Another person to be particularly watchful of is the chronic liar. Some people will lie when placed under pressure or to protect another person's feelings; others will lie because they are afraid of being punished. The chronic liar is a maladjusted person who lies frequently, even when there is no reason to do so. Experience shows that many people who lie also steal. This person is a high risk.

The Model Executive

Many retailers today are unknowingly victimized by employees who misappropriate funds. Why? Because we are reluctant to believe a person placed in a trusted position would steal. An executive cannot imagine how a buyer on his staff could be slipping phony invoices through his accounts payable each month. He won't believe a warehouse manager in his operation could be in collusion with truckers to pass phony bills of lading. To top management, it is difficult to suggest that any of its upper-echelon staff might be stealing. The result is that the happy embezzler has found a home, at last, in retailing.

Who is he? How can you smoke him out? The Continental Casualty Company of Chicago conducted a study of the embezzlement cases it had handled. It found that the average embezzler is about 35 years old, male (93 percent), has been employed nine years, worked in the store about six years before starting to steal, and usually steals three to five years before discovery (if discovered at all). This description is confirmed by the Surety Association of America. It describes a typical embezzler as about 36 years of age, married with two children, and someone who has served his present employer for about five years with apparent honesty.

The embezzler, Mr. X, is well thought of, trusted, and often does his job with expert skill. He is praised as a top-notch administrator and model executive. In most companies, the embezzler is never caught. In fact, he receives the usual gold watch at the end of his many years of "faithful" service. But if management does stumble onto his machinations, the reaction is unfailingly the same: "I just can't believe it. Why, Joe is a solid citizen if there ever was one. I never dreamed . . . I never suspected a thing." Of course not! If anyone had suspected Joe, he wouldn't have been able to fleece the company of thousands of dollars each year.

Here are 10 danger signals that Mr. X, the embezzler, may flash:

1) He doesn't take his vacation. (He can't risk having some substitute person stumble over his manipulations.)

2) Often you find that he gambles a lot—cards every week at the country club for high stakes, a weekend now and then at Las Vegas. Frequently he is unable to cover his losses with his regular income.

3) He is often critical of other people, feels that most people steal but may show great dislike of dishonesty in others, may claim extreme personal honesty, and may often appear to be a religious fanatic.

4) On the other hand, he may be a man who drinks excessively, or he may often frequent night clubs. Perhaps you've heard rumors about his associating with some undesirable characters around town.

5) He may use "business channels" to get his car, house, appliances, and so on, either at low prices or as "gifts" from resources dealt with by the company.

6) Sometimes the clue is that he borrows small amounts of money from fellow associates, often not repaying them. You may run across some of his unauthorized I.O.U.'s in the change fund or his personal checks—undated, post-dated, past-dated. He may even request others to "hold" his checks.

7) He may be the man you can't coax into giving up the custody of his records. He works overtime regularly and may take records home to work on at night. He may be excessively neat and fastidious in his bookkeeping. Watch out for funny business if he rewrites records under the guise of "neatness."

8) Sometimes he gives himself away by bragging about his exploits or by carrying unusually large sums of money in his wallet.

9) He's the fellow who tells you to butt out. He is irritable and hostile. He gets overly annoyed, even at reasonable questioning.

10) Mr. X may seem "big league," have an unusually large bank balance, buy heavily in securities, or claim he has a higher standard of living because he receives a large sum of money from an estate.

The Employee with Undesirable Associates

Another type of person who should be watched is the employee known to have undesirable associates. The employee may himself be neat and presentable in appearance, yet have friends visit him in the store who are obviously of a different sort. For example, they may be members of a local motorcycle gang or may have criminal records. When managers see that an employee has undesirable associates, it is wise to have him watched. Only too often these undesirable "friends" are putting pressure on the employee to steal. In order to retain his status with the group, he may do as they demand.

Teenage Employees

Frustration is handled more successfully by most people as they grow older. From the experience of living, they find ways to face and to solve their problems. Because younger people are often unable to handle frustration well, they are most likely to find emotional release in antisocial behavior, frequently in crimes of theft.

This age group makes up a large percentage of a theft classification known as the "casual pilferer." This is the employee who steals because he sees an opportunity to do so without being caught—the money or merchandise is near at hand and available. Besides, everyone is doing it, and the store won't miss it.

Motivation for these individuals may vary. Sometimes they have an urgent need to prove themselves to their peer group, to show how smart they are or how much courage they have. Sometimes they steal just to impress their friends with their ability to get something for nothing or to experience the excitement of trying to get away with the theft. Stealing for the casual pilferer starts on a small scale, but may accelerate as time goes by, especially if the fact that his actions are undetected gives him confidence that further thefts will not be discovered.

Checklist for High-Risk Employees

Here is a checklist of the 14 signals that can help you spot the high-risk employee. You may want to keep this checklist in your desk and occasionally take it out to review it. Ask yourself, "Do I have anyone on my staff who fits into one of these categories?"

1) *Living beyond means*: there must be an "outside" source of income—it could be your profits!

2) *Emotionally unstable*: maladjusted employees often steal as a reaction to strong feelings of depression.

3) *Heavy drinker*: people who drink heavily are often under financial pressure; liquor may be used to quiet nerves, making stealing easier.

4) *Drug user*: impaired moral sense and judgment remove psychological barriers to theft.

5) *Gambler*: the compulsive gambler is more willing to take a chance—with horses, numbers, store merchandise, and cash.

6) *Overly attentive person*: deliberate efforts to ingratiate himself with his boss hide the employee's real activities.

7) *Long-time worker*: he may know the loopholes and methods to make stealing easy.

8) *Rule violator*: if he'll ignore store regulations, he may also show a lack of responsibility in handling store money and merchandise.

9) *Serious debts*: the employee will have to find a way to satisfy creditors, often at the expense of store profits.

10) *Family problems*: home emergencies and marital difficulties may bring on financial pressures that lead to theft.

11) *Chronic liar*: experience shows many liars also steal.

12) *Top-notch executive*: the ideal employee leaves clues to his dishonesty but is rarely suspected and even more rarely caught.

13) *Questionable associates*: store merchandise can easily find its way outside to a friendly "fence" via undesirable companions.

14) *Teenagers*: high potential for frustration makes for high-potential thieves.

If you have employees working for you who seem to fall into the categories listed in this section, have them tested several times by honesty shoppers, check their packages carefully when they leave the store, and keep an eye on them before they become a supervisory headache. But a word of caution about these characteristics: they are only *clues*. Not every person with these characteristics is dishonest. In the final analysis, each case must be weighed on its own merits.

4

METHODS OF EMPLOYEE THEFT

In spite of their best efforts, many stores find themselves unable to stop the spiraling costs of internal theft. The question is "Why?" One answer is that management really does not know *how* employees steal, and therefore cannot effectively set up counter-measures.

Security specialists estimate that there are over 4,000 methods of employee theft from retail stores. Fortunately, only a limited number of these are repeated techniques. Many of the others in this endless list are merely variations of fundamental methods. Most employee dishonesty involves cash register thefts, direct merchandise thefts, collusive thefts, embezzlement, and fraud.

Discovering a Method of Theft

It is often asked how employees discover a method of theft. They do so in several ways. The first is *by accident*. For example, an employee may discover a $5.00 bill lying behind a register drawer. He reasons that the register must have been short $5.00 perhaps a week ago, a month ago, or more. Since neither his manager nor anyone from the accounting department has indicated that the sum is missing, he concludes that management either is careless or considers the loss unimportant. The employee then decides to test out his theory. The next day he withholds $5.00 from the register. He is careful, however, to keep the bill handy so that he can claim it must have fallen behind the waste basket in case anyone should question him about it. But, of course, in most stores a shortage of this size is not noticed; and when he sees that management again makes no point of the missing money, the employee finds that he has discovered a successful method of theft.

A second way in which employees discover a method of theft is *from other employees*. To many members of the staff, successful stealing is something to be proud of. Fellow workers tend to admire the employee who can "beat the system." This sets up the problem of theft contamination, a condition that has long plagued retailing. Some thieves even become heroes in the minds of other workers. Methods of stealing are openly discussed by the staff over their soft drinks or coffee in the employee lounge, just as casually as one might discuss yesterday's shopping expedition or a movie seen the night before.

A third method, of course, occurs *through observation of weaknesses in the store's control systems or in the quality of its supervision.* When a dishonest employee discovers a loophole, he moves in to beat the system, securing the cooperation of other employees if necessary. He also learns a lot by watching other dishonest workers; and if he is unfortunate enough to have a dishonest supervisor, then soon not only he but most of his co-workers will also be stealing.

The following are some of the general categories of theft in supermarkets and other retail stores and a few sample cases to illustrate the forms they have taken. By reviewing some of these methods of theft, the manager has an important tool to help him locate and evaluate loopholes in his systems and to measure the effectiveness of his staff.

Altering Cash Register Records

Manipulating cash register records is a frequent method of theft. In one food store, a cashier stole successfully for many years. Three nights a week, the assistant store manager was on night duty until closing time at 9:30. Usually around 7:30, however, he left by the back receiving door and did not return until the next day. The employees accepted this good-naturedly as a prerogative of the man in charge. One cashier, however, saw it as an opportunity. As soon as the assistant manager left for the night, she immediately removed the tape and balanced the cash receipts, just as though she were closing out the register for the day. Then she reopened the register with a fresh tape and rang up sales until closing time. Before leaving, she destroyed the final tape and pocketed the money from these sales.

Because the store did not audit the cash register transaction numbers on the tapes or the cumulative register readings to assure continuity between each day's sales, the cashier avoided discovery for several years. Finally, a new controller audited the tapes and discovered her scheme. Based on the interrogation and on the limited evidence available, she confessed to stealing $81,000; but her actual thefts greatly exceeded that figure.

In another food store case, the doubling of the shrinkage problem in one large supermarket prompted management to call in an outside security consultant. After some investigation, his suspicions finally centered on the store manager, a man obviously living far above his income. Yet, when put under surveillance and watched every minute of the working day, there was no indication that he was doing anything wrong. In fact, his attitude was outgoing, and he appeared to be a normal, honest, hard-working store manager. The consultant's only clue to the theft was that the suspect never left the store directly at the close of day. Though store managers ordinarily work later than their subordinates, this manager appeared to be overzealous, putting in long hours every night of the week.

His curiosity aroused, the investigator took up a concealed location near the store and watched the store manager's activities after closing hours. At first, the observation didn't indicate any questionable activity. The manager looked as though he were checking out the registers, pulling tapes, and doing the routine tasks connected with tallying the day's receipts. It wasn't until the second or third night that the consultant suddenly realized what was happening. The manager was not counting the day's sales receipts. He was actually taking the detail tape for the day out of one of the 17 registers, putting in a fresh tape, and then reringing the day's sales. But he was shorting the register. This gave him a fresh detail tape which balanced to the penny minus the $20.00 to $50.00 he stole from the register. He turned in the phony register tapes and destroyed the originals.

Accepting Vendor Kickbacks

Another frequent type of employee theft is the kickback, a form of dishonesty almost traditional to American thinking. Many firms shut their eyes to the problem of vendor kickbacks or pretend that it has no solution. But it is actually quite prevalent, both at store level and among headquarter's staff.

At store level, vendor collusion is common on store-door deliveries. Working with a dishonest store employee, the dishonest vendor's representative may inflate the invoice by making a deliberate error in multiplying price extensions or in totaling the bill. He then splits the overpayment with the employee.

The deliveryman can also charge for 15 dozen loaves of bread and deliver only 10, selling the balance to another store and splitting the income with the dishonest employee. One enterprising meat manager in a large Boston supermarket developed a very profitable sideline. He would sign for meat that was never unloaded from the delivery truck, permitting the driver to sell it to various small markets. He and the driver would split the proceeds, a tidy $10,000 a year.

Other variations of vendor collusion at store level include: 1) delivering the correct number of items and then removing some of them under the guise of taking out stale merchandise, 2) removing merchandise that is actually stale and shorting the store on the credit due for such returns, or 3) stealing other store property from the back room or sales area.

To control such deceptive practices, some stores make it a rule to receive new merchandise at least 20 feet from the display. Receipts are not signed until the merchandise is actually counted and delivered; and all invoices are paid by check and mailed, rather than by cash from the store's funds, after having been verified by the accounting department.

At the supermarket headquarters level, buyers of perishables are often corrupted by dishonest suppliers who sell second-grade products at first-grade prices and offer kickbacks in return. Because of normal variations in the quality of perishable items, such kickbacks to meat and produce buyers are usually not detected. In some cases, the buyer himself assumes the responsibility for inspecting incoming merchandise. In other situations, he simply forces the receiving clerk to accept the substandard perishables to satisfy the supplier giving him his monthly kickback.

Rigged invoices are another typical buying-office fraud technique. One common method is for the buyer to approve an inflated invoice and to get a kickback from the supplier on the overpayment. But the kickback can also be made in the form of merchandise. One such manipulation devised by a men's clothing buyer resulted in substantial losses to a New York department store. Although he was employed by the New York store, the buyer opened his own men's specialty shop in suburban Long Island, New York. His enterprise proved quite profitable, principally because the invoices for his merchandise were placed through the company that employed him on Fifth Avenue. For many years the Fifth Avenue store unwittingly paid for all the clothing stocked in his private retail concern. To retain the business of the large department store, the vendors were compelled to divert some of the shipments to the buyer's private enterprise. If they refused, the buyer merely threatened to cancel their Fifth Avenue account.

In another instance of headquarters fraud, the executives of a major retail chain became suspicious that its buyers and top management were receiving substantial kickbacks from some manufacturers. The rumor was circulated that the buyers were receiving their kickbacks in the form of government bonds. So the head of the company hired a team of investigators and provided them with the names of all the buyers, their secretaries, wives, and family members. The investigators were then sent into the New York City marketplace where they spent many weeks going through the public records of people's names and addresses who had been assigned such bonds. The research was arduous, but it paid off. The investigators discovered the names of seven of the company's highly paid merchandising executives who had received more than $200,000 in kickbacks from manufacturers.

Selling Below Retail

Giving special prices to family and friends is a common method of theft. This is a difficult method of theft to detect, and it leads to the loss of millions of dollars in profits annually. In one food store, a cashier had her friend go through the checkout lane two and three times a day with $20.00 and $30.00 worth of groceries for which she charged him only $2.00. When she was finally caught, she admitted that they had stolen $16,000 in merchandise.

In supermarkets, meat is always a high-theft item. More than one store has discovered the head of the meat department passing out choice steaks and other prime cuts to his relatives and neighborhood friends at reduced prices. One meat man had his wife visit him almost every day in the meat department. He would wrap a package of expensive meat in brown paper, dash a crayoned price of 89 cents on the package (the hamburger price), and she would dutifully go through the checkout lane paying 89 cents for $20.00 worth of meat. Stores that have discovered this particular type of ruse now have the meat department use cellophane bags so the cashier can see the meat that is being paid for at the checkout counter.

Selling merchandise below retail among employees is also a costly method of theft in non-food stores. Many employees, in fact, do not look upon this practice as a form of dishonesty. They feel the store can easily afford these "discounts." One saleswoman in a basement candy department admitted stealing $1,500 in cash on sales and also confessed that she had purchased stolen merchandise, such as jackets, blouses, dresses, and jewelry, from stockboys in the store. Although she recognized that both these activities were dishonest, she did not feel she was being dishonest in selling candy to her friends at reduced prices. Although the candy retailed for $1.00 to $1.50 a pound, she sold it to her friends at the rate of five pounds for 10 cents!

Once discount selling starts among employees, the speed of such contamination is unbelievable. In fact, it sometimes reaches the point where every employee in the store automatically gives special discounts to other employees, even when the employee is not a personal friend. They may also take large discounts when writing up their own sales. In a typical case, a salesman purchased several shirts worth $13.95 each and wrote up a sales check charging himself only 55 cents each.

Giving Out Free Merchandise

In addition to discount selling, many employees feel that "free" merchandise is a fringe benefit to which they are justifiably entitled. At a New York supermarket, for example, the checkers were in league with the managers of the meat and dairy departments. Each manager was stealing about $10.00 worth of merchandise from his department on a weekly basis and giving an equal amount to others in the group. The loot was being passed through the checkout lanes by the children of the thieves, and the loss was between $7,000 and $9,000 a year.

In a Chicago discount store, records were distributed free to other employees. Stockboys, restaurant employees, salespeople from other departments—any store employee could obtain records without paying for them. Whenever a co-worker purchased one record, the clerk would always stuff the bag with half a dozen "gift" records. In return, these co-workers handed out merchandise stolen from their stock. One of the saleswomen in records had obtained 15 stolen cashmere sweaters in exchange for several albums. She also received a weekly package of stolen cosmetics from the salesclerk in the cosmetic department in return for the records.

In another case, two saleswomen used the locker room to exchange stolen merchandise. One worked in the blouse department and often stole several blouses for her friend which she would put into her accomplice's locker. The other woman, who worked in the handbag department, did the same with handbags. The lockers became their own private post office box.

Issuing Fraudulent Refunds

Stealing cash is an easy matter for any employee who has access to both the cash room and a refund book. One supermarket manager supplemented his salary by writing phony refunds, totaling about $50.00 a week. It was a simple matter for him to write out a fraudulent refund slip every night after the cash room employees had gone home and to remove that sum from the store's cash fund. Fortunately, however, in an effort to improve customer relations, the company mailed questionnaires to all customers who had received refunds during the previous six-month period. The number of returned questionnaires marked "addressee unknown" alerted management to the phony refund slips, which were easily traced to the store manager.

Many dishonest discount and department store employees have also found fraudulent refunds to be a profitable route to easy cash. One service representative working at a refund desk admitted that, during the past four years, she had written over $42,000 worth of fraudulent refunds. She used the money to decorate her house and to buy new furniture, clothes, and a car. The service representative's scheme was to have a customer sign for a legitimate refund. After the customer had gone, she would add several fictitious items of merchandise to the signed refund and would pay herself the additional money out of her cash drawer. The store had a poor refund control system. It should not have allowed the person writing and authorizing the refund to have access to the cash for payment.

Another saleswoman admitted that, over the past year, she had defrauded the store of $6,000 by writing phony refunds. She used the name and address of a customer who ordered merchandise to be sent C.O.D., wrote a fictitious refund for the identical merchandise, forged the customer's name, and then took the phony refund to the credit desk and received the cash.

Committing Early and Late Thefts

Often supermarket store managers and their assistants are given a lot of liberty to enter the store when it is normally closed. In Houston, Texas, for example, one manager came in on Sunday and worked on records relating to the purchase of merchandise, on payrolls, and on other items of this nature. During the two or three hours in which he worked, his wife and two children took shopping baskets and rolled them around the floor of the supermarket, filling them up with food and other merchandise which they loaded into the family car.

This man's thefts might have been discovered earlier if the store had kept records of employee purchases. Such records would have revealed that, although he was the manager of the store, he never purchased any groceries. The only possible explanations were that: 1) he was buying food in some other store, or 2) he was stealing food rather than buying it.

After discovering this theft, the company took a unique approach to closing the loophole. To encourage employees to shop in the store they instituted employee discounts. They also assigned someone to check out all employee purchases. After totaling the order and figuring the discount, which is approved by the manager, the checker writes the employee's name and payroll number on the receipt tape, which is filed by date. It is then an easy matter to review the receipt tapes when thefts of merchandise by an employee are suspected. By doing random checks, this method of control also enables the company to learn why honest employees who shop elsewhere find their own store unsuitable, despite the discount available to them.

Food stores are particularly susceptible to employee thefts because of the long hours they are open. Many stores do night stocking, yet over and over again night stockers are found to be stealing on a large scale. Often these groups are poorly supervised and have the full run of the store. During the late-night hours, street traffic is at a minimum, so they feel secure in removing bulky cartons. One store discovered that the night stockboys were throwing wild parties and inviting their friends into the store at night. They barbecued store steaks in the parking lot and feasted on store beer and other snacks.

More serious are the organized rings of night stockers who clip the store for thousands of dollars worth of merchandise. One company found the stockers were taking out stolen steaks in empty boxes of soap powder; in addition, they were loading their car trunks each night with a variety of store foodstuffs. One group of stockers even went so far as to pull up in a rental truck and load it to capacity.

In another case, a security specialist was called in to investigate supermarket losses. He discovered a whole night crew working together to steal $14,500 worth of goods over an 18-month period. The method they used took advantage of a loophole in the store's security system. Every night the central alarm system was turned off for 15 minutes to allow the night crew to enter the store. That quarter of an hour was sufficient, however, for the crew to pass in and out several times carrying away armloads of merchandise.

In department stores, early and late thefts can take other forms. One department store that left the day's change bank in the cash registers overnight began to get regular complaints from cashiers on the day shift that the bank was short $5.00 or $10.00 when they opened the registers for the day. At first, the manager thought the cashiers going off duty were stealing the money at night, but finally suspicion centered on the night stocking crew.

Observation was impossible, so the store manager had a simple electrical switch built into the registers. If the drawer was opened at night after the registers were locked, the switch would be tripped, operating a camera concealed above the manager's cash office at the end of the checkout lanes. Three days after he installed the device, he found on entering the store in the morning that the camera had been tripped. He rushed the film to a developing studio and received an 8 x 10 inch photo of the night stocking supervisor with his hand in the till.

Investigation disclosed that the night worker had found a key in a variety store across the street that opened the panel on the back of the register, allowing him to pull the side trip lever springing the drawer open. The thief was caught before his thefts got out of hand; his apprehension also led to the removal of suspicion from several of the late cashiers and to management's having more suitable locks installed on the back panel of the registers.

A man who worked in a sporting goods department in another store, when finally caught, admitted that his method of theft was to select merchandise early in the morning before the other employees arrived, to conceal it in a drawer behind his counter, and to put it in a bag during the day. He would then take it out of the building in the evening using a customer exit not authorized for employees. His thefts amounted to many hundreds of dollars worth of merchandise before he was finally caught.

In another department store, a salesman stole merchandise for himself by wearing it out of the building or concealing it in his pockets. His method of theft required him to come into the store an hour or so before the usual store opening time in order to wander through the selling areas and pick out the merchandise that he wanted to steal. The store obviously was overpermissive in allowing employees to roam through the dim selling floors before the normal store hours. If employees must work in the store before or after hours, then the premises should be fully illuminated and proper supervision should be provided.

Stealing from Cash Registers

Cash register thefts take many forms. Here are only a few. A woman working in a store's pantry shop, where purchases were rung up in the department, admitted that over the past eight years she had stolen $16,000 in cash from sales. She stole by underringing approximately $5.00 on each customer purchase. A review of her register tapes revealed that she never rang up more than $2.00 on a sale, although the merchandise she sold often totaled far higher. The lack of a proper auditing system enabled her to do this successfully for eight years, with neither the department manager nor the buyer nor anyone in the auditing department ever aware that the amounts on her register tapes differed greatly from those rung on other register tapes in the same pantry shop.

In one chain of food stores in Southern California, there was a particular store that had shortages greatly in excess of the other five stores in the chain. This store was given special attention by a security consultant, and it was found that where cashiers in the chain's other stores were averaging no more than one or two voided sales slips per day, in this store checkout supervisors often signed for as many as 20 or 30. The store did not have a policy that the supervisor had to see the customer involved in such transactions, and employees would save their "void" slips and give them to the checkout supervisor at the end of the day. Dutifully and meaninglessly, he would initial them. It did not seem strange to him that his employees were making so many errors. When caught, the employees admitted thefts by the phony "voided" sales of $26,000 over a six-month period.

Another variation of cash register thefts involves the use of register receipts. To accomplish this, the checker retains the sales receipt on a sale, rather than giving it to the customer. When another purchase is made for a similar amount, she pockets the money from that sale without ringing it up and gives the second customer the withheld sales receipt from the first customer. Sometimes customers are careless with their sales receipts and drop them on the floor by the checkout counter or leave them on the checkout stand. This provides the dishonest checker with a golden opportunity to substitute that receipt on a later sale of the same amount. The dishonest supermarket checker is best able to use this technique on single-item sales and is apt to steal in this manner on such high-ticket items as cartons of cigarettes.

No listing of employee cash register thefts would be complete without recalling the ruse perpetrated by a supermarket manager and his assistant in a large Illinois food store. This store was part of a large chain of supermarkets, and for several years it had been a "problem store" to company management. It consistently came out of each inventory period with unusually large shortages. Every effort by management to uncover the source of the trouble failed. Security audits were made; investigators were placed in undercover jobs in the store; special controls were placed on credits and invoices, but all to no avail. A few minor thefts were uncovered among employees, but neither the arrest of these thieves nor the arrest of a large number of shoplifters had any marked effect on the shortages.

Then, one day, a new assistant controller who had become

intrigued with the shortage problems of the store decided to spend a few days just observing the operation. He wasn't looking for anything in particular. In fact, he didn't know what he was looking for, but he hoped he'd recognize whatever it was when he saw it. And he did.

On the third day of his vigil, he was standing at the front of the store casually watching the checkers working on the registers with their lines of customers. Everything seemed routine, but the assistant controller sensed that something was radically wrong. He had an intuitive feeling that he was at that very moment looking at the cause of the store's high losses, but he couldn't put his finger on it. Then it hit him. He couldn't believe his eyes. Slowly he counted them again. Yes, that was the answer! The store had 13 checkout lanes, but the company had installed only 12. And each day the store turned in register tapes and sales receipts for only 12 cash registers. The thirteenth "ghost" register was the key to the store's staggering shortages. Further investigation revealed it had been installed by the wily manager and his assistant.

The thirteenth checkout lane was operated only a few hours each day. After all, the thieves didn't want to be too greedy. But when it was in operation, every sale rung on the thirteenth register went into the pockets of the manager and his assistant. The diabolical duo had constructed their own extra checkout lane, purchased their own cash register, and opened up their own gold mine. These men had stolen for years before the assistant controller detected the extra cash register. Their thefts were estimated at better than $80,000 a year.

Although this case appears to be unique, three other supermarkets in various parts of the country have also found that their store managers had installed money-making machines in the form of an extra checkout aisle and privately owned cash register. The moral is obvious. Periodically count your cash registers!

Using the Back Door

The back door of the store is a common route for theft. Cartons can be shoved near the rear exit and quickly tossed into an employee's car when no one is watching. Small merchandise, such as hosiery, is often stolen by sliding the items under the receiving door after it is closed for the day. The thieves then drive around behind the store and snatch the items off the dock after the store closes.

At a Long Island, New York, supermarket which required all rear doors to be locked, employees complained of poor ventilation, so the manager agreed to leave a back door open. One clerk, apparently needing more fresh air, made frequent trips outside—each time carrying a case of merchandise with him. He deposited the cartons in his car, which was always parked near the receiving door, another infraction of the rules. Over a period of nine months, he hauled away $14,000 worth of goods. He was, it turned out, the chief supplier of his grandfather's corner grocery store.

Food warehouses suffer from similar thefts with cartons of merchandise being tossed over a protecting fence to be later retrieved by the thieves. In other cases, merchandise has been left in a railroad car which supposedly had been unloaded and is then pulled out of the protected area into a nearby siding. The thieves return to the car in the dark hours of early morning and retrieve the cartons.

One particularly audacious theft involved a distribution center protected by a high wire fence and a uniformed guard at the gate. The center was closed from Saturday noon until Monday morning, but a guard was at the gate at all times. The employee thieves moved in by sending a man disguised as another guard to relieve the man at the gate. Dressed in a uniform that had been stolen from the outside guard agency and knowing the name of the guard's boss, it was easy for the impersonator to persuade the man on duty to go to another assignment several miles away. As soon as the real guard left the premises, five employees in the theft team moved in. Using the company's tractors, for which they had obtained duplicate keys, they systematically removed four company trailers, which were lined up at the receiving bays, loaded with merchandise for the Monday morning delivery.

Writing Phony Bottle Refunds

Although individual thefts may be small, the cumulative loss from fraudulent claims for bottle refunds is often staggering. Many stores are careless in handling their bottle refunds. They allow the checker to write the bottle refund slip, put it in the register, and pay the customer a cash amount for the bottle or credit the bottles to the sale. The dishonest checker soon finds she can write phony bottle refunds, put them into the register, and pocket the cash with little fear of detection.

Avoiding Package Controls

Unlike department stores with multiple exits, customers enter and leave most supermarkets through doors at the front of the store where the checkstands are located. Since this area is generally supervised by the manager or an assistant, most supermarket employees are required to leave the store through the customer exits where they can be observed, rather than through a back door. This helps to control thefts that are caused by employees who try to remove stolen merchandise from the store. But employees who are bent on stealing can be quite resourceful.

One meat man in a Michigan supermarket carried several steaks out of the store in the evening two or three times a week by concealing them under his hat. He had been doing this successfully for 10 months and probably could have continued his deception indefinitely, except for a packaging defect. His game was up one night when the store manager noticed a streak of blood running down his cheek.

In multiple-exit stores, employees are usually not allowed to use customer exits, but must enter and leave the store through a door that is supervised and reserved specifically for employee use. Yet, even though the employee exit is supervised, employee package control systems are notoriously weak because checkers fail to compare the contents of the employees' packages with their sales slips.

A typical example of this type of theft involved a saleswoman who worked in the hosiery department of a discount store. She would buy a small, inexpensive item of merchandise and then use the sales check to take a large package of costly hosiery out of the store. In one instance, she bought an inexpensive pair of gloves for 98 cents. She then accumulated several boxes of hosiery in the drawer behind her counter. She slipped her stolen items into a paper bag and on leaving the store in the evening she used the 98 cents sales receipt from the gloves as verification of her purchase.

Using the same ploy, another saleswoman would first purchase one phonograph record and then make up a package containing several expensive albums. With the sales check from the purchase of the single record, she was able to take the bag of record albums out of the building at night. In this same department, one stockboy was found to have stolen a record collection of 1,500 albums in this manner, while a relatively new employee admitted possessing 150 stolen records and 26 stolen albums. Small merchandise such as this can also be easily stuffed into a jacket or pockets.

A saleswoman in the jewelry department stole by duplicating a customer's purchase. In one instance, a customer charged a necklace and pair of earrings. After the customer had left the department, the employee wrote an identical sales check and used it as authorization for wrapping a duplicate set of jewelry for herself. She then took the items out of the store at closing time, successfully defeating the employee package control system.

In another case, an employee shoplifted sweaters by taking them into a fitting room and concealing them beneath her clothes. She also accumulated other stolen merchandise in her locker. To get these items out of the store, she made a package of stolen goods and left at 5:30 on a Monday when there was no door check of employees because the store did not close until 9 P.M.

For the same reason, package controls of part-time employees are complicated. Their hours don't correspond to store closing times, so the store neglects to provide an adequate security check on their packages.

Some employees go so far as to flaunt the controls openly. In one store, an undercover agent discovered after many weeks of investigation that the man employed to manage the return goods room was stealing the returned merchandise. He had stolen clocks, radios, irons, rugs, and literally hundreds of other items of merchandise for 17 years without being detected. He simply took the stolen merchandise out an unauthorized exit at the warehouse either on his lunch hour or at warehouse closing time and put it in the trunk of his car. Because of his status as a supervisor, the employees guarding the warehouse exit were afraid to challenge him when he walked past them carrying his stolen merchandise.

Mailing Out Merchandise

Dishonest employees who mail merchandise out of the store are not uncommon. In Portland, Oregon, for example, a leading department store had a post office branch located in the selling area of the store. One buyer had been mailing suits, topcoats, overcoats, and even yards of men's fabric on a daily basis over a period of years to contacts in Los Angeles, San Diego, and other key centers in the West. The extent of his thefts has never been accurately measured, but it amounted to several hundred thousand dollars.

Another example of the mail-out theft occurred in Kansas City, Missouri, where an employee in the shipping department of an auto supply company mailed packages of merchandise to his roommate via parcel post. When apprehended, the goods recovered amounted to $30,000 and included television sets, radios, tape recorders, typewriters, tires, tools, and electrical appliances.

In another store, a package sorter hired as a part-time Christmas worker admitted opening packages that were supposed to be mailed to customers. He destroyed the wrappings and confiscated small merchandise, such as wallets, jewelry, and hosiery, by putting them into his pockets.

Pocketing C.O.D.'s

Department stores often have C.O.D. theft problems. For example, the management of a department store in Detroit woke up one day to discover that many C.O.D. payments went unpaid for three to six months, and, in some cases, the money had not been paid in for as long as two years. Records did not show that the merchandise had been returned to the store.

It took only a minimal amount of investigation to uncover the fact that the delivery drivers were pocketing C.O.D. money because the store had failed to control these transactions. As is true in most employee theft situations which are allowed to continue over a period of time, contamination had already set in. It was found that 28 of the store's 75 drivers were stealing cash on their C.O.D.'s. The amounts involved varied from several hundred dollars to several thousand dollars.

The store was faced with a crisis. Moving in to arrest the thieves would mean wiping out a third of the delivery operation. This would disrupt the entire company and cost a million dollars in customer sales. In addition, the store wanted to avoid the unhappy newspaper publicity which would follow any such wholesale firing of personnel. It had no choice but to take the loss and tighten its auditing and control procedures on C.O.D.'s.

Cashing in on Layaway Transactions

The layaway department has been one of the most susceptible to theft. Control records and procedures are usually poorly designed or are not enforced. One employee in a layaway department said he took cash from some transactions where the layaway merchandise was missing and an adjustment credit had been written. If the merchandise later showed up, he kept the cash equivalent to the adjustment credit. He also admitted taking accumulated parcel post charges and accumulated C.O.D. service charges. He estimated his thefts at $1,600.

Perpetrating Service Department Thefts

Collusive thefts by employees represent some of the most complex cases. In one California department store, carpet sales had fallen off considerably due to cancellations from customers who complained of slow deliveries. This was particularly disturbing to one vice-president, because he knew that the carpet installers put in a tremendous amount of overtime. He approved their overtime hours each week as the sheets crossed his desk. Eventually, this vice-president became suspicious of the situation and decided to have a study made of the firm's systems and procedures to see if there were any loopholes in his controls.

It was discovered that the company had a competitor stealing the store's customers. Once an order for carpeting was received and the exact measurements were taken by one of the store's employees, the manager of the carpet department would delay installation until the exasperated customer would call and cancel the order. The rug department manager would then promptly call the customer back, posing as a representative of an entirely different company with a fictitious name and address. He would offer to install the same carpeting the customer had ordered, immediately, and at a much lower price. He explained that he had heard about the problem the customer was having with store "A" from a friend who worked in the rug department there. He knew they were behind in their orders and were having difficulty in getting stock. He could offer this merchandise at a lower price because he operated from a warehouse and had low overhead.

His explanation sounded logical, and, of course, the customer was pleased and relieved at the possibility of finally getting some action on the carpet. She was also delighted at the fact that the price was considerably lower than she had originally expected to pay at the store.

The manager who phoned from the fictitious company was, of course, telling the truth. He could sell the carpet at a very low price because he didn't have very much overhead. In fact, his overhead was nonexistent because both the carpet he sold and the labor charges for installing the carpet were paid for by the store. By the time the manager and his staff of 16 installers were arrested, the store was out more than $250,000 in merchandise and another $200,000 in overtime pay spent in installing the stolen carpets.

In discount stores, where carpet installations are more often made by outside contract firms, losses can occur through excessive labor charges, stolen goods, or a combination of both if a store employee is working in collusion with the outside contractor.

Similar dishonest activities occur in many service and repair departments. One aggressive appliance deliveryman would make his deliveries in the morning and then use the company truck and appliance parts to make repairs during the day. Unsuspecting customers, relieved to have their equipment repaired promptly and at a reasonable cost, would eagerly follow his instructions to pay him in cash or to make out a check payable to him. The customers' names, of course, were obtained from company records. Fortunately for the store, his extra-curricular activities were discovered one day when he failed to make a service call and the impatient customer called the company to complain.

Stores that service television sets often suffer serious inventory losses on replacement parts that are stolen by repair personnel who moonlight during evenings or weekends, or who run their own private businesses during company hours. Here, again, the dishonest employees get their customers from the company's records, being sure to avoid those customers who are covered by a service contract.

Creating False Markdowns

Theft by marking down merchandise to "as is" prices is a common occurrence. In one warehouse, an employee who wanted an expensive item, such as a refrigerator, would put a small scratch on it. Then, when the buyer made a tour of the warehouse, he would point out the scratch and suggest that the price be reduced because of the damage. The buyer would write a markdown, and the warehouse employee would later purchase the merchandise at the reduced price.

In this same warehouse, another dishonest employee would send a stockboy to the store selling department to ask for a markdown sales check on a particular item he wanted. The thief would write on the note that the buyer had marked down a damaged carpet sweeper to $1.50. The messenger that he sent to the store would go to the appliance department where the carpet sweeper was sold, give the note and $1.50 to the salesperson, and receive a sales check. This sales check would be used by the thief to pass a new carpet sweeper out of the warehouse.

A variation on the markdown ruse occurs in many stores when the company allows rolls of blank price tags to be kept in selling departments. This enables dishonest employees to write their own prices on merchandise, far below the correct retail price. The employee attaches the fraudulent price tag to the merchandise and buys it or sells it to friends who come into the store. This careless control of price tags can be a most costly practice. One clerk who did this, when finally apprehended, admitted thefts of merchandise amounting to $27,000. With her removal from the scene, the inventory shortages in her department dropped 31 percent.

Misusing Salvage Receipts

Some stores are careful in controlling salvage, but others are not. In one store, salvage slips intended to be used for taking home old lumber and discarded fixtures were used by dishonest employees as a pass for removing packages of new merchandise. The man who approved the salvage slips was shown a pile of salvage lumber or a discarded display unit, and he would then sign a salvage slip, assuming that it would be used to take that particular item from the warehouse. Instead, ladders, picnic tables, beach umbrellas, bicycles, and other merchandise were removed. In some cases, the employees paid a dollar or two for the salvage goods; but more often they paid nothing.

Other variations on the use of salvage sales to conceal thefts of new merchandise are also possible. One stockboy obtained a book of blank salvage receipts from the supply department and used them to put himself into business. He would steal new merchandise from stock and sell it to his friends at discount prices, pretending it was salvage goods. He issued forged salvage receipts so that his friends could take their merchandise out of the building. He then pocketed the money from these sales.

Although this employee had no authority to quote prices or to sign salvage receipts, he was able to operate his private store for many months, unnoticed by management, because the store did an inadequate job of auditing and supervising salvage sales. When management finally uncovered the operation, it decided to prevent future instances by selling all such merchandise to an outside salvage contractor.

Tapping Pneumatic Tubes

Although the pneumatic tube which carries money to a central cash room for making change is not as common as it used to be, some stores still use it. In a certain Midwestern store, one of the maintenance men discovered that the cash room tube went through the top of his supply room. At first, he paid little attention to this fact; but later, as he listened to the sound of the tube whooshing through the pipe over his head, he had an idea. With only a few minor adjustments, he calculated, he could add a branch office to the store's cash-handling system.

One evening, he stayed late and constructed a diverting tube. By pushing a lever he could redirect the tube so it would drop down into his supply room. Each day on his lunch hour, he sat in the room and, as the tubes came by, he pushed the slot causing the cash carrier to drop down into his personal cash box. He then removed the sales slip and stamped it with a paid stamp which he had stolen from the office supply department. The stamp, of course, carried the correct date and looked legitimate in every way. The engineer then returned the sales slip to the change tube and sent it rocketing back up to the selling department. When change was necessary, of course, he provided it. Over the years, working on his lunch hours, he was able to steal an estimated $181,000.

Chances are he would still be stealing if he hadn't taken a vacation. While he was on vacation, a relief worker discovered that the door to the supply closet was locked, so he went to the guard and got a master key to the room. When he opened the door, he was astounded to discover the extra cash tube and the change tray which had been so cleverly devised by the maintenance man.

Because the store moved too hastily into the case and did not catch the thief in the act of stealing, it was unable to prosecute him. So they made a deal. The thief paid back $71,000 to the store from his "savings." The store generously allowed him to keep his $55,000 home, his luxury car, and his boat. He still lives in Florida in quiet retirement, enjoying a leisurely life made possible by his personal pension plan.

Falsifying Employee Discounts

Stores that have small concessions selling high-ticket items sometimes find themselves being cheated by a dishonest salesperson. In one instance, a dishonest clerk sold a customer a set of matched gold coins worth $100 for cash. He charged the customer the full retail price. After the customer left the store, he wrote the sales check as an employee purchase and took a 20 percent discount (which was the normal discount given store employees). He then pocketed the 20 percent cash difference on the sale. The store procedure was weak because employee discounts didn't have to be authorized by a supervisor.

Stealing Charge Plates

A woman employed in the store's credit office admitted stealing charge plates returned by customers. She took them off the desk of the credit office manager and used the stolen plates to shop in branch stores. Sometimes she gave them to her friends and family, who made thousands of dollars worth of fraudulent charge purchases in all of the company stores. When finally caught, the total amount involved was over $67,000.

In another store, a salesclerk in the women's glove department admitted stealing a customer's charge plate and then using the plate to make fraudulent charges. On her day off or during the evenings when she was not working, she visited the company's branch stores, returned the merchandise, and received cash refunds for it.

Embezzling Funds

Embezzlement is a form of theft which involves the fraudulent appropriation of cash, checks, etc., which have been entrusted to the employee's care. The most vulnerable areas are the bookkeeping department, where checks are disbursed, and the cash office.

Forging checks is a form of embezzlement found in many companies. According to W. E. Rose, an authority on crimes involving bank clerks, "employees have used more than 800 different ways of defrauding their companies with bank checks." One of the most common methods is for an employee to make out a company check to his own name. The employee takes the cancelled check out of the incoming mail from the bank and destroys it. Usually, he conceals the theft by raising the amount on several legitimate cancelled checks.

Other methods of check disbursement thefts include: 1) seizing a check payable to the company and forging the company name so it can be cashed, 2) seizing a check payable to a resource and forging the resource's name, 3) raising the face amount of a check or changing the name of the payee, 4) paying an invoice twice and appropriating the second check, and 5) stealing a check made payable to cash.

Thefts committed by dishonest bookkeepers and cashiers are usually very costly because they are unlikely to be uncovered until considerable damage has been done. The bookkeeping and cash offices also provide the opportunity for many types of fraud.

Impostered charges, delaying or shorting bank deposits, setting up a dummy resource firm so that the checks paid by the store on the dummy invoices can be cashed, padding the employee payroll by adding phony names, cashing unclaimed wage checks, and so on, are just a few of the more common techniques of embezzlement and fraud.

Others are: overloading expense accounts, inserting fictitious ledger sheets, stealing incoming payments, covering petty cash thefts with phony I.O.U.'s planting postdated bank checks in petty cash funds, and making false bookkeeping entries.

A dishonest employee can get away with any one of these types of crimes in a company that lacks adequate controls on inventory, cash, payroll, and expenses.

Manipulating Computers

This type of theft holds promise for greater exploitation in the future. Many companies make up their payroll by computer. In one particular food store chain with central offices in the Midwest, an assistant manager was studying computer programming at night in a local school. After several months of study, he came into the building one Saturday and told the guard at the door that he was going to do some work in his office. First, he made sure that no one was on the sixth floor where the computer room was located; then he went in and spent about half an hour manipulating the computer program tape. He "tipped" the computer so that from that week forward his salary, which was then $155 a week, was punched out by the computer on a computer-written bank check as $355 a week—a very neat raise of $200.

It might be supposed that the food chain would soon catch on to this type of embezzlement, but it was more than two and a half years before the auditors, trying to locate the discrepancy in payout figures, finally uncovered the culprit. By that time, he had embezzled more than $27,000 from the firm.

Computer crimes of this type are becoming more and more frequent; and as retailing becomes more sophisticated and the equipment becomes more complex and less understandable to general management, there will be increasingly serious crimes related to manipulation of computer records. This young embezzler was a pioneer in the field of computer thefts. It will not be long before thieves have the capacity to wipe out entire retail chains by using the firm's own computer programs to embezzle millions of dollars.

Duplicating Keys

Keys must be carefully protected against theft or duplication without the knowledge of management. One careless manager, for example, left his store keys on a stockroom shelf. A sharp-eyed stockboy "borrowed" the keys and had duplicates cut while on his coffee break. He then sold the duplicate keys to a neighborhood gang of hoodlums. The following weekend the gang rented a truck, backed it up to the rear platform of the store, and cleaned the store out. Loss: $56,000.

In Portland, Oregon, a shrewd porter managed to steal a key to the outside street door of the store. He slipped into the maintenance department one lunch hour, opened the maintenance supervisor's locker, and took the key off the ring. He had it duplicated at a nearby store and replaced the key on the supervisor's key ring before he returned from lunch. As a result, the porter was able to steal merchandise successfully for many months. His technique was simple. He unlocked the customer exit, parked his car near the door, and filled the trunk nightly with store merchandise. One evening, a passing police patrol car became suspicious of his actions and reported him to management.

It was only a matter of days before they had the porter under arrest.

Following his apprehension, all locks were changed and a new keying system was installed. Tighter controls were put on the keys, and periodic inventories were taken to insure keys had not been lost or misplaced. Each key was also stamped "Do Not Duplicate." Carelessness with keys can be costly.

Steps to Take

Employee thefts are usually the result of weaknesses in supervision or weaknesses in control systems and procedures. But, probably, we should also take some personal blame. As retailers, we are extremely conscious of operating costs. In recent years, we have substantially reduced our supervision, our training, and considerably reduced and weakened our control systems and procedures. While we are tempting the general public by displaying our merchandise openly and unprotected, we are also tempting our potentially dishonest employees by providing them the opportunity to steal with little fear of being caught.

These few cases mentioned here are largely the day-in and day-out types of employee dishonesty, but they represent only a small sampling of the variety of theft techniques used by dishonest employees. When one sees one or two types of dishonesty, it is easy to believe that "if you've seen one method of theft, you've seen them all." Although this is easy to assume, it isn't necessarily true.

Stand at your employee exit door one evening and watch the people leaving. Everything looks fine. There is no visible sign of stealing, yet somehow, unconsciously, you will get the feeling that at least one of them must be stealing. The question is "How?" Perhaps one night as you watch a cashier leaving the store, wearing a new mink coat, you secretly wonder if it was paid for out of your store's profits. On another occasion, you glimpse Johnny, the stockboy, sneaking out across the back receiving dock toward his car during the lunch hour when the back room is deserted. As he walks across the lot, you notice a substantial bulge under his jacket; and as he opens the car door and gets in, you wonder if possibly that bulge under his jacket could be stolen merchandise.

If you've ever had these thoughts, you are not alone. Store managers across the country share these same doubts and concerns about their people. The big problem is always the same. Where should you put your control emphasis? How do you determine what areas need attention? There is no easy way, but of prime importance is a good knowledge of the methods of employee theft. Knowing these methods can help to alert the manager to any unusual employee activities. It can raise questions in his mind when he sees a situation that should be investigated. It alerts him to behavior that betrays dishonesty. It can indicate where there is a need for a surprise register audit, where there is a need for a spot check of an employee package, or where some other investigative technique is required.

Knowing how employees steal is also useful in training key personnel on their way up the administrative ladder so that they better understand the purpose of certain control procedures and the reason why they are supposed to enforce store rules. In other words, the store manager needs to know how dishonest employees use accomplices to conceal their thefts, why ''void'' sales receipts are dangerous to authorize without investigation, how a dishonest bookkeeper can embezzle store funds, and so on. Supervisory attitude is often the key to control. Usually dishonesty is not caused by faulty control systems and procedures but rather because the controls were not properly enforced.

By occasionally reviewing this chapter concerning the methods of theft, a manager will soon learn how to spot those loopholes and weaknesses in his systems and procedures that need to be tightened and corrected. Analysis is the vital first step in reducing internal thefts, and reviewing your company's control systems in light of the more common methods of employee theft is a good place to begin.

Of course, just knowing the more common methods of employee theft is not sufficient in itself to stop such activities. But it can serve to guide the manager in his search for areas of his operation that need to be investigated. In the end, it is the supervisor of each individual department who has the tremendous responsibility of being alert to the dishonest employee theft problem. It is important that every manager constantly tries to remember not to be too complacent or too smug about the security of his operation. Internal theft is a very real danger in every single department in the store, no matter how well it's managed. It requires continuous attention and continuous monitoring to keep employee theft under control.

Counter-measures to employee theft cannot be designed unless you know *how* employees steal. The store and department manager should be familiar with the frequently used methods of theft. This knowledge will help each to detect and prevent such thefts. It is knowledge that gives you an important edge in the battle to control theft attacks by your store's unknown and invisible opponents.

Catching a dishonest employee serves little purpose if nothing is done to change the conditions which led to the dishonesty. Each dishonest employee case needs to be carefully reviewed and the causes determined. The weaknesses in the control systems and procedures, the breakdown in supervision, or whatever has allowed a particular type of theft to flourish should be located and corrected. Each case is an important lesson to help you improve the security of the store.

PART THREE

Applying Investigative Techniques

5

HONESTY SHOPPING

The testing of salespeople and cashiers by honesty shoppers is a proven method of investigation. By posing as customers and making cash purchases throughout the store, these detectives are able to test the integrity of the company's employees. In department stores, this method of investigation probably uncovers more dishonest employees than any other single security effort. It is also effective in stores with checkstands and in discount operations where registers are centrally situated in departments throughout the selling areas.

Theft of cash on sales is a major cause of high inventory shortages. Dishonest employees often prefer money over merchandise because it is simpler to steal and easier to remove from the premises without detection. Thefts ranging from $40.00 to $150 a day per dishonest worker are not uncommon, and it is easy to see how a substantial theft figure can be reached in a short period of time.

In addition to being the most effective means of curtailing such losses, honesty shopping is one of the few security efforts in which the money recovered generally exceeds the store's financial outlay in apprehending the culprits. For example, one large department store, using its own shoppers, was able to conduct 3,195 tests at a cost of 60 cents per test. While this represented a total investment of $1,917, the resulting cases allowed the store to recover $3,583. The following year, management nearly doubled the number of shopping tests to 6,108, increasing its costs from $1,917 to $3,664. The returns justified the decision. Cases increased by 451 percent, and recoveries soared to $19,780.

Though shopping is usually profitable, it is still valuable even when the cost of running the tests is not justified by the immediate cash return. Each time a dishonest employee is identified and discharged, the amount of his admitted and recovered theft is important, but not so important as the potential amount he might have stolen if he had not been apprehended. The salesclerk, for example, who admits stealing $80.00 a week on sales gives the store a large cash recovery. But the loss might have been much greater when you consider that, statistically speaking, he could have been employed some 12 more years with the store. By detecting the thief, the honesty shopper may well have prevented future thefts of over $50,000.

There are other important reasons for instituting honesty tests. First, by uncovering errors in the ways cash is handled by employees, honesty shoppers can show management how well the store systems are being followed. An excessive number of errors or a failure to give customers their sales receipts, for example, usually indicates poor supervision or poor training.

Shopping tests are also useful because they set up a psychological barrier to theft in the minds of employees. If new members of the staff are informed that honesty shoppers will test them frequently for accuracy as well as for honesty, this warning alone may serve to prevent a borderline person from stealing.

The Basic Types of Shopping Tests

Several basic types of shopping tests have been developed over the years to detect dishonesty. Most of these techniques require the shopper to pay either *even money* (the exact amount of the sale plus tax) or *uneven money* (an amount greater than the total sale plus tax). Often used in combination, the even-money purchase allows the shopper to depart without waiting for a sales receipt, leaving the clerk with cash in hand and no record of the transaction. The purpose of the uneven-money purchase is just the opposite. It is used to obtain a sales receipt so that the clerk can be identified and the honesty test purchase can be located on the register tape.

Shopping Department Stores

In department stores, five basic techniques are utilized. These consist of: 1) The "single buy," 2) the "combination buy," 3) the "double buy," 4) the "exchange buy," and 5) the "refund test buy." Of course, variations of these basic types of purchases can be devised, and an imaginative shopper will work out new ways of combining and applying these techniques to make them even more effective.

The 'Single Buy'. To carry out a "single buy," the shopper goes into the selected department, e.g., the glove department, and spots the clerk she wants to test. After trying on several pairs of gloves, she carefully chooses one pair which costs $5.95. Next, she strolls over to the adjacent counter and looks at some bracelets in a display rack. Again, she tries on several, viewing them in the mirror, and doing what a customer normally does when shopping for jewelry. Finally, she decides on one of the bracelets priced at $1.95. She now mentally adds the cost of the two items together, plus sales tax, for a total sale of $8.30.

The shopper digs into her handbag and takes out a $5.00 bill, three $1.00 bills, a quarter, and a nickel. She notes the amount of the last sale recorded on the register by reading the window at the top of the machine. Now, she hands the money and the merchandise to the salesperson she wants to test, saying, "I've decided to take these gloves and this bracelet. You don't have to wrap them. I'll just drop them into my shopping bag."

The shopper places the gloves and the bracelet in her bag, says "thank you," and leaves the department without waiting for a sales receipt. She does not look back to see if the clerk rings up the sale, but she may listen to hear whether the bell rings on the register. The shopper soon moves out of sight, so the salesperson can feel safe either to ring the sale or to pocket the money.

If the shopper in this test situation has been working with a partner, the partner will be nearby observing the entire transaction. Should the clerk not ring up the sale, the second shopper will make an uneven-money purchase a few minutes later to obtain an identifying sales receipt. The next day, the shopping manager will take the shopper's violation report and check the cash register tape to see if the test sale appears correctly on the tape.

The "single buy" can be carried out by one shopper or two. If one shopper does the test, the amount of the previous sale recorded on the register will serve to locate her test sale on the tape. This will not be difficult to spot because the combined price of this two-item purchase will provide a total that does not appear too often on the tape.

One great advantage of the "single buy" is that a dishonest salesperson is less suspicious of an even-money sale when the customer selects two items of merchandise. A single-item purchase and the exact amount of money will often cause the clerk to suspect the verity of the transaction.

The 'Combination Buy'. The "combination buy" is similar to the "single buy" with one exception—the shopper buys two items but does so in two separate transactions. As with the "single buy," she gives the clerk an even amount of cash for the sale, places the item in her bag, and leaves the department without a sales receipt. In a few minutes, however, she returns and purchases a second item, saying she just reminded herself that she needed it, or offering some other appropriate excuse if one seems necessary. Again, she gives the clerk the exact cash amount and puts the item into her bag. This "combination buy" presents a dishonest clerk with two opportunities to pocket the customer's money. The clerk may not pocket the first sale because she is cautious, but when the second opportunity arises on top of the first, she will often give in to temptation.

If shoppers are working in pairs, the shopper who is observing the salesclerk will watch to see if she rings up both sales. If she does not ring up one of the sales, the second shopper will move in for her uneven-money purchase to get an identifying sales receipt. As with the "single buy," if the shopper is working by herself, she must keep a record of the last sale shown in the register window prior to her purchase. Later the tape can be examined to see if both sales were properly recorded.

The 'Double Buy'. As the name suggests, there are two parts to the "double buy." The *first* part of the purchase is made to identify the clerk. In this part of the sale, the shopper buys one or more items and pays the salesperson an *uneven* amount of money, requiring the clerk to give her change and a register receipt. This sales receipt identifies the salesclerk and establishes a control figure for locating the subsequent "test" sale on the register tape.

After browsing around the department for several minutes, the *second* part of the "double buy" is made for *even* money. This, of course, is the honesty test. The shopper appears to make an impulsive decision to buy an additional item over and above those already purchased. In buying this extra item, she pays the sales person the exact amount of money plus tax and says, "I'll just stick this second item into my bag along with the others." The shopper then moves out of the department. The tape is checked the next day to see whether the salesclerk recorded the even-money sale.

In the "double buy" situation, the honesty shopper has to use common sense in maintaining some measure of price consistency between the two purchases. It would not be normal, for example, to come into a men's shop and purchase a handkerchief for 39 cents and then, before leaving the department, impulsively buy a pair of cufflinks for $10.00. A real customer would more likely come into a department for cufflinks, buy a $10.00 pair, then, as he started to leave, remember he needed handkerchiefs and buy some on impulse.

It's also important not to blur these two purchases by intermingling them in any way. The first purchase, the more expensive one, should be a complete and separate transaction. A few minutes should elapse before making the second purchase. Under no circumstances should the second part of the "double buy" be made until the first part is completed. This means the sale is rung, and the merchandise is packaged and given to the customer.

Shoppers, like good chess players, should always plan their move in advance. For example, they should try to select a sufficiently large item for the first part of the purchase to require a bag that will also hold the second even-money purchase. It would make little sense to buy cufflinks and then to select a man's shirt as the impulse item, unless the shopper is already carrying large packages. The honesty shopper should also try to locate merchandise for the second purchase that is some distance away from the cash register, so she can leave before the cashier has time to return to the register.

It is often helpful on the "double buy" if the shopper can select two or three units and add them together for the even-money sale. In this way, the dishonest clerk may either keep all the money or ring up part of it, pocketing the difference. For example, let's suppose the shopper has made a purchase in the jewelry department. She then wanders up to the counter and asks the clerk to show her some earrings in the showcase. Next, she stops and looks at some bracelets. After some discussion and comparison, she finally selects a bracelet and slips it on her wrist, telling the saleswoman that she has decided to wear it. She gives the earrings to the clerk to be wrapped in some tissue and suggests they be put in the bag with her first purchase—the uneven-money buy which was made to get the identification receipt.

The shopper gives the suspect even money in denominations that allow her to separate the two sales so she can ring up just the earrings of just the bracelet and then pocket the balance of the sale. Of course, since the total is an even amount, she may choose to pocket the entire sale. There are obviously many ways to vary the "double buy." Many shoppers feel it is one of the best types of shopping tests.

The 'Exchange Buy'. In this test, a shopper hesitates between several items of merchandise and finally decides to take the least expensive of the selection. She gives the salesclerk an uneven amount of money, requiring her to ring up the sale and to provide a sales receipt. When the salesclerk has given the shopper her change and the packaged merchandise, the shopper returns to the items she has been undecided about and tells the clerk that she has changed her mind. She has decided to take the higher-priced item. The shopper then gives the salesperson the exact cash difference between the two items.

For example, she has been shown scarves at $2.95, $3.95, and $4.95. She hesitates but finally decides on the one for $2.95. She gives the saleswoman a $5.00 bill. The $2.95 plus tax comes to $3.10, so the clerk rings it up, gives the shopper her change, and puts the scarf into a bag. Now the shopper reconsiders. She is obviously still torn between whether to buy the $2.95 scarf which is the correct color or the $4.95 scarf which she particularly likes because of the design. She has been looking at the $4.95 scarf while the sale is being rung up. As the clerk hands her the bag, the customer smiles and apologizes, saying that she hates to be a bother, but she has decided to splurge and buy the $4.95 scarf, after all, instead of the one she originally selected.

The $4.95 scarf comes to $5.20 with tax, and since the clerk has already received $3.10, the shopper hands her $2.10, the exact amount of the difference between the two scarves. She then removes the $2.95 scarf from the bag and puts in the more expensive one. The clerk is left with the even-money difference between the first purchase and the second purchase as the customer quickly walks out of the department, leaving the clerk to decide whether or not to pocket the $2.10.

In this type of shopping test, the shopper should be careful not to make the difference in value between the two items excessive. For example, it would be unlikely that a normal customer would purchase an item for $4.50 and then decide to substitute a $22.50 item. This would also put an excessive amount of money into the hands of the suspect which may prevent the theft by making it seem too risky.

The "exchange buy" is particularly effective in certain departments where it would be difficult to make a "double buy" without arousing suspicion. For example, it might appear odd for a customer to buy one pair of shoes and then impulsively buy a second pair. The same might be true in millinery and some ready-to-wear departments, but in these same departments it would not be unusual for the customer, on impulse, to upgrade the amount of her purchase.

The 'Refund Test Buy'. An honesty shopper is constantly seeking methods of testing which encourage belief in the mind of the salesperson that the shopper is an ordinary customer. The "refund test buy" is a successful method for throwing the thief off guard.

The shopper brings a piece of merchandise with a sales check into a department and claims to have purchased it a week or so previously. She explains that the item does not fit her, that it's the wrong color, or that she has received a similar item as a gift. The shopper insists on getting cash for the merchandise since she does have the sales check. Upon receiving the cash refund, she then makes an even-money purchase in the department.

The fact that she came in for a refund helps establish the shopper as an ordinary customer. Once this confidence is instilled in the clerk's mind, then either the "single buy," the "double buy," or the "combination buy" may be used as a test of the suspect. Usually in this situation, an identifying purchase is not needed because the clerk's identity is on the refund.

A similar method can be applied in stores that use charge accounts. In this case, the shopper is given a charge plate, usually under a fictitious name and address. After entering the department and spending time looking at various pieces of merchandise, talking to the clerk about the size, color, and her needs, she finally comes to a decision and purchases an item by charging it to her account. The clerk goes through the normal process of writing up the sale, having it approved by the charge office, and having the customer sign the sales receipt. This usually takes a few minutes, and during this period the shopper is browsing through the department.

As the clerk completes the sale and is ready to hand her the package, the shopper selects another item. She says she has decided to take this particular merchandise also, but she doesn't want her husband to know, so she'll pay cash for it. She then hands the salesclerk the exact amount for the second item and puts it into the same bag with the charged item. This second transaction should be undertaken some distance from the cash register so the suspect is given an opportunity to walk over to the register with the money while the customer walks out of the department.

It should be noted that in using the "refund test buy" or the charge plate method, the store gains added benefits. The clerk can be observed to see if she checks the name and address on the charge purchase against the imposter "wanted list" and whether she phones the charge office to get an okay on the sale. The clerk can also be observed to see if she follows the proper refund procedures. Thus, the store is provided an opportunity to discover if important control procedures are being followed.

Shopping Checkout Stores

Honesty shoppers have been used for years in stores where cash registers are located in the sales area. But in recent years, supermarkets and other retailers with checkout operations have found that shoppers can be an effective security tool. There are two basic methods used in shopping a checkout store. These are: 1) the "impulse sale," and 2) the "sandwich test."

The 'Impulse Sale'. In this test, the honesty shopper wheels a basket of merchandise up to the checkout counter. The checker rings up the order, totals it, hands over the receipt, and gives the shopper her change. As soon as the merchandise is packed, the shopper reaches over and impulsively grabs a magazine or some other item at the checkstand, saying, "Oh, by the way, I think I'd better buy this too." She then hands the cashier the exact amount of money for this impulse item, sticks it into her package, and walks out of the store with her bag of groceries.

The grocery sale provides the transaction number and the amount of the sale so the head of the shopping department can later check the register tape to see whether the impulse purchase was rung on the register. If the sale is missing, it is assumed the clerk probably pocketed the money.

The 'Sandwich Test'. A second type of shopping device to test checkers is called the "sandwich test." The shopper selects a small item of merchandise which can be easily carried unbagged out of the store. She then digs out the exact amount of money required for that particular item and watches for an opportunity. When a customer is in the middle of having her sale rung up, the shopper pushes her way past the other customers in line, apologizes, and hands the salesclerk the exact amount of money for the single item she's carrying in her hand. She says something to the effect: "I hope you will forgive me; I don't mean to be rude, but I'm rushing to pick my husband up at the airport," or a similar explanation. She then moves rapidly out of the store without looking back to see what the clerk has done with her money.

In this type of test, the cashier must finish ringing up the first customer's sale before she rings up the payment for the single item of merchandise that the shopper has given her. Often a second shopper, working as a partner to the first, is located at a point where she can see whether or not the sale is rung up after the present transaction is completed. The second shopper also notes the total amount of the sale presently being rung so the register tape can be audited the next day to see if the test sale was properly recorded.

Accuracy Tests. Honesty shoppers can also serve supermarkets in other ways. First, they can test the checker for: ringup errors by price and by department, items not rung up, guessing at unmarked prices, change-making errors, and so on. For example, the shopper can select an assortment of items from different departments, some taxable items, some advertised specials, less than the full multiple on a multiple-price offer, as well as items involving coupon redemptions. She can also select three different cans of merchandise that appear identical and place one with the price face up and the others with the price face down to see if the checker takes the time to turn the three cans over to determine the correct cost of each. Or, while the checker is in the process of ringing up the order, the honesty shopper can take an unrung item from the feed belt, pretending to examine it, and then place the item on the discharge belt with items that the checker has already processed.

If a store does enough of this type of shopping, it can discover what percentage of its losses is being caused by cashier errors, and it can identify cashiers who need retraining or closer supervisory attention. In some instances, a cashier may simply be unable to ring up sales accurately because of a lack of finger coordination. In such cases, management has little choice except to replace her with a person who is more capable of doing the job.

Another valuable use of honesty shopping in supermarkets is to have the shopper bring a cart of merchandise to the checkout counter, with one or two items on the lower shelf of the basket, to see if the clerk checks the shelf and charges the customer for this merchandise. Findings on this particular type of testing have sometimes been most revealing. In Iowa, for example, a chain of nine stores became concerned about the problem and ran a series of shopping tests. It discovered that 40 percent of the time the honesty shopper could walk out of the store with merchandise that had not been paid for because it was on the bottom shelf of the cart.

Accuracy tests may also include the handling of trading stamps. The shopper will make a purchase to see if she is given trading stamps and if the stamps she receives are the correct number for the amount of her sale. In addition to errors, trading stamps often pose a problem because the cashier can intentionally withhold them or pocket those which customers refuse to accept. There is also the possibility that the cashier will shortchange the customer on trading stamps and will later keep the difference.

In reviewing these strategies, some readers may feel that the shoppers are unfair in the way they set up opportunities for employee theft. Although the situation may occasionally appear this way, the fact remains that if the employee is honest, these strategies will not tempt him to steal. On the other hand, if the employee is dishonest (and this is the type of person you are trying to ferret out of your operation), he is extremely gun-shy and has to be provided a reasonable opportunity to steal. You are trying to get the suspect to steal from trained shoppers in situations you can control, rather than from customers on sales transactions you are not even able to observe.

Where to Look for Shopping Suspects

There are two methods of locating shopping suspects. The first, *general shopping,* uses a random shopping technique or a shotgun approach. It will occasionally uncover a thief; but it is inefficient, and a large number of tests are wasted. Used periodically, it is a good method, but only if the cost of blanketing the store with tests is not excessive. A more effective approach is *shopping specific suspects*. This is the rifle-bullet approach. If suspects are carefully selected for shopping, there will be a high return for the number of tests made. The following are some of the means for identifying dishonest employee suspects.

Leads from Honesty Shoppers

One of the best ways of locating employee suspects is to depend upon the experience of your honesty shoppers. A top shopper has a knack for spotting suspects, and she produces a high number of cases. For example, she will notice that a particular saleswoman or cashier is wearing a suit with pockets. Experience has taught her that a large percentage of employees who wear suits or skirts with pockets do so to facilitate stealing cash on sales. She is also particularly alert to the salesman who suggests that her purchases be placed in the bag she is carrying and to the saleswoman who takes her handbag behind the counter. Of course, all of these actions may be innocent, but the fact that she selects such suspects to shop gives her a higher case score than if she merely worked by random selection. It is therefore advisable to allow the shopper free rein in selecting her suspects. She should be encouraged to shop such persons three or four times before being certain of their honesty.

Dishonest employees seldom steal every day or every time they are tested. Each person has his particular *modus operandi,* and he may only steal on one type of sale or only at certain times. This may be the day before payday when he needs money, a particular time of year when he wants to buy Christmas or birthday gifts, or just a particular week when he has overspent his salary. Therefore, a suspect should be tested on different days, at different hours of the day, and under different test conditions.

Leads from Supervisors

Experience shows that when supervisory personnel provide a suspect, it is a hot lead. Usually, a manager does not report one of his own people unless he has some positive indication of theft. So if he says he is suspicious of someone on his staff, that person's name should be placed in a suspect file, his packages should be examined periodically, and he should be given some attention by the security staff. Often the manager is right when he thinks one of his people is stealing, whether the employee is caught by the shoppers or not. Instead of stealing money, he may be stealing merchandise.

Many managers resent being asked to report any of their employees as possible leads for shopping tests. Those who are insecure or immature may even take steps to cover up dishonesty rather than to help bring it out into the open and cure it. Some may even attempt to defeat the honesty shopping tests.

These feelings are understandable. The supervisor wishes to avoid embarrassment over dishonesty found in his department and is afraid it may jeopardize his own job security. One way to overcome this attitude is to persuade him that he is management's representative in the department and that he has a responsibility to the company and to the entire work group. If he is able to uncover dishonesty, it is a factor in his favor. On the other hand, if dishonesty is found in his operation and he has not reported it, this may suggest that he is *not* a competent manager.

Naturally, the supervisor of a department is in a strategic position to spot dishonesty among his staff. If he is a competent manager and has been working closely with his people, he knows a good deal about them and their problems. He can often spot the employee who suddenly goes sour on the job or who suddenly seems sulky and depressed or angry and oversensitive.

Therefore, it is important to let the supervisor know that his efforts to spot dishonesty among his staff are appreciated. After he has provided a lead, the shoppers should move in rapidly and do a series of tests. A supervisor will not continue to provide this type of information if management isn't responsive. Let him know the results of the shopping tests to assure him that his information has been acted upon. If the information leads to the apprehension of the thief, management should go out of its way to let the manager know what a real service he has done for the store. In addition to personal congratulations, a note of commendation should be put in his personnel folder to make him aware that this type of help will favorably affect his merit review.

Employees Suspected of Undercharging

When management has uncovered evidence that some of its employees are selling merchandise below its retail value, honesty shoppers are faced with a difficult task. To detect these individuals, the shopper must be completely familiar with the prices of merchandise throughout the store. After a few weeks, many well-trained shoppers can tell you the exact price of almost any item of merchandise. Obviously, if a shopper is waiting behind another customer and knows the value of the merchandise being purchased, then notices that the clerk has undercharged the customer when ringing up the sale, the shopper has spotted a suspect. With further surveillance, a case can be built against this employee.

Management is often unaware that employees are undercharging, even when this practice is widespread. For example, in one recent incident, a shopper standing near a salesclerk was astonished to note that the clerk sold a $19.95 electric iron to an employee for 82 cents. In another instance in the same store, a salesman was discovered selling men's shirts to his friends for 25 cents each. Another salesclerk in the linen department had a neighbor who frequently visited her there. On one occasion, the woman purchased six sets of sheets and pillow cases retailing at $34.95 for the very nominal price of $1.68.

This type of undercharging is common in stores of all types; food stores, discount stores, variety stores, drug stores, specialty stores, and department stores. It is difficult to detect, and it is one of the most contaminating types of dishonesty. The employees involved usually don't look upon themselves as thieves but as "smart operators." Once this type of dishonesty gets a foothold in a store, it spreads like a brush fire and is almost impossible to stamp out.

In one large department store, in less than three weeks, shopping tests and interrogations uncovered 37 employees who confessed to selling merchandise to other employees far below the retail value. The investigation could have continued indefinitely, but management called a halt when it became apparent that the store would soon be without any staff. The only logical solution was to set up stronger controls, to hold meetings with employees, and to make it clear that in the future controls on employee purchases would be tightened.

Co-workers of Dishonest Employees

Additional shopping suspects are often revealed by dishonest employees during their interrogation. But even if they are not, chances are that when one employee in a department is stealing, there will be other dishonest individuals in the same department. Management often finds it difficult to understand how a method of theft can be passed around to a wide group of employees, much less from one store in the chain to another. But executives tend to look at dishonesty differently from the way employees do. The executive reasons that, if he were to steal, he would be secretive in order to avoid discovery. The dishonest employee, on the other hand, feels a certain sense of victory when he discovers a successful method of theft, and he brags about it to other employees over coffee during the relief break. Rather than look down on the thief, his co-workers often admire his skill and resourcefulness and want to emulate him.

Contamination is a problem that should concern every manager. Eventually it leads to collusive planning and even to collusive thefts which are far more devastating than thefts by employees working alone. It means that a "mop-up" operation is required whenever a dishonest employee is arrested.

However, if you catch a clerk stealing cash on sales, it might not be advisable to send the honesty shoppers back into that department for two or three days. Within a week, it certainly will be safe to begin systematically testing the other salespeople on the counter. However, since there is no way of predicting how long the other clerks may refrain from stealing because of fears generated by the apprehension of the first employee, it is wise to go back a second and even a third time before assuming the leads are dead ends.

Employees with Below-Average Cash Sales

Another successful technique is for the controller's division to select a high-loss department and average out the cash sales for each salesperson over a period of three or four weeks. This average should be prorated for the number of hours that each employee worked.

In department stores, it is wise to select departments, such as cosmetics, gloves, handbags, or jewelry, where the great number of smaller cash sales provides an ideal opportunity for clerk thefts. Larger merchandise, such as furniture, often requires a send sales check, making cash theft more difficult. Once the audit is made, you may find that one salesman is running daily sales of $20.00 or more below the department average. He is obviously an excellent shopping suspect or else a good candidate for retraining or replacement.

Employees with Above-Average Cash Sales

Experience shows that the person stealing may also be the top-producing salesperson in the department. The successful thief is noted for his strong drive and aggressiveness. In fact, he is often looked upon by management as one of its best employees.

A typical example of the successful employee stealing cash on sales was a salesman with an outstanding sales record who had worked in the store for several years. When he was finally caught, the personnel manager asked him: "Mr. Jones, you sold in our store for over seven years, and have one of the best selling records. Naturally, we were surprised to find that you were stealing cash on sales. We are certainly disappointed to lose your services because you are obviously a good salesperson, but your confession here shows that you stole an average of more than $30.00 a day for the past two years. The thing that is difficult for me to understand is how you could steal this amount and yet continue to run the highest cash sales in your department?" The dishonest salesman smiled sympathetically at the personnel manager and said, "That just proves what a good salesman I really am." How true!

Employees with Patterns of Overages and Shortages

Individual cash register overages and shortages should be recorded in a way that will allow members of the security staff or management to examine them for irregular patterns. Security men know that a pattern of overages is more apt to represent stealing than is a pattern of shortages. When there is individual drawer responsibility, a shortage is more likely to be an error. Overages, however, frequently represent theft manipulation.

Watch for employees whose daily register receipts show overages of $.25, $.75, $1.50 or $2.00 followed by a sudden overage of $15.00 or $25.00. What is happening? Often the dishonest employee is under-ringing sales and withholding a sales receipt from the customer. At the end of the day, the thief is frequently afraid she has made an error in her mathematics. Thus, if her figures show that she has built up a reserve of unrecorded sales totaling $15.75, she will take the $15.00 and leave the $.75 to prevent a shortage. She believes a shortage will cause suspicion but that an overage is reassuring to management. Naturally, the knowledgeable manager is just as suspicious of overages as he is of shortages.

Eventually, the pattern of small overages will show a larger overage of, let's say, $25.00. This occurs when the dishonest employee has built up a "bank" of stolen money in the register but encounters a situation that prevents her from removing it. Perhaps the boss decided to hang around and watch the day's receipts being counted, or the department buyer is conversing with another employee and is standing next to the register. Whatever the cause, the dishonest employee is unable to get the stolen cash out of the register before closing it out for the day. As a result the money is included in the day's receipts and shows up as a substantial overage.

Shortages can also indicate dishonesty, particularly if they are found in a community-drawer register. Watch for a series of even-dollar shortages, such as $1.00, $2.00 or $5.00. Cash register errors seldom occur in even amounts.

If an employee is stealing cash directly out of the register, this does not mean he or she won't steal from an honesty shopper. Some employees steal cash from the register because of limited opportunities to steal even amounts of cash from customers. But they will steal such sales when offered. A thief is often quite greedy for money, and an even-amount sale is just another opportunity for theft.

When overages and shortages occur in a cash register with a community drawer, it is difficult to locate the logical suspect to be tested. Sometimes all the cashiers using the register are shopped, but a better method is to try to eliminate some employee suspects by reviewing their days off. Obviously, if a series of three shortages appears on a cash register in a period of three weeks, and two of the people who use the community drawer were not working on those days, they can be eliminated as suspects.

At this point, it is sometimes advisable to reassign each of the remaining suspects to a different register. In this way, further analysis of their register tapes will soon uncover the thief, as one of the registers will continue to show patterns of overages and shortages. Management can then move in with honesty shoppers.

The employee who has a continuing pattern of overages or shortages on the register should be shopped two or three times each month for a period of three to six months. Chances are that such a person is stealing, and the fact that the honesty shopper does not observe a violation only indicates that she has somehow not hit the employee at the right time or that she has failed to set up the conditions that the employee requires to trigger a theft.

Employees with Excessive 'No Sales'

When an employee stumbles upon a "clever" method for stealing, he invariably passes along the technique to other employees. For example, when a store audits tapes and finds excessive "no sales," it will usually find that as many as 50 to 60 percent of its employees are running excessive "no sales."

The first tendency of management when it sees such a large number of "no sales" is to dismiss the idea of dishonesty and assume the clerks are opening the registers to provide change for customers or for some other legitimate reason. In general, however, excessive and unauthorized "no sales" indicate a theft suspect.

A really productive method of locating employee suspects is for the auditing department to review two or three months of tapes to locate any workers who have an excessive number of "no sale" rings. Management is often astounded to discover that many cash registers are running 20 to 40 "no sale" transactions a day; it wrongly assumed that the clerks handling the tapes were examining them for this type of irregularity. But unless an unusually talented clerk is handling these tapes, such irregularities will not be discovered.

Whenever you come across a register tape with an excessive number of "no sales" on it, chances are that you have stumbled across a dishonest employee. The cashier or clerk who is stealing cash on sales, particularly if she is underringing on the register, must keep track of the total amount she has underrung during the day in order to take out the exact amount of money she has stolen. Being very nervous and worried about the theft, she will often ring a "no sale," open the cash register, and count the cash. She thus reassures herself of the amount she has underrung.

Management should establish guidelines as to the number of "no sales" that can be rung while still providing adequate customer service. Under optimum security conditions, the wise store manager will not allow an employee to open a register on a "no sale" for any reason except when opening the register for the day and closing the register for lunch, for the relief break, or in the evening.

Employees with Excessive 'Void' Sales

Management must realize that the so-called "void" sale can easily be misused by a dishonest employee to cover up a cash theft from the register. Some stores are so lax in this regard that they do not even require authorization of a void transaction by the supervisor. Other stores require authorization but do not require the supervisor to see or talk to the customer. When a supervisor approves a "void" sale after the customer has left the store, this creates a significant loophole in the control procedure. Merely signing the voided sale is of little benefit in terms of preventing employee dishonesty.

Frequently, the dishonest employee will bring a cash register receipt to a supervisor and will offer one of a variety of excuses for the voided sale. She may say she hit a wrong key or she had to re-ring the entire transaction. She may claim the customer decided not to make the purchase after she had rung it on the register or the customer found out she had too little cash with her and decided to make the purchase later. In stores that handle both charge and cash transactions, the excuse may be that after the sale was rung on the register as a cash transaction, the customer changed her mind and decided to charge it to her account.

No matter what the explanation given for the voided sale, it is important that the department supervisor verify the clerk's story. If the customer is still at the register, then the supervisor can get direct confirmation. But even when the customer has left the store, it is still sometimes possible to check the cashier's story. If, for example, she says the customer decided to charge it to her account, then the supervisor can check the charge office to see if the sale was actually charged. But when management's control over voids is lax, the cashier with register tapes showing an excessive number of voids is a prime suspect and should be shopped.

It is surprising how voids can get out of hand. A discount chain in Southern California made a security analysis of one of its high-shortage stores and discovered that some employees had 20 to 40 void transactions *each day*. Tests of these cashiers by honesty shoppers soon uncovered the fact that most of them were stealing. They not only stole the shopper's money, but they also took cash from the register, concealing the thefts by phony "void" sales. Putting a void slip in the register meant that their cash balanced at the end of the day, enabling them to pocket the stolen money without fear of detection. The investigation revealed that employees had used fraudulent voids to steal $26,000 in the six months prior to the security study.

Temporary Employees

Prior to the Christmas season and before Easter, many stores take on large numbers of temporary sales help. The temporary employees often lack the loyalty toward the store felt by permanent workers. During these peak seasons, there is little time for properly screening the people who are brought in as temporary help and even less time for keeping an eye on them. In some stores, the temporary Christmas and Easter employees make up 35 percent of their year's total dishonest employee apprehensions.

Because temporary employees are a generally higher risk, additional honesty shopping tests of these people should be scheduled during these peak periods. Some stores triple the number of tests made during the months prior to Christmas and the six weeks prior to Easter. This additional effort pays off handsomely in cutting seasonal shortages.

Remember not to neglect permanent employees during this period. The financial pressure of Christmas gifts and the general confusion, as well as the lack of supervisory attention which results from the peak customer traffic, serve to increase temptation for most employees. Dishonest employees who are already stealing will often double or triple their thefts at this time. Thefts are easier because cashiers are handling more money each day than they do during slower sales periods. So have shoppers test your regular workers as well as your temporary staff during these holiday seasons.

Signs of Dishonesty at the Register

Indications of dishonest activity at the register come in many forms. A security consultant reviewed the operation of a large department store in Washington, D. C. On the first day of his study, he made a tour of the store and noticed that a great number of cash register drawers were not completely closed. The drawers appeared to be shut, but the experienced eye of the consultant spotted the fact that they were not closed far enough to latch. He recognized that when a salesperson does not completely close the drawer on the register, this makes it easier for her to take money or to make change without ringing the sale.

After walking through the store and noting the general condition of the registers, the consultant went back a second time and jotted down the 22 cash register numbers where this was occurring. He suggested that management make honesty shopping tests of the salesclerks. After two weeks of tests, 19 salespeople had been apprehended for theft of cash on sales. Store management took corrective action to see that in the future cash register drawers were completely shut after each sale, and any register found open was promptly recognized as a potential sign of dishonesty.

Another sign of dishonest activity at the register are scraps of paper with figures written on them. These scraps represent personal banking notes. By jotting down each amount underrung and adding them together, the thief feels more confident that she will take out the correct amount of money at the end of the day. She doesn't want to take out more than she has underrung and thus create a shortage—this is a source of major concern to her.

In one case, a clerk had hidden a series of matchbooks in the drawer underneath her register in which individual matches in each book had been bent over at a right angle. Investigation revealed that this was her method of bookkeeping; each bent match represented one dollar underrung on sales. In another instance, a woman kept pennies in the drawer underneath the register, and she shifted these pennies into a line along the edge of the register drawer. Like the bent matches, each penny represented a dollar she had underrung.

High-Shortage Departments

Another way of spotting suspects is to look over your inventory shortage figures. Select those departments which show an abnormally high shortage or those which have shown a steady increase in shortages over the past few inventories. In this situation, shoppers should be programmed to make a minimum of three or four shopping tests of each of the employees in the high-shortage department. Spread the tests out over a period of three months. Periodic night audits of the change drawers in your registers may also reveal shortages that can be followed up by shoppers.

Inventory shortages, of course, can be caused by many factors, including paperwork errors and failures to keep accurate accounting records. But a basic cause is often theft of cash on sales. One, several, or even all of the employees in the department may be stealing. Honesty shopping tests will resolve this question for management.

Another approach is saturation shopping of a high-shortage department. As the name suggests, shoppers blanket the department. There have been situations in which every customer on the floor was an honesty shopper. This method can quickly give management an answer to the department's cash theft situation and prevent the severe losses which might occur during a long period of investigation.

Poorly Managed Departments

Look for suspects in the poorly managed department where there is laxity in enforcing store systems. This type of manager often thinks he is in a popularity contest; he believes that if he is liked by his staff, then he is running an efficient operation. He also believes that if he is kind and lenient to them, they will be loyal and honest in return. Yet, psychological studies have repeatedly shown that employees do not favor this type of supervision. They may pretend to be pleased with the liberties they are granted, but underneath they are dissatisfied by the lack of leadership.

Employees, by and large, want to be proud of their department, their boss, and the company for which they work. This pride stems from a tight operation and from a supervisor who requires each employee to live up to his fullest potential. In the poorly supervised, lax operation, dishonesty will often be uncovered.

A failure in supervision may also occur if the manager is authoritarian. This attitude is likely to cause considerable frustration among his staff, and employees may steal as a transfer of their feelings of hostility against him and the store. So be sure honesty shoppers periodically test workers in poorly managed departments.

Offbeat Departments

Whenever you set up shopping coverage, the supervisor should include the offbeat selling areas, places which are normally neglected by shoppers. The very fact that they are offbeat departments means they often have poor control systems and inadequate supervision. These conditions breed employee theft. Here are a few typical offbeat departments: 1) shoe repair, 2) barber shop, 3) employee cafeteria, 4) cut flowers, 5) baked goods, 6) gourmet foods, 7) parking lots, 8) warehouse store, 9) salvage sales, 10) employee store, 11) snack bar and hot dog stand, 12) popcorn concession, 13) outpost departments, 14) boutiques, and 15) service departments.

This list will probably suggest other offbeat spots in your own operation—the delicatessen, liquor department, or pastry shops for example. Certainly, you should make your list as complete as possible. Some of these offbeat departments are service centers without merchandise, and are usually overlooked by shoppers because management does not regard them as sales areas. Because they are seldom tested, the people working in them often feel free to steal; and it is astounding to see how much cash can be stolen from a department like the shoe repair or baked goods shop.

Perhaps the most neglected major theft area is the store's paid parking lot. Store managers and headquarter's executives seldom visit the lot or spend any time observing its operation. They don't drop in unexpectedly during late-night hours or during early morning hours when many parking lot thefts occur. Laxity in supervision, combined with inadequate control procedures, lead to heavy cash losses.

Employees who work in the parking lot often conceive clever dodges in order to steal cash paid for parking. In one large store in Detroit, 22 parking lot attendants, including the manager and the assistant manager, successfully stole $100,000 over a period of six years. The manager admitted stealing more than $25,000 of the total. Some stores do not have adequate controls over the measuring and recording of customer parking fees. But even where stores have elaborate control systems, ingenious parking lot attendants often figure a way to defeat the cash-handling procedures.

Many stores today have a soda fountain or a restaurant. Historically, these operations have been among the most vulnerable to cash theft on sales. The fountain or the restaurant should use prenumbered customer checks to improve control and to aid honesty shoppers. An experienced shopper will keep a mental record of the number on her customer check, and her audit of the checks will show whether it is in the day's receipts or has been destroyed. If the employee later claims that the money she pocketed was a tip from a customer, her alibi is discredited by pointing out that the prenumbered customer check is not in the sales checks for the day.

One reason for high losses in offbeat areas is that management regards them as nickel-and-dime sales. It thinks of the hot dog and the soda, for example, as a 75 cents purchase and feels that it is hardly worth worrying about. But knowledgeable security men know that you can be nickeled and dimed to death. Even in such offbeat areas, thefts can amount to thousands of dollars.

Every department should have a suitable cash register that is designed to hold the individual clerk accountable for his sales transactions. Some stores try to economize by having adding machine-type registers in such locations. These machines often have no register tape, and when they do, it is seldom a detail tape. Any attempt to economize in this way is penny-wise and pound-foolish. Investment in a proper register serves two purposes: first, it enables the merchant to achieve accountability for money and sales handled by a specific clerk; and second, it encourages the employee to discharge his duty and to properly account for the funds entrusted to his care.

Developing a Shopping Program

When a company has decided to use honesty shoppers, several questions arise. Should the store hire an outside agency or should it develop its own shopping staff? What are the relative costs and problems of these two alternatives? How does a store work with an outside agency and what should its expectations be in terms of performance? If it decides to use its own staff, how does a store go about setting up an internal shopping department to perform honesty tests? Here are some practical answers to these questions.

Outside Agency vs. Internal Shopping Staff

The decision whether to use an outside shopping service or to develop an internal honesty shopping department is based heavily on considerations of store size and financial resources. In a smaller store, where there is no security department and where the store staff is too limited in size to handle its own honesty shopping operation, the outside shopping service can be effective, providing the agency works closely with management. This means that management must regularly give the service a list of suspects to be tested, including such information as the descriptions of the people, details of clothing being worn on that day, and the locations of the registers assigned to them. Too often, the store allows shoppers to operate on a random basis instead of zeroing in on specific targets. This means that there is little chance the store will get a high return for the money invested.

An outside shopping service should be expected to meet a production standard. To determine the relative effectiveness of the service you are using, compare the number of shopping tests it has performed with the number of cases it has developed over any given period of time. This approach can apply both to the outside agency and to the store's own shoppers. For example, one outside service may average a single dishonest employee case in every 465 shopping tests. Another may produce one case in every 260 shopping tests. This does not compare favorably with the standards set by stores that have instituted their own honesty departments. Some internal programs average one dishonest person in every 70 tests. A reasonable standard to expect is an average of one case in every 150 tests.

Outside agency tests can cost anywhere from $2.25 to as much as $15.00 per test, but the most typical cost will be about $3.50. You will find that the cost of tests when using an outside agency will be considerably higher than it is for stores which use their own shoppers, especially if the outside shopping service combines service shopping with honesty shopping. In order to submit a service-shopping report, the outside agency must make a test buy on every sale in order to identify the employee. This results in a high number of nonproductive test purchases in addition to higher costs. In a department store, an honesty shopper can average six to eight tests per hour and a firm that pays its own staff on an hourly basis can average a cost of $.60 to $1.40 per test. Shopping tests in supermarkets usually take longer to complete and involve more traveling time between stores, so that an honesty shopper will usually complete only one or two tests an hour, resulting in an average cost range of $2.50 to $3.50 per test for a supermarket company that uses its own staff.

Some companies prefer to pay outside agencies on the basis of a percentage of the amount of restitution recovered. This is a very risky practice because it can lead to such dishonest practices as tricking honest employees into stealing, using duress to obtain inflated figures of admitted thefts, and so on.

It is also important in working with an outside firm that there is a clear agreement with the agency as to what is to be considered a "shopping violation." Most companies with a security department will require at least two clear-cut thefts of cash on two separate sales transactions before an employee is interviewed. Some outside firms persuade management to take a person off for a single "policy violation," such as a failure to give the customer a sales receipt. Although management may want the service to report this oversight, this is not an acceptable standard for determining an employee's honesty, and it should not be construed either as proof of theft or as evidence that the shopping service is effective. A "shopping violation" should be a theft of cash on sales. Failure to give a sales receipt often means only that the cashier is careless, needs to be retrained, or needs better supervision.

There should also be agreement as to whether the store or agency is to interview dishonest employees. Quite often, the outside firm can do a better interview job because it specializes in handling such cases. Even so, a member of management should sit in on the interrogation as an observer. You should also ascertain whether the service which is legally operating as an agent of your company is sufficiently insured and includes your company as being co-insured on their policy.

Some companies purchase outside shopping services because store management likes the fact they will also provide a service-shopping report on tested employees. The manager feels he is getting two types of tests for the price of one, and this seems to justify the higher cost of the agency tests. But store security specialists know that an honesty shopper must devote her full time and attention to the problem of detecting dishonesty and other causes of shortages. When she is required to observe the service aspects of the sale and must write a full, detailed report on how the clerk handled the sale, she cannot do an effective honesty shopping job. It has been found repeatedly that when a shopping test combines a service-shopping test and an honesty test in a single buy, the honesty test loses its value. Service shopping must be maintained as a separate function.

For many stores, the outside shopping agency is the logical answer to the problem of checking cashiers and salespeople for thefts of cash on sales. The agency usually has experienced employees who understand the store's theft problems. But when a company has a chain of stores or a store is fairly large, management would be wise to consider setting up its own honesty shopping department. Not only is the cost lower, but there is also greater flexibility. Shoppers are available whenever needed to test a particular suspect. These shoppers also tend to be more interested, to put in additional effort, and to show more imagination in their methods of shopping. They are not out to achieve a certain number of tests, and they are more productive in terms of the number of cases developed. Since these shoppers identify with the company, they look on the store as a personal responsibility. For them, the dishonest employee becomes a challenge, and they make a special effort to devise new methods for uncovering such infractions.

Department stores that use their own shoppers and that can keep the cost of shopping tests at a moderate level usually find they can recover from $3.00 to $5.00 for every dollar invested. While the percentage of dollar returns will be somewhat lower in supermarkets, because of the higher shopping test costs, nevertheless, honesty shopping is also profitable in food stores. What is particularly advantageous is that management can experiment by increasing shopping tests until they reach a point of diminishing return.

The question of whether your own shoppers will become known to the employees is frequently raised. This will be determined largely by the care you use in selecting them and by the way you train them. The risk of being identified is always present, and a shopper may be betrayed by some careless action on her part or by a careless word passed down the line by management. But there is no reason to reveal the shoppers to any store employees at any time. One store had housewives shop every day on a part-time basis, some of whom had been on the shopping staff for 10 to 15 years. Production records proved they weren't known to employees, and experience sharpened their skills over the years. These long-term shoppers turned in three and four times the number of cases of newer staff members.

As long as precaution is taken not to reveal the identity of your shoppers, there are some advantages in the fact that the shoppers become known to your employees as customers. A talented honesty shopper may strike up a personal relationship with a suspected clerk, throwing the dishonest employee off guard. There is far less likelihood that this shopper will be suspected than a stranger who comes into the store. It has been found in the past that the smart dishonest employee will *not* steal from a stranger. The thief feels it's safer to steal from a regular customer.

In some areas, stores that do not have the resources to set up their own internal shopping departments have found it practical to form a shared shopping staff with a number of other stores in the area. Many have found that in terms of cost and flexibility, this arrangement has advantages over employing an outside agency.

Selecting Your Shopping Department Manager

When management decides to set up its own honesty shopping department, the first step is to hire a full-time shopping supervisor. If the store has a security department, the honesty shopping operation should function under the security director. If not, it is usually headed by the operating vice-president, or the personnel manager, or, in some cases, by the store manager.

A full-time shopping supervisor is an important element in making the whole operation successful. Some companies try to hire a shopping supervisor who has had two or three years experience working as a shopper or as a team manager for an outside shopping agency. Such a person is familiar with shopping techniques and with the records and routines involved in setting up the operation. He or she is also in a position to set up adequate controls for the shopping test merchandise and the money involved to avoid errors and losses caused by carelessness, negligence, or inadequate controls. If an individual of this type is not available, the company should select a mature person who shows aggressiveness, good judgment, initiative, imagination, and a proven background of good character and personal integrity.

The person selected to head the shoppers should be adept at mathematics and record keeping, careful on details, thorough, accurate, conscientious, and should possess a good understanding of human nature. These qualities will be necessary in handling such responsibilities as balancing shoppers' cash banks, locating "specials" and identifying them for shoppers, returning shoppers' merchandise to stock, and making refunds on these items, among other responsibilities. Quite often, a woman who has spent some time in actual shopping and has worked her way up to become a supervisor in the field combines these needed qualities.

Recruiting Honesty Shoppers

Honesty shoppers vary considerably in their ability to detect dishonest employees. Certain people have a special talent for spotting dishonesty. Over the years, it has been found that one detective will produce eight cases a day and another will not produce a case in three or four months. The existence of special detective ability has been proven by a detective selection test which successfully isolates the high case producers. This test has proven itself useful not only in selecting floor detectives, but also in choosing people for the store shopping staff.

In time, a really good honesty shopper will develop a whole range of "suspect indications" which will help her spot good suspects. Often, she will work on an intuitive basis. That is why interviews with top case producers are always frustrating to the person with a logical mind. When asked why she selected a particular person to shop, she is unable to offer any specific reason.

In addition to natural detective ability, honesty shoppers need to have some mathematical skills. It is advisable when screening people for this position that a simple arithmetic test be given to show whether the shopper is able to handle figures easily and whether she is accurate and observant.

Good candidates for honesty shoppers fall into the following categories:

Housewives. Stores that recruit their own honesty shoppers usually rely heavily on part-time housewives and pay them on an hourly basis. It is surprising how many housewives find honesty shopping an interesting and exciting occupation. They enjoy the challenge and the lack of direct supervision that the job offers.

On the average, the part-time shopper will work 8 to 12 hours each week, shopping two or three days a week for two to four hours. Stores find no difficulty in recruiting people for this work. Many women would like a change or simply want to earn some extra money. Stores that give employees a discount provide the shopper with an added inducement.

College Students. Male shoppers can often be found by contacting the employment office in local colleges where there are young men studying law, retailing, or business administration. These college men find that a few hours of retail work each week is profitable not only because it gives them some extra spending money, but because it broadens their knowledge and enlarges their understanding of the business world.

Airline Hostesses. Some stores have very successfully recruited airline stewardesses. They find that their outgoing personalities enable them to chat easily with a salesperson and that their flight costumes throw the clerks off guard. They show considerable imagination and are persuasive and convincing in their customer role.

Older Women. Some older people make the best shoppers. When selected with care, these women can successfully play the role of a grandmotherly type who loves to gossip and chat. It is surprising how easy it is for these elderly women to persuade a salesclerk that they are legitimate customers. Often a cashier feels that the elderly person is an easy mark for a theft. They are garrulous, seem easily confused and naive, and are less likely to demand a sales receipt. Often they lead the culprit on by deliberately appearing unintelligent.

One particularly successful shopper wore a babushka, was about 70 years of age, talked with a thick accent, and gestured a lot with her hands. She always seemed unable to understand the prices of merchandise and often lost things in her large over-stuffed handbag. But she was a consummate actress; underneath her guileless face, she had one of the sharpest minds in the profession. It was not surprising that she caught more dishonest employees than anyone else on the staff.

A Variety of Types. In lining up an honesty shopping staff, usually a considerable number of shoppers, perhaps 10 or more, should be put on the payroll as part-time workers to provide a wide variety of customer types. The larger the pool of trained and experienced shoppers available to draw upon, the more flexibility and the more impact you can achieve.

It is a mistake, for example, to use *only* airline hostesses, or *only* college students, or *only* young people. Your shopping staff should consist of teenagers, people in their twenties and thirties, middle-aged housewives, and elderly people. You should have black shoppers and white shoppers, men and women, Irish, German, Polish (you name it), kids in long hair and dungarees, and white-haired women with gnarled hands.

Not only should there be many types of people on your shopping staff, but they should play different roles depending on their appearance and background. A woman may come in dressed in a nurse's uniform, or she may pose as a manicurist from a nearby barber shop out on her lunch hour. She might come in dressed in a mink coat and look like a wealthy customer. The college student might look like a hippie or like an ambitious young lawyer.

All the locally dominant ethnic groups should be represented on the staff. If your particular store has a large Jewish, Irish, German, or black customer clientele, these should be in your shopping group. By having 15 or 20 shoppers to draw upon, you can create this variety, thereby increasing case production and reducing the risk that a shopper will be spotted by an employee.

Scheduling Shoppers

Shoppers can be scheduled in two ways. They can be called in each week for three days and work five hours each of those days, or a group of shoppers may be called in for a similar period every three or four weeks. Whatever the system of rotation, it is important to keep a variety of shoppers moving through your stores.

Let us say, for example, that you have 24 shoppers, divided into four groups of six. You bring in the first group of six for a full 40-hour week. You have them work in pairs and shop several stores. The next week, you schedule the second group of six shoppers, and you continue to rotate the pool on this basis. At the end of four weeks, you are now ready to start again with the first group of six shoppers. The advantage here is that since the shoppers would be in the store doing honesty tests only once in four weeks, they will be fresh and alert, and the salesperson is unlikely to identify them as shoppers.

Shopping has to be done on a continuing year-round basis. It is not effective if it is done spasmodically at the whim of a member of management. To be effective, it should be planned, calculated, and continuous, using logical methods that will give a high return on the investment. In addition, a good program will eliminate the risk of serious employee cash thefts flooding the store before they are discovered.

Setting Up Suspect Files

It is advisable to set up a suspect card file. The simplest way is to keep a 3 x 5 card on each suspect, filed alphabetically. Assign honesty shoppers to specific suspects and keep notations on the name card regarding the date of each shopping test and the results. If the results are negative, then the word "negative" should be written on the card. If there is some doubt about the situation or if the suspect acted in an unusual or suspicious manner, record these details. If detailed reports develop, then open an "employee suspect folder." Whenever you get a violation but want to delay the apprehension until several thefts have been witnessed, the file should be moved to an "active" file drawer. This group of active case folders should be kept in another part of the file cabinet.

Detailed reports on the testing of these people should be reviewed periodically to see if everything is being done to keep the suspect under proper surveillance. This review will show management whether shoppers are neglecting any particular suspect. It also allows a file to be closed when sufficient testing has cleared the suspect of suspicion. If the person is a very high-risk suspect, then other types of investigative techniques may be applied before the person is eliminated as a possible thief. Periodic review and cleaning out of dead-end leads will keep the files up to date.

The suspect file card and investigation folder serve to aid the interrogator when the suspect is finally caught. To refresh the interrogator's memory, it is helpful to put some details in the file on the reason the person was originally suspected of stealing and any other facts that might be useful to the interrogator. These leads can help the interrogator uncover further theft activities by questioning the subject about other people he knows to be stealing from the store.

Establishing Shopping Priorities

After developing a list of suspects, it should be arranged in some order of priority to insure the maximum return for a minimum effort. The following is one suggested way of grouping suspects in order of priority:

1) Employees known to be stealing.

2) Employees who are considered to be a high risk.

3) Employees working in offbeat sales locations, such as parking lots and the shoe repair department.

4) Temporary employees.

In addition, random shopping tests for overall coverage throughout the store should be worked out on a yearly schedule. Management should be assured that every employee in the store has been tested at least once or twice on a random testing basis during each 12-month period. There will always be some dishonest employees whose names never show up in the suspect files, and unless both the rifle-bullet and the shotgun approaches are used, there will not be a well-rounded shopping program.

Designing and Utilizing Proper Forms

The shopping department requires three types of forms. The first form, a special suspect form, gives a detailed description and location of the "special" who is to be tested. The second is a shopper's violation report that records the details of the shopping test when there is a policy or theft violation. The third form, a return-to-stock form, is used to keep track of the shopped merchandise for balancing against the cash, for writing up refunds, and for moving the merchandise back into stock.

The Special Suspect Form. The first form, requesting a "special suspect" shopping test, should contain the following information:

1) The number of the department in which the suspect works.

2) The floor, if the store has several floors, or the location by compass point, such as the north corner of the store, southwest corner, etc.

3) The cash register number.

4) The reason why the employee has been selected as a "special". This gives the shopper a way of evaluating priorities on "specials" and of determining how frequently the person should be shopped. Often, the reason for the request can indicate the type of purchase that may prove successful.

5) A description of the person to be tested, including age, height, weight, color of hair and eyes, and the particular clothes being worn on the day of the test. Any distinctive details should be noted (glasses, scar on left hand, etc.). The important goal is to provide the shopper with sufficient information to enable rapid identification of the clerk to be tested.

6) A place for the name of the person submitting the shopping request.

7) A section for a continuing record of the dates the suspect is shopped, the name of the shopper making the test, and whether a violation resulted from the shopping test.

8) Space to detail any unusual information that might have value later if the employee is interrogated. For example, on one particular test, the clerk may have rung up the sale, but waited 20 minutes before doing so. This type of information is helpful during the interrogation because it indicates the subject's method of theft.

An example of a standard shopping request form is illustrated in Figure 2.

The Shopper's Violation Report. The second form, the shopper's violation report, should provide space for the shopper to describe in exact

SHOPPING REQUEST

To: _____

Please Shop _____

Dept. Number _____ Floor _____ Register Number_____

Reason for Request _____

_____

_____

_____

Description of Person to be Shopped:

Age   : _____   Style Clothes : _____

Height   : _____   Style Hair   : _____

Weight   : _____   Other   : _____

Color Hair   : _____

Color Eyes   : _____

Color Clothes : _____
                                        Submitted by _____

SHOPPING RECORD

Dates Shopped	By Whom	Violation (yes-no)
_____		
_____		
_____		
_____		
_____		
_____		

(Any additional information, use other side)

DISPOSITION _____
(PULLED OR NOT)

Figure 2. Special suspect form

detail the facts relating to the shopping test which resulted in a violation. Whether the violation ultimately turns out to be a policy violation or a theft does not alter the need for details at this point. The shopper, of course, should make out her violation report as soon as she returns from her shopping tour, while the facts are still fresh in her mind. This report should contain, among other information:

1) The name and the payroll number of the person being tested.

2) The date of the shopping test.

3) The department and its location.

4) The cash register number or, if a sales book was used, the sales book number.

5) The name of the shopper.

6) A space for the name of the shopping supervisor with a statement saying that her signature verifies that the shopping supervisor has pulled the tapes of the suspect, has audited her day's work related to the test, and has confirmed the violation.

7) A section devoted to the identifying purchase and a second section allotted for the violation purchase. The identifying purchase may occur before or after the violation. If the person has a previous shopping violation, then the identifying purchase quite often can be made 20 minutes to a half hour before the violation test. It the suspect has no previous violations, then the identifying purchase will be made only after a violation test occurs. It is both costly and unnecessary to make an identifying purchase until a test purchase arouses the suspicion of the shopper that a violation has occurred. In either case, however, the identifying and violation transactions should be separate parts of the shopping report, but they should *both* contain:

   a) The time that the test was actually made.

b) The merchandise purchased.

c) The retail value.

d) The sales tax.

e) The total amount of the sale.

f) The exact money offered to the clerk on the sale. For this purpose, squares on the form can be filled in showing a $10.00 bill, $5.00 bill, $1.00 bill or other denominations, and similar squares showing $.50, $.25, $.10, $.05, $.01, with a space at the far right for the total amount tendered. This detailed information is extremely important if the suspect should be "pulled" immediately for interrogation. The interrogator should know what types of bills and what specific coins he should look for in her handbag or in her pockets. These will have an identifying mark or prerecorded serial numbers.

g) Sufficient space for the shopper to write out a fully detailed narrative report on the violation purchase. Of particular importance in this section are the facts concerning what the salesperson did with the money, how he handled it, whether he held it in the back of his sales book, whether he stuffed it in his shoe, whether he put it into the register without ringing it, or whether he rang a "no sale." It should also include a description of the clothing the suspect wore (to aid in positive identification), and an exact description of each item of merchandise purchased (color, style, and so on).

h) Finally, the shopper's violation report should answer two other questions: 1) Did the salesperson give a receipt? and 2) Was the sale correctly recorded? Before writing a violation report on an employee's failure to give a sales receipt, a shopper should be careful to check the merchandise and the bag to be sure the receipt wasn't included. On every purchase, the shopper should note the price tag and the amount of the sales receipt. She should not assume that just because the item was rung on the register that it was rung at the correct price.

A sample form is illustrated in Figure 3.

The shopping manager should keep an overall report on the total number of shopping purchases made and the departments tested. Separate folders should be maintained on the "specials." These facts should be summarized in the form of a monthly report to store management.

During the day when shoppers are working on the selling floor testing employees, the shopping manager will be busy in the bookkeeping department following up on the previous day's violations. Shoppers will have written violation reports which show that a clerk didn't give a sales check, or failed to ring the register, or performed some other irregularity concerning the sale. The shopping manager checks out these possible violations by going into the auditing department and pulling the cash register tapes for the registers involved. She also pulls the clerk's sales receipt tallies, the sales checks, and any other materials pertinent to the violations that need to be checked out and evaluated. A careful examination of the auditing materials against the shopper's report helps determine whether a theft or a policy violation has occurred. If it is a policy violation, this report may be sent to the head of personnel or to the training department. The salesperson may then be interviewed and reminded of store policy.

The Return-to-Stock Form. The return-to-stock form is used to protect the shoppers and security personnel from charges that the merchandise "disappeared" or was "never returned to the selling department." This form should include the number of the department selling the merchandise; the type of merchandise and a description of each item (size, color, style, etc.); the retail price of the item; and a legible signature of the buyer, assistant buyer, or head of stock who receives the merchandise being returned from the shopping tests.

The form should also be dated as to the day goods were returned to the store or to the selling department, and the name of the person

Employee's Name: _____ Payroll Number: _____ Date: _____

Dept: _____ Register: _____ Salesbook: _____ Floor: _____

Report Checked by: _____

Shopper: _____

IDENTIFYING PURCHASE: Time: _____

(List and itemize merchandise)

Purchase #				Amount		Sales Tax		Total	

Money tendered	10.00	5.00	1.00	50¢	25¢	10¢	5¢	1¢	Total

VIOLATION PURCHASE: Time: _____

(List and itemize merchandise)

Purchase #				Amount		Sales Tax		Total	

Money tendered	10.00	5.00	1.00	50¢	25¢	10¢	5¢	1¢	Total

Did salesperson give receipt? _____

Was sale recorded? _____

Remarks:

Above violation has been verified (tapes examined, tally checked, etc.) by shopping supervisor.

Signed: _____

(Shopping Supervisor)

Figure 3. Shopper's violation report

returning them should also be recorded at the bottom of the form. See Figure 4.

Location of Shopper's Office

Reasonable caution in protecting the identity of your shoppers implies that the office they use should not be located in the store or in any nearby location. If employees on their way out to lunch or relief spot a shopper going into a nearby building two or three times, they will become suspicious. Locate your shopping office off the premises, preferably several blocks away from the store. Have shoppers take their purchases to their cars in the store parking lot, like any other customer, and then drive to the shopping office in some other part of town.

Never bring shoppers into the security office for questioning, if the security office is located in the store, or allow a store detective or store executive to approach them on the selling floor. When a shopper wishes to report information to management, it is best for her to go to a pay telephone and phone in the report, using a private number that does not go through the store's switchboard. Management, in turn, can then make a decision as to whether they want the shopper to continue to observe the subject or whether they will wait until another test is made on another day.

If, for any reason, the honesty shoppers do have to be contacted in the store, some concealed and out-of-the-way spot should be found. This can be a back room in the warehouse or an office upstairs at the rear of the store. It is important to use great care, however, if, for some compelling reason, the shopping office must be situated inside the store. Don't locate it near an employee locker room or rest room or near an elevator where employees might observe the shoppers entering or leaving. Employees are sharp, and they will be quick to spot shoppers.

Developing a Shopping Manual

When setting up your own honesty shopping department, it is advisable to develop a shopping manual which describes the rules of the department, the company's basic policies, and the shopping records and testing methods. This manual should include the legal requirements necessary for the development of a larceny case against the employee. For training purposes, the manual should also contain a detailed, easily understood explanation of the various basic techniques of honesty shopping tests.

Date _____

Dept. Number	Type of Merchandise	Merchandise Description	Price	Received in Stock by:

Merchandise Returned by: _____

Figure 4. Return-to-stock form

The new shopper should be given the shopping manual as part of her basic training. The manual may then be carefully reviewed with the help of the shopping supervisor so the new person fully understands the information in it. To learn the methods of testing described in the manual, the trainee should then be assigned to work on the selling floor for several weeks with an experienced shopper.

In addition to testing methods, the manual should detail how the shopper is to handle her cash bank, how she is to write up shopping reports, how she must balance her cash and merchandise at the end of the day, and how the return-to-stock merchandise is to be listed and totaled. A copy of the manual should also be available in the shopping office for reference.

Providing an Adequate Bank

The manager of the shopping department should supply an adequate cash bank for her shoppers. It is important to provide sufficient money so that shoppers are not limited to testing only those departments with lower-priced merchandise. If funds are too restricted, dishonest employees may be successful in stealing large amounts of cash from departments selling dresses, suits, luggage, electrical appliances, and other higher-priced items because shoppers don't have the money to test these departments.

The result is that both shoppers and management are misled into believing that most shopping thefts occur in departments with lower-price merchandise. They are convinced that they are doing an excellent shopping job, when in fact they are concentrating on only one-tenth of the store's departments and on the least productive ones in terms of substantial cash thefts. The apprehension of a dishonest employee in the better coat department, who steals $95.00 on a sale, is equivalent to 32 honesty shopping detections of $2.95 each in the jewelry department. It is therefore advisable for the shopping manager to provide a somewhat larger bank than may be needed so that if an additional purchase seems advisable, the shopper is not hampered by a shortage of funds.

The shopper's bank should also have a sufficient variety of coins and bills so that she can easily carry out even-money sales for tests. It may be difficult to judge how many pennies, nickels, dimes, quarters, and dollar bills are needed in order to have proper money for a test, but so long as change is available from the shopping manager, shoppers will be able to obtain the denominations they require.

It is unwise for the shopper to get change from the store's cashiers more than once or twice. Frequent trips to the cashier will reveal that she is not an ordinary customer. It doesn't take long for the employee grapevine to spread the word and to reveal the honesty shopper's identity.

The shopping department's cash bank should be balanced daily by the head of the shopping department. She should count the total funds in the bank at the start of the day, keep a careful accounting of the money given to each shopper for making purchases, and balance the purchases made with the money returned by the shopper at the end of the day. The amount of money spent on the purchases and the cash returned by the shopper should be equal to the original fund given her at the start of the day. Periodic surprise audits of shoppers' on-hand cash and merchandise should be made by the internal audit department. But keep in mind that some merchandise may not be on hand because it is being held aside as evidence while shoppers attempt to get a second violation on the employee. These items should also be counted.

Returning Merchandise to Stock

A major point to be considered is how and when shoppers' merchandise is to be returned to stock. In some stores, shoppers' goods are returned directly to the selling area. This is a poor practice, especially when deliveries are made by a member of the security department. Certain salespeople have an amazing memory for faces, and they can associate a customer's face with an item of merchandise she purchased. The next time the shopper comes into the store, the salesman will remember her and will point her out to the other employees.

Another disadvantage to returning shopping merchandise directly to the selling department is that the clerks get to know how frequently honesty shopping tests are being made, the days of the week the shoppers are in the store, and even the hours during which the shopping tests are performed. Obviously, this helps the dishonest employee outsmart the shoppers.

To avoid this problem, two steps can be taken. First, on any theft violation, hold the merchandise until the second or third theft violations occur and management interrogates the employee. Once the statement is taken or the case is brought to court, the merchandise can be returned to stock. Second, hold the routine merchandise that doesn't represent any theft violations for at least three days and then *gradually* feed the items into the return goods system. Use a variety of fictitious customer names and addresses so that the credits attached cannot be traced to the honesty shoppers. When a store has a "return goods room," this provides an excellent way of returning shoppers' merchandise, because it can be processed in such a way that employees in selling departments cannot distinguish the shoppers' purchases from those of regular customers.

The Skilled Honesty Shopper

Honesty shopping requires special skills. It takes talent to play the role of a normal customer and to put the suspect at ease while making a test purchase. The shopper must also be thorough and careful in other aspects of her job. For example, she must be accurate in writing violation reports, and careful in observing the handling of the sale. The following are some of the characteristics of an effective shopper:

Guards Her Identity

Good shoppers are careful not to reveal their identity to anyone. They do not even tell their friends outside the store about the type of work they are doing. People like to gossip, and it is surprising how rapidly information can spread in a community. Before you know it, the news can reach the ears of someone who works in the store.

Keeps Shopping Money Separate

It is unwise for shoppers to make any private purchases during working hours. It is much too easy to mix personal money with shopping funds or to mix up personal and store merchandise. When they are at work, many shoppers prefer to place their own money in a locked safe in the shopping office and to carry with them only the store money furnished for the shopping tests. In this way, there is no danger of confusion if the two become mixed.

Acts Like a Normal Customer

The skilled shopper tries to win the confidence of the employee by creating a belief in her mind that she is an ordinary customer. Some shoppers use shopping bags from other nearby stores to give the impression that they have just been shopping there. Little details like this are helpful in calming the fears of the dishonest employee who always suspects every customer of being an honesty shopper.

The effective shopper remembers that the average customer asks many questions. Is she getting good value for her money? Will the merchandise wear well? Will it suit her needs? Can it be laundered without fading? Does the color match her other accessories? Is it well made? What type of guarantee does it carry? And so on. The talented shopper incorporates these types of questions into her shopping contacts with salespeople.

A real customer would not accept the first item of merchandise shown her by the clerk, hand over the cash, and run. If she were buying hosiery for herself, for example, she would not just ask for her size, but she would also ask questions about the product and compare it with other brands at different prices. In other words, *she shops,* and the honesty shopper must *also shop.* If the shopper is buying a pair of gloves and the salesclerk does not have her size in a particular style, she should not take a smaller or larger pair of gloves because a normal customer would not do so. She must select something else.

Suppose that a salesperson overcharges the shopper. The shopper should respond the way a normal customer does and call this to the clerk's attention. She shouldn't make a particular fuss about it, of course, but it is important that she makes out a violation report after her day's work, notes this overcharge by the clerk, and informs the shopping manager that the clerk should be shopped again to ascertain whether the overcharge was deliberate.

What if she is undercharged by the clerk? Here, again, the shopper should respond the way most customers would and not call the undercharge to the salesperson's attention. (Some customers do, but the majority do not.) She does, of course, note this undercharge in her shopping report.

Dresses the Part

The shopper learns to dress so that she blends into the crowd of the department she is to shop. For example, if a shopper is going to test a teenage "mod" shop, then she should dress and look the part of the young mod customer. This type of symbolic clue suggests that the customer is not an honesty shopper.

Remains Inconspicuous

The effective shopper is not too distinctive in her dress or appearance. She does not wear bright, overly stylish clothes; particularly distinctive hats; or large, unusual pieces of jewelry. She is careful not to use excessive makeup. Bright colors, conspicuous jewelry, and unusual styles would make her stand out from the crowd, and this is not desirable. She also avoids speaking too loudly or being too aggressive and extroverted. It helps if she is quiet and unassuming in her manner and avoids noisy or too animated conversation with salesclerks (although some conversation is vital for convincing the employee that she is a normal customer). In sum, she should not do or say anything that attracts unusual attention to herself.

Varies Testing Methods

The effective shopper tries to vary the type of purchase she makes and the method she uses in testing clerks. In one case, she may use the "single buy" or the "double buy." She may also use the "combination" or the "exchange" buy. As described earlier, there are several basic shopping methods, and the good shopper varies and combines these tests to suit the particular situation. She doesn't get into the habit of making only one type of purchase.

Avoids Soiled Articles

Purchases of soiled, damaged, or perishable goods, unless they are the only type of merchandise available, are normally avoided by the effective shopper. Purchasing such items may result in difficulties in trying to return them to stock. A shopper should, for example, avoid buying white goods in most cases because they quickly become soiled in handling. Only when she is directed to do so should she buy yard goods which have to be cut from the bolt, instead of buying remnants. The same rule would apply to trimmings that are sold by the yard, to chain that is sold by the foot, and to electrical wiring that is sold per foot and is cut from a large roll.

It is also unwise for the shopper to buy the last of any item in stock. She tries to select merchandise that is fresh, in good condition, and not "sale" merchandise. Shoppers should also be careful not to soil or damage purchased merchandise so the store will not suffer a markdown loss.

These rules, however, should be broken at times to avoid establishing patterns which will identify the customer as an honesty shopper. In the retail food business, for example, strict avoidance of perishables for honesty purchases may reveal the shopper's identity.

Knows the Product Being Shopped

Wherever possible, the shopper knows the product being shopped and makes herself familiar with the types of goods she buys. For example, if a woman is buying socks or clothing for a young child, she should give the clerk the child's age and be sure that she knows what the correct size for that age would be. If a man is doing shopping tests in the hardware or paint department, he should know exactly what he is buying. He should be able to recognize a moly-bolt, for instance, and he should have a story prepared before he enters the department as to why he needs the items.

Memorizes Details

When the clerk appears to have stolen the money, the good shopper makes a special effort to remember the clerk's clothing and face so she can write an accurate description in her report. She looks for any distinctive physical characteristics: height, weight, stooped shoulders, facial scars, rough hands, extra-short fingernails, glasses, and so on. She also notes anything unusual about the suspect's clothing or jewelry.

She is even careful about small things, like noting whether the date on the sales receipt issued by the register is correct. Some cases have been lost in court because a forgetful department manager failed to change the date on the cash register, and the cash register receipt used to identify the clerk didn't have the same date as the violation report. Small details can be extremely important if the case should go to court.

Another detail good shoppers note is the exact time of each test purchase. When the salesclerk goes to lunch or relief, for example, she will be closing out her register temporarily, and there will be a "no sale" on the tape and another "no sale" when she returns and reopens her register. If the shopper's sale is made at 3 P.M. for a total amount of $9.17, the next day the shopping manager may find a sale on the tape for $9.17. This suggests the suspect did record the test purchase. But if the $9.17 on the tape appears in the morning hours before the clerk left the register to go to lunch, then the $9.17 on the tape can be ruled out as the shopper's purchase, and it can be assumed there was a theft.

Shows Good Judgment

There are many areas in honesty shopping which require good independent judgment on the part of the shopper. For instance, whenever making a shopping test, the shopper must provide a reasonable opportunity for the clerk to steal the money. If the suspect is waiting on two or three customers at once, or if a department supervisor is standing next to the cash register, the good shopper postpones the test until the situation is more suitable. Sometimes shopping a suspect during the lunch hour or relief period, when there is less floor coverage, provides the opportunity to steal that the thief has been awaiting.

Experienced shoppers often case a department carefully before they move in to do the actual shopping test. They look over the merchandise and select the particular items they plan to buy. One of the things they try to do is to select merchandise that does not require them to hand a large number of coins to the clerk. In other words, if a sale with tax totals $9.15, this is excellent. But if the sale totals $9.84, the clerk may not steal on this particular transaction because it is harder for her to conceal this number of coins. As in any specialty, small points such as these distinguish the professional from the amateur.

Marks the Money

After receiving the day's bank, the experienced shopper assures herself that she has the proper amount of coins and bills to match the tally slip provided by the head of the department. She then lists the serial numbers of her bills and puts a small pencil mark on the border of each one for identification. She also makes a small scratched ''X'' (or some other recognizable mark) on each coin. These marks and the serial numbers of the bills will be vital when the dishonest employee is interrogated.

In many stores, no apprehension is made until an employee has stolen cash on at least two sales, but the exception is when the employee has been observed stealing and has hid the shopper's cash in any location where money would not normally be carried. Under these circumstances, if the employee is kept under constant observation, the employee can often be pulled off the floor for interrogation. Therefore, the experienced shopper takes no chances and uses marked bills on every shopping test.

Honesty shopping is, as we can see, a specialized and complex field that requires special talents, special skills, and alert and imaginative people. It requires the same type of enthusiasm and creativity that characterizes top-notch security investigators and productive floor detectives.

Scientific Devices for Honesty Shoppers

The question is sometimes raised as to whether any of the newer scientific devices can be applied to honesty shopping to improve its effectiveness. Most scientific devices have no application in honesty shopping tests, but there are several which have been used at times for specific applications.

Ultraviolet Lights

First, there is the use of invisible ultraviolet marking pencils for identifying shopping money. Actually, the ultraviolet light marking presents little improvement over traditional marking methods, as it still requires the shopper to record the serial numbers of the bills and the interviewer to be in possession of this record when he starts questioning the suspect. But the ultraviolet pencil can be used effectively to gain a fast admission of guilt from the dishonest employee. The invisible markings can cause the suspect to undergo an emotional jolt which can disorient him and make the investigation more effective. In addition, the fact that the markings are invisible suggests that the store is using scientific devices to detect dishonesty. This causes psychological fear in the mind of the thief. He feels there is no use in lying to the interviewer because he already has the evidence against him.

How can this emotional impact be achieved? Let's suppose you have a dishonest salesman who is regularly stealing cash on sales. The shopper who is going to test him prepares the money in the usual fashion by listing the serial numbers of the bills and putting the pencil mark on the edge of each one. In addition, the shopper also marks each bill with the ultraviolet pencil. The marking is invisible so long as the bill is in normal light. It will only show if the bill is placed under ultraviolet light.

The shopper tests the salesman and gives him the marked money. As expected, the man doesn't ring the sale but, instead, holds the money in back of his sales book. After the shopper leaves the department, an observer sees the employee slide the money out of the sales book, fold it, and slip it into his pocket. A few minutes later, the supervisor of the department is contacted, and he escorts the suspect to the manager's office.

After a few minutes of preliminary discussion, the manager asks him to empty his pockets onto the desk. This, of course, includes the marked money. The manager then spreads the bills out across the blotter so they don't overlap, and asks the salesman point blank if all of the money is his. He states emphatically that it is. The interviewer may ask him the same question again, saying "Are you really sure?" The thief again states unequivocally that the money is indeed his. The manager asks if any of it was taken from the cash register, and the salesman again denies it. When the interviewer feels the employee is completely committed to his statement that every bill on the desk is his own personal money, he quickly snaps on his desk lamp with its ultraviolet light and illuminates the bills spread out on the desk. As the black light hits the ultraviolet crayon markings, the word "STOLEN" suddenly appears on three of the bills. The dishonest employee, faced with this type of dramatic evidence, invariably experiences the emotional shock necessary to break down and confess his guilt.

It has been argued that the employee will undoubtedly admit his dishonesty in any event if the case has been properly prepared, and this is true. But it also is true that he may not confess or that it may take a considerable amount of time and talk before the employee is persuaded to admit his guilt. The use of the ultraviolet marking is a dramatic way of obtaining a fast admission of guilt. In addition, its ability to disorient the thief allows the well-trained interrogator to follow up with questions concerning the length of time the person has been stealing and the amount of his thefts. He can also explore questions relating to why the employee started to steal and to his knowledge of other employees who are also stealing. The black light has given the interviewer a psychological advantage which he can often use to gain in-depth information of the thief's activities, more than he might obtain in a usual type of interrogation.

Stop-Action Cameras

A second type of scientific device suitable for honesty shopping is the stop-action movie camera. In this case, when a register is being hit by shortages and a clerk is suspected of stealing, a stop-action movie camera is placed in a concealed location where it can photograph the amount rung on the register and the hands of the clerk using the register. This camera is connected electronically to the cash register and operates whenever a sale is rung. Opening the register automatically starts the camera, and it continues to run until the sale is completed and the drawer is closed. In this way, the camera observes the amount recorded on the register and the action of the clerk's hands putting in the money and taking out change.

One problem with such technical devices is concealment. A second problem is removing the film each day and loading it with fresh film without being observed by an employee. There is also the necessity of getting the film developed and reviewing the pictures—a time-consuming job. Stores often use these cameras for a short period of time and then abandon the project because it is too much work.

Closed-Circuit Television

Closed-circuit television cameras can also be concealed and used in a similar manner. In many ways, they are more practical than the movie camera. No film or developing is involved, and with today's television tape recorders, a permanent image of the scene may be obtained. The tape recorder unit can be located in a locked closet in the manager's office or in some other remote location, and the camera itself is small, silent, and not difficult to conceal. As it requires little servicing, clerks are unlikely to discover that the cameras are in operation.

It is advisable, however, to exercise some caution in setting up the camera. Outside specialists should be employed to put it in operation at a time when the store is closed and no employees are on the premises. Care should also be taken to keep the closet that contains the television tape recorder locked at all times. No employee should be aware that a concealed television camera is being used. Once any employee knows, there is simply no way of keeping the information confidential.

If the store manager wants to use the television equipment to prevent thefts, that is another matter. In this case, he would let all employees know they are being watched by television cameras. Such an approach, however, can cause serious morale problems. Any decision to use such cameras as a psychological barrier to theft should be carefully weighed and evaluated. It is possible that such a decision could lead to a serious breach of confidence between personnel and management.

Closed-circuit television does have advantages. It allows continuous observation of the salesclerk and cash register for an extended period of time, either from the manager's office or from some other location in the store. It does not require fresh film daily, nor does it require any particular attention. It is light and easy to move to various locations.

But using television for problems involving thefts of cash on sales has limited applications. It is excellent when a clerk is stealing directly out of the register, particularly when a community drawer register is involved. It is possible to locate the thief, and if a thief is spotted, the entire theft operation can be permanently recorded as evidence on a television tape recorder. But if the employee is stealing cash on sales, is underringing on the register, or is pocketing even-money sales, the television camera provides no advantages over the usual honesty shopping operation. In fact, it is a liability because of the excessive amount of time that must be spent with eyes glued to the television monitor before a theft can be spotted. Even if a theft is seen, it is not a desirable theft situation because the clerk is stealing from a normal customer and the money is not marked and cannot be identified as stolen. There is no way the store can move in on this situation and make an apprehension.

In the end, television can discover a suspect, but the employee must still be tested by honesty shoppers. As a method of developing shopping suspects, the television camera is a time-consuming and costly approach. Shoppers are far more productive, less expensive, and more efficient in terms of time and effort.

Electronic Cash Registers

The new electronic cash registers with optical scanning devices hold great promise for ultimately stopping most cash thefts. While developers have thus far concentrated on their capability for providing merchandising information to management, attention is also being given to the accounting and auditing potential of this electronic equipment. However, until improved electronic accounting devices are established throughout retailing, management will have to continue to use prevention and detection methods.

Shoppers Are Indispensable

The least expensive and most productive approach for controlling cash thefts is to prevent them from occurring in the first place. This means better screening of personnel, more adequate register training, tighter control procedures, and greatly improved supervision. But with even the best management, there will continue to be cash thefts. Therefore management will still need detection techniques to find the criminal, and honesty shoppers will remain a valuable weapon. Second only to the undercover agent, they comprise the most productive detection technique available to retail management for eliminating internal theft.

6

UNDERCOVER DETECTIVES

Have you ever wondered if . . .

—Your cashiers are giving special prices to their friends?
—Your stockboys are slipping merchandise out through the back door?
—The night crew is filling its car trunks with store goods?
—Your employees are signing for goods not received?
—Your salesclerks are writing phony refunds?

These types of questions often trouble store managers, because each represents the kind of crimes that are occurring in retail operations today. And yet, while many firms continue to spend large sums of money on floor detectives to fight shoplifting, they neglect the most potent weapon available to protect themselves against internal theft—the *undercover detective*.

The undercover detective is a person schooled in investigative techniques who poses as a regular employee to uncover internal theft activity. He is usually assigned to a specific job and department and is given clearly defined investigative objectives. In many ways, his role is similar to that of the floor detective who pretends to be an average customer and mingles with other customers to detect shoplifters. The undercover agent instead pretends to be an average employee and mingles with other employees to detect dishonest workers. Both detective positions require individuals with special skills and special training.

There are, however, certain major differences between the two. When the floor detective gets tired of pretending to be a customer, he can leave the sales area and have a cigarette, chat a few minutes with one of the salesclerks, or drop into the corner coffee shop with another employee. The undercover detective is by contrast a loner. He has none of these moments of escape from his role. He must act out his part from the time he enters the store in the morning until he leaves at night. In many cases, his dual activities continue long after working hours.

The undercover agent is a person hired as a "warehouse stockman," "receiving man," "stockboy," "bagger," "cashier," and so on. He does the job normally expected of a person hired for one of these positions, but he also works to gain the intimate confidence of his fellow employees. If his co-workers are stealing, his goal is to persuade them to cut him in on the action. He must then establish their method of theft and determine the kind of merchandise being stolen. If possible, he also tries to ascertain how the merchandise is being disposed of.

The agent's job requires a high level of intelligence, analytical skill, puzzle-solving ability, and the talent to act out a role in a believable fashion. Most important, he must be an expert in human relations, a quality that will enable him to win acceptance as a member of the work group and will help him to gain the confidence of dishonest employees.

Management Reluctance: Cost and Ethics

Some people in management shy away from using undercover operators because of the cost involved. Good agents can be expensive. Salaries for the service of really capable detectives range anywhere from $150 to $300 a week, but an experienced agent is well worth the investment. Cost should always be related to cash recoveries, and the recoveries when internal thefts are disclosed can run into thousands of dollars. In many cases, the expense of employing an undercover operator is trivial when compared with the money recovered from a single theft case.

In terms of potential profit returns on dollars invested, one undercover detective is a better investment than a whole staff of floor detectives. The average shoplifter case varies from $3.50 in a supermarket to $50.00 in a top-quality department store. But the dishonest employee case frequently runs from $850 to a half million dollars or more.

Although most supermarkets and other chain stores are extremely vulnerable to shoplifting because of the large quantities of exposed merchandise, this form of theft usually averages 25 to 35 percent of their total theft losses. The primary problem is *internal theft*, which usually accounts for 60 to 75 percent. Therefore, in spending the security dollar, it is wise to allot 60 to 75 percent of the security budget to theft detection carried out by undercover detectives.

In addition to their concern over cost, some executives are reluctant to use undercover agents because of the question of ethics. Naturally, most of us hate to be "spied upon," but management has the right to know what's happening within the company. The word "ethical" is defined as "in accordance with formal or professional rules of right and wrong." So long as the undercover program is restricted to company objectives, none of the formal or professional rules of right and wrong will be violated. Management has no desire to probe into the personal affairs of employees that have no connection with the business. Further, the honest employee has nothing to fear from such a program. It is not a question of "fair play," because dishonest employees are unethical and immoral and have no sense of "fair play" whatsoever. In short, management is as justified in using undercover detectives to ferret out dishonesty among employees as it is justified in using floor detectives to ferret out dishonest customers.

The Value of Undercover Investigation

When and where the agent can be used to best advantage is limited only by your imagination. Some of the ways in which the undercover agent can serve your operation are to:

1) Detect thefts that cannot be prevented by supervision or by the usual control systems and procedures.

2) Detect thefts in nonselling areas, such as the receiving room or warehouse.

3) Uncover thefts in after-hours operations.

5) Resolve the problem of the "suspected" employee by either clearing or incriminating him.

6) Uncover systems loopholes being used by dishonest employees to steal.

7) Probe departments or stores in which high shortages cannot be explained.

Both in matters of direct theft investigation and in exploring areas related to theft, the undercover detective is invaluable to retail operations. The above list represents some of the many ways in which undercover operatives can serve your store by identifying the criminals, by amassing the needed evidence, and by exposing the control weaknesses or the underlying problems that made the theft possible. Let us look at each area in more detail.

Thefts Not Prevented by Controls

Even the best manager and the best control procedures cannot always prevent employees from stealing. Take, for example, a baffling case that occurred in one discount operation store. Walter Marcus, the store manager, had found his attempts to stop the theft of cigarettes in his store extremely discouraging. He had been working on the problem ever since his assistant brought the matter to his attention six months earlier. Walt had tried everything he could think of, but each week cigarette inventory figures continued to show a mounting loss.

Finally, in desperation, he decided to start from scratch. He hired a carpenter to build a special stockroom for the cigarettes, complete with a heavy oak door. Then he went to the local hardware store and bought an expensive padlock, made of heavy steel and guaranteed to defy even the most experienced lock picker. As a further precaution, he took the two keys that came with the lock and had them stamped

"Do Not Duplicate." Finally, he entrusted one key to his assistant and kept the other on his own key ring clipped to his belt.

Walt also set up a new control procedure for the cigarette stock. Under this system, only his assistant could remove cigarettes from the stockroom. A running inventory record pad was tacked inside the stockroom door, and whenever cigarettes were removed from the locked area, the exact number of cartons by brand name and by quantity were noted on the pad.

Eight weeks later, as Walt walked to the stockroom to check the inventory, he was optimistic. He had gone over the control plan in his mind many times. There was no possible loophole he could see. The stock simply had to balance. But would it?

Reaching the stockroom door, he first carefully examined the lock. He could find no scratches or other signs of a "picked" or "forced" entry. He bent over and carefully examined the hasp and the edges of the door. Still no telltale marks. Walt smiled to himself. It really looked as though he had licked the thieves this time. Soon he was busy checking the stock against his inventory sheets. He was careful and thorough, counting each opened carton twice to verify the accuracy of his survey. He even opened several of the larger boxes to be sure they were filled with the correct number of individual cigarette cartons. It was 40 minutes before he had completed his inventory count. Finally, he took down the inventory withdrawal pad, snapped the heavy padlock shut, and carried the two sets of figures upstairs to his office.

Once seated at his desk, he pulled over the small adding machine and totaled each inventory list. Then he subtracted the number of cartons removed by his assistant. He stared at the figure in amazement. His inventory showed 47 cartons of cigarettes were missing. Impossible! In spite of the tight controls he had put over the stockroom, the new door, and the heavy padlock, the thief had somehow managed to rob his stock again. There simply seemed to be no answer to the problem.

Later in the day, Walt and his assistant reviewed the implications of this latest inventory count, trying to decide what else could be done. Suddenly his assistant snapped his fingers. "I've got it!" he said. "Let's put an undercover agent in with the stockpeople."

Walt was hesitant, "I don't know."

"Look," he argued, "we've tried everything, and there's no way to find out what's happening."

Walt finally approved the suggestion and phoned a local detective agency. Three days later an undercover agent was hired by the store as a stockboy. The young man was soon accepted as one of the regular workers, and it wasn't long before the thieves offered to cut him in on the loot. The case was rapidly solved.

It turned out that the gang wasn't deterred at all by the sturdy stockroom and fancy lock. In fact, they weren't concerned about the lock at all. Their only interest was in how the stockroom door was mounted. The hinges were on the outside, and using a hammer and a large nail to tap out the holding bolts the door was easily removed. In this way, they were able to enter and leave the stockroom without disturbing the lock.

The agent also learned that the gang was stealing other items as well as cigarettes. They had taken several tape recorders and portable radios from a locked showcase. Again the locks were meaningless. The thieves simply used a quarter to pry up the edge of the glass counter top.

In this example, as in many other cases, stock records indicated serious losses, but neither systems nor supervision could detect the culprits or stop the thefts. The only logical answer to such security problems is the use of competent undercover agents.

Thefts in Receiving Operations

Because serving customers is a primary responsibility, management attention, quite naturally, is often directed more to selling areas than to nonselling departments. Ironically, however, many of the major theft problems are in nonselling operations. Receiving areas are particularly vulnerable to thefts. They are usually confused and haphazard operations, often made worse by poor housekeeping. And because all store merchandise passes through this one physical area, it is an ideal spot for individual and collusive thefts. With proper receiving control records, losses may be detected; but stopping them is often a different matter.

One store in the Midwest, for example, was suffering from high shortages in its dress department. Investigation of the records traced the losses to the receiving operation, but management was baffled as to how to identify the thieves. The company employed a number of receiving people who worked on different shifts, so there seemed to be no way, in terms of control systems, to pinpoint the individuals involved. Finally, the operations vice-president decided to hire an undercover agent.

The agent, whom we shall call "Jack Briggs," was employed

through the personnel office and assigned to work as a receiving department employee. During his first three weeks on the job, Jack could find no clues indicating dishonesty among the dock workers. In fact, he found the receiving men, by and large, to be of good character and integrity. Yet, the control records left little doubt that the dress thefts were occurring in the receiving department.

Then, one day, the detective was returning to the store after lunch and stumbled upon the answer. Here's how he explained it in his own words:

"As I approached the store, I stopped for a moment at the edge of a sidewalk crowd and squinted to focus my eyes on the receiving dock. I thought I'd stand and watch it for a few minutes. I wasn't looking for anything in particular; I was just doing my usual job of observing to see if there was anything special happening. At first I watched a lone delivery truck as it ambled down the alley away from the store, pausing at the curb as the driver looked for a hole in traffic. So far there was nothing of interest.

"The truck finally got an assist from a friendly cab driver and turned into the street. The alley leading away from the store was now deserted. Then suddenly I saw something. I caught a movement in the shadows at the back of the alley. A moment later, a man emerged from the darkness and walked briskly across the receiving dock. Under his arm he carried a large dress box. Suddenly I got that funny feeling you get when you know you're on to something. Perhaps it was his actions or the fact he was carrying this big box; but whatever it was, I was sure this was the man I had been seeking.

"As I watched my suspect climb down off the dock, I felt sure that I knew him, but I had to get closer to make a positive identification. As he slouched down the alleyway toward the street, hugging the box to his side, I soon got a better look at him—a tall man with a large paunch and flattened nose. There was no mistaking that face! The man was the head of the receiving department.

"Even as I watched, he shifted the package to his other arm; the box was obviously heavy with merchandise. I had to duck back quickly at one point because he stopped to look up and down the alley, as though afraid someone might be following him. Once he had looked around with that look of fear so common to the thief, I was sure he was the man I wanted."

The undercover agent reported his observations to the store manager. The next day, shortly before noon, the manager parked his car on the main street around the corner from the store's receiving alley. Patiently, he waited. An hour passed, then another 40 minutes. There was still no sign of the suspect. Then his patience was rewarded. The same employee emerged around the corner from the receiving dock with a large box under his arm. It was like a rerun of the previous day's episode. The thief stopped for a moment to look up and down the street, then he walked rapidly south toward a nearby bus station. The manager who had been watching him quickly got out of his car and, hugging the building walls to be sure he wouldn't be seen, slipped quietly up behind the receiving manager. "What do you have in the box, Harry?"

The thief wheeled in fright to look into the eyes of the store manager. Knowing he was caught, he froze in panic, unable to speak.

"Is this the first time you ever did this?" continued the store manager.

Shaking with shock, the frightened culprit answered in a barely audible voice: "Yes, I don't know why I did it. Today is the first time. Really it is! The first time." He repeated this phrase insistently as though somehow that fact justified his actions.

"Well, let's go back and talk it over," said the store manager, gently taking him by the arm. Seated in the manager's office, Harry was at first evasive and hostile; but as the interview continued, he finally broke down and confessed. He admitted that he had been stealing from the receiving room for the past seven years.

"It was easy," said Harry. "I'd just stuff a few dresses into a box and walk out the receiving dock and down the alley."

"But what if you were asked about the package?"

"Oh, I was stopped twice. I just said it was merchandise I was dropping off at a vendor because it was damaged."

"What do you do with the merchandise? Where is it now?"

"I sold it."

"To whom?"

"To some of my buddies, you know, guys in the store and their friends. You see, I take the stuff over to the bus terminal and check it in a public locker. Then I take the key and later have lunch with some of the guys. After lunch, we hold a raffle for the key to the locker that has the box of merchandise. Sometimes the key goes to the highest bidder or sometimes everyone just chips in, and then we draw slips out of a hat for the key."

"How much would you get?"

"Usually about ten or fifteen dollars. It depends on how much money the guys have on them on the particular day we raffle off the key.''

No one will know the full extent of Harry's thefts. With seven years of stealing behind him, he couldn't begin to remember all the merchandise he had stolen. But he did sign a statement admitting $50,000. Police later estimated the actual figure was many times that amount. The store manager regretted he had not put an undercover agent on the dock long ago. Although the store had controls, they weren't sufficient to detect or to deter the thief.

Similar thefts from receiving docks, stockrooms, warehouses, and transfer trucks occur daily in stores across the country. Neither control procedures nor alert supervision can get at the core of all of these thefts. Often, the only way to eliminate them from the company is through the use of an undercover agent.

Warehouse and Transfer Thefts

Many large thefts of merchandise involve the store warehouse or transfer operations. Thefts from transfer trucks are a common occurrence, and losses can reach staggering proportions. For example, in a large city in the Northwest, management of a 12-store chain found that over a period of eight years seven of their warehouse and transfer employees had been stealing from the firm's transfer trucks. These thefts averaged $1,000 worth of merchandise daily. The fact that these thefts continued for so many years before the culprits were discovered shows how serious and how difficult it is to control store transfers of merchandise. In this particular case, the store admitted a loss of $250,000 in merchandise, of which $35,000 was recovered from the homes of employees at the time of apprehension. Police investigating the case said that probably the actual losses were closer to one million dollars. In any event the thefts were substantial.

Warehouses are also the frequent targets of large thefts. This is probably due to several factors:

1) The warehouse is usually isolated from store management both physically and mentally.

2) Management neglects the operation because of its tendency to put attention where the action is; namely in the store.

3) Although detectives are put in the selling departments, no undercover detectives work in the warehouse, and security is inadequate.

4) The physical layout of the building often aids the thieves. There are numerous uncontrolled exits, aisles are not straight, and lighting is poor. Even in a well-run warehouse, there are periods of peak activity in which housekeeping is neglected. During such periods of merchandise movement, thefts are easily concealed by the confusion of the overall operation.

5) The warehouse manager may become a serious obstacle to preventing theft losses. He often does not feel that he is part of the management team. Sometimes he feels he's been isolated and neglected. His reaction is to build a personal dynasty and to become overprotective toward his operation and his personnel. Therefore, he often resents any security restrictions and misinterprets any attempt by store management to improve security controls in his operation.

6) The warehouse is often a sensitive labor area. If it is not unionized, management will usually do everything possible to keep the union out. This means keeping the workers happy. The end result is often lax control and little or no meaningful security in the entire operation.

The warehouse, as in other nonselling operations, needs undercover agents to detect employee dishonesty. It is the only effective method available to locate internal thefts. Psychologically, guards can prevent many thefts because they impose a climate of control over the warehouse. But to the real criminal, a guard is easily defeated. Systems and procedures can also prevent thefts as well as pinpoint the fact that theft losses are occurring. But procedures cannot uncover the methods of theft being used or the thieves. Even strong supervision is limited. A warehouse supervisor cannot be in all places at once. He can often spot a high-risk employee and have him removed from the operation, but he is powerless to stop the real criminal and can seldom detect group thefts.

Because management is usually customer-oriented and therefore primarily concerned with store problems, it can easily overlook the security vulnerability of the warehouse. Based on past experience in many companies, this can be a costly mistake. For example, a large Midwestern chain learned through its control procedures that serious losses were occurring in its warehouse. After considerable debate, management decided to put three undercover men into the operation. The findings of these agents were not only startling, but revealed the extent of dishonesty that can occur without discovery under the very eyes of management.

The agents reported that collusive employee thefts began three years earlier. At that time, two nighttime employees at the warehouse began to steal. Soon the whole group was involved in the thefts. At first, their thefts were on a small scale; they stole merchandise and put it into the trunks of their cars. Then one of them suggested that they could make some money on the side by selling stolen goods to friends. The men began to approach some of their acquaintances and got a favorable response. At first, they took orders for merchandise and delivered it to the homes of their friends. As time passed, they became more daring. Soon members of the theft ring began to invite friends into the warehouse at night to select the merchandise they wanted. Naturally, they charged their friends only a fraction of the retail price.

Soon the nights were busy as the employees helped their customers to cart the chairs, sofas, refrigerators, pool tables, air conditioners, and other goods to their cars and pickup trucks. Traffic leading in and out of the warehouse each night began to resemble the line of cars at a drive-in movie. Business was good. But the thieves were not satisfied. How could they get more customers? Suddenly one employee had a brainstorm. "Why not advertise?" he suggested.

"Of course," agreed the other thieves. After all, the warehouse office had a mimeograph machine and the wife of one of the night workers was a secretary. In less than a week, the group put together a 30-page catalogue of items carried in the warehouse stock, but with the *special prices* being offered by the group. A $200 sofa was offered for $85.00; $75.00 chairs went for $20.00; $350 air conditioners cost only $120, and so on. The men not only mimeographed the catalogue, they also included sketches of some of the merchandise. These drawings were made by a friend of one of the men, a commercial artist. Once the catalogue was mimeographed and stapled together, the night crew divided its work into two groups: one group took care of filling the night orders and loading the trucks, while the second group took copies of the new catalogue and toured bars and restaurants in the neighborhood soliciting sales.

Business was really booming! Soon it was decided that the group should provide their customers with an added service—the delivery of merchandise. So they began to forge customer's-own-merchandise sales checks, using them to send the stolen items out through the store's normal delivery channels. But business was too good and management began to notice the losses.

Once the undercover agents had developed a legal case against the dishonest employees, the store notified the police and they moved in on the thieves. They closed up the racket, but the final tally of losses suffered by the company was a painful blow. In only three years, the thieves had stolen $350,000 worth of merchandise. Only a few hundred dollars of it was ever recovered.

How could warehouse employees get away with these thefts for such a long period of time? Why wasn't management at least aware that losses of this size were occurring? Because the firm's inventory figures never reflected the warehouse losses. Of course, the people who took the inventory checked the merchandise in the warehouse each year at inventory time, but the crew working the warehouse outsmarted them. The dishonest employees stole the merchandise but left the packing cases that the goods came in stacked on the warehouse floor. No one suspected they were empty; the clever culprits had nailed them to the ground.

Thefts in After-Hours Operations

If not well supervised, workers on early and late schedules often steal. In fact, most major gang thefts in retailing are committed by after-hours workers. Typical of this problem was a case in a large store in New Jersey. Five bakers came into the store each day at 6 A.M. to bake bread and pastries for the store restaurant and bakery department. Over a period of time, this group formed a collusive theft operation.

After two years of organized and systematic thefts, the store became alarmed by the growing inventory shortage figures and began an extensive security investigation. The study revealed that the merchandise was being stolen during the night. Repeatedly, employees coming on the job in the morning reported merchandise missing which had been seen on the selling floor the night before. Management finally decided to put undercover agents into various nighttime operations. One agent was planted in the porter group, another in the control division where the night clerical staff and computer employees worked; then, with some reluctance, because they felt this was a complete waste of time and money, the company also added an agent to the early morning baking crew.

In less than a week, the undercover agent discovered the source. Management was awed by the extent of the bakers' thefts. For two years this group had been stealing on a large scale from the store. Their operation had become so professional that they had even rented a warehouse on the other side of the city to hold the stolen merchandise. When the store president visited the clandestine warehouse, he was shocked by the amount of goods the bakers had stolen. Although it represented only a small part of the group's total thefts, 23 large furniture vans were needed to bring the stolen merchandise back to the store.

Night cleaning crews are also a major nighttime theft group. Large thefts by such groups are uncovered so frequently that one wonders why stores continue to neglect proper precautions. Such thefts often result from a failure to screen the night porters properly before putting them on the job. Many stores depend upon the outside cleaning agency to do the screening and often find out too late that the agency doesn't do so. In addition, night workers are often poorly supervised. The porter groups are usually free to steal with little risk of being caught.

Professional thieves recognize the lack of management controls over night porters and move in to exploit this weakness. The professional thief will often contact night workers by striking up a conversation in a nearby bar or coffee shop where the crew hangs out. He offers the porters immediate hard cash for the wanted stolen merchandise. Soon the porter group's thefts become systematic and substantial, with theft the main order of business and cleaning only an incidental consideration.

Even after a gang of thieving porters is caught, this still does not insure a solution. The outside professionals will soon be at the coffee shop or bar recruiting larcenists from the new porter staff. Over the years, this repeating pattern of thefts by night porters has become so common that security directors continually urge management to assign at least one undercover agent to the night cleaning crew. Management, on the other hand, tends to wait until specific thefts have occurred before taking action. In most cases, they wait far too long. The store often suffers a serious and unnecessary loss because of the company's slowness in acting to uncover the thieves.

Often, the after-hours porter thefts are well organized and even ingenious. The executives of a large store in Miami, for instance, heard rumors that a man was approaching bar patrons in the district and asking them if they would like to purchase an expensive brand of men's suits carried exclusively by their Miami store. The man claimed that the manufacturer had overproduced a tremendous quantity and had decided to sell them privately as seconds through a special "wholesale" outlet in each state. As the Florida representative, he could offer them the suits at approximately one third of their original retail price.

The story sounded believable and some of the bar patrons took advantage of the offer, ordering suits of specific styles, fabrics, and sizes. If the customer didn't know what size or color he wanted, he was instructed by the "salesman" to go into the department store that carried these suits, to pick out the suit he liked, and to copy down the style number, color, and size from the label. He told the prospect that his company's selection of suits was so large that he could be reasonably sure they would have an exact duplicate in their wholesale stock. Of course, the customer's selection was simply stolen from the store.

After several of these stories had reached the ears of store management, it was decided to put an undercover worker into the porter group. Both store management and the security director were completely baffled by these reported thefts. They had competent supervision, and the store security department had tight controls over the porters when they left the building at 2 A.M. The security director was sure the porters couldn't get the suits out of the building in phony packages or concealed on their persons.

How did they steal? A porter would push his trash truck into the stockroom of the department, making his usual pickup of refuse. After glancing around to be sure he wasn't being watched, he would remove several men's suits, hangers and all, and drop them into his cart. When his trash truck was filled with refuse, he would dump its contents down the chute to the store's baling room. There, another member of the gang would put all the stolen suits into one trash bale and then put an "X" on the bale so it could be easily distinguished. At the end of the shift, all the bales of trash were taken up to the street loading dock and put onto a trash truck. The man driving the truck, although he worked for an outside concern, was also involved in the thefts. He would stop his truck at a predetermined place on the edge of town and throw the bale under some trees in a ditch. The porters, after being checked off their night shift by the security guards, would drive to the isolated spot in a pickup truck, recover the bale, take it to a garage, and remove the stolen merchandise. In addition to men's suits, the gang was also stealing radios, tape recorders, stereo equipment, dresses, and other merchandise. The stolen items were all stored in a large cellar in the home of one of the porters.

The undercover agent discovered that the theft operation was set up by a professional syndicate operating along the Eastern seaboard. This gang of professional criminals specialized in organizing store employees of various types. The group recruited the employees, then taught them various ingenious methods of theft. Losses from these inside groups of thieves were estimated to be about $5,000 a week or a quarter of a million dollars a year.

If the store had heeded the advice of security specialists and recognized the vulnerability of night operations to theft, an undercover agent might have been planted as a permanent member of the night porter group. In this way, the syndicate would never have gained a foothold in the company.

Collusive Theft Rings

Not all employee theft rings, of course, are found in nonselling areas or in after-hours operations. They can turn up in any part of the store. Group thefts by stockboys, receiving men, checkers, markers, and similar gangs are uncovered daily. In recent years, the shift from individual to gang thefts has obviously created a serious threat to store profits. It reflects a change in employee attitudes. Several years ago, for instance, most internal thefts were the work of a lone thief. In those days, if one employee discovered another stealing he would report the thief to management. This type of moral responsibility has practically disappeared from retailing. Today's retail employee not only keeps the thief's secret but often joins up with him.

Many employee thefts may also involve outsiders, such as resource truck drivers. Professional criminals have been known to approach the drivers at diners where they congregate and offer to buy any merchandise the driver can salvage from his deliveries. Once the dishonest trucker is given the opportunity to unload stolen merchandise and to receive on-the-spot cash in payment, his next logical step is to persuade a receiving employee to put merchandise on the dock where he can steal it, or to sign for merchandise that is not delivered to the company. A dishonest receiving dock employee may sign a receipt for six cartons and receive only five. The truck driver keeps the sixth carton and sells the merchandise to a fence. He then splits the money with his accomplice on the dock.

A similar situation can involve deliverymen and vendors' representatives. The dishonest employee assigned to check in the merchandise delivered to the selling floor can be working with the deliveryman and can sign an inflated invoice. The store again pays for merchandise never received. Some merchants feel such thefts are nickel-and-dime losses of little importance, but in many companies they become quite substantial.

In Seattle, Washington, for example, a vendor's representative was finally caught and jailed after admitting he had cheated a single chain of more than $47,000 worth of merchandise. These thefts occurred because dishonest employees signed for merchandise never received. A deliveryman who serviced bread and pastries in a chain of Chicago supermarkets was able to build a 12-room house on his share of the proceeds from illegal charges made to his supermarket customers —charges that often could not have been made without the aid of dishonest employees working with him. Uncovering these types of thefts requires close supervision, tight checking procedures, and the use of undercover agents.

Clearing or Incriminating the Suspected Employee

One of management's real nightmares is to have an employee on the staff who is suspected of stealing and, yet, have no factual evidence to determine the validity of this suspicion. Is the employee stealing or not? Human nature being what it is, once a person is suspected of dishonesty, the tendency is to believe the worst. But often these suspicions are unfounded.

A typical example involved two packers in a large store. Night after night, the assistant store manager noticed them leave the store with large shopping bags full of packages of merchandise. Each package had a colored seal indicating an employee purchase. The assistant manager couldn't believe these packers could make so many personal purchases day in and day out. He therefore suspected them of stealing. Finally, to resolve the problem, he placed an undercover agent in the packing department. After three weeks of close observation, the agent reported that in every instance the suspected packers had bought the merchandise they carried out of the store. There was no evidence of stealing.

The work of the undercover agent in this case not only relieved the mind of the assistant manager and removed the cloud of suspicion from the two packers, but it had an ironic twist. In the course of his observation, the agent uncovered a ring of three other packers, not suspected by management, who were stealing large quantities of merchandise. The thefts of this trio might have continued indefinitely if management had not placed an agent in the operation. Uncovering the real theft ring was a bonus, but it points up the need to put an undercover agent periodically into each nonselling operation.

Unfortunately, the employee suspected of stealing does not always turn out to be honest. One case in which a department manager's suspicions were confirmed involved a saleswoman who was suspected of stealing merchandise. The department manager was suspicious because of the woman's nervous manner whenever he unexpectedly came up behind her. But he couldn't determine how she was stealing the merchandise; she seldom took a package out of the store. Finally, an undercover agent was put in the department, and the manager soon had his answer.

The salesclerk was working with accomplices from outside the store. An accomplice would come into her department during a busy period, pick out an item of merchandise, and give it to the clerk. She would then appear to write a sales check for the merchandise, wrap it, and hand the package to her "friend," so it looked like the usual sales transaction. But the sales check which she appeared to write was not a sales receipt check, it was an "even-exchange" sales check. Sometimes she would vary the technique and write a fraudulent "uneven-exchange" check. In one instance, for example, she gave the accomplice a $19.95 bedspread and had him pay the difference between that and the fictitious $14.95 bedspread supposedly brought back for a credit. Once the department head was informed of the method of theft being used by the saleswoman, he was able to move in on the problem.

Thefts Involving Systems Loopholes

One of the questions raised in every employee theft case is what method of theft is being used. The undercover agent, because he gets directly involved in the action, is able to supply this vital information. The store benefits in two ways: first, the thief is eliminated; and second, the control system or procedure can often be redesigned to prevent similar thefts in the future.

Many control procedures fail simply because they aren't properly enforced. It is also true, however, that some control systems have built-in loopholes which allow dishonesty. The undercover operator, by investigating thefts and working directly with the thieves, can advise headquarters if a manager is lax in enforcing control procedures or if there are control loopholes that need to be corrected. Discovering weak spots in store controls is important. Management must never underestimate the ingenuity of the thief. Whenever a store control procedure has a loophole, you will invariably find that one or more dishonest employees are using it.

The case of the dishonest saleswoman who was stealing merchandise by writing fraudulent even-exchange sales checks is a typical example of a systems loophole being used by a dishonest employee to beat the company. The loophole in this case was the fact that even-exchange sales checks did not require a customer's name and address nor an authorizing signature by the department head. Once management recognized the problem, it was a simple matter to close off this method of employee theft.

A book could be written about the number and variety of procedural loopholes spotted by undercover investigators. Systems design weaknesses occur in nearly every store and are usually unique to that particular store's procedures. Once the thefts are uncovered, better procedures or stricter enforcement can prevent future occurrences of similar thefts.

Probing Departments with High Shortages

Inventory shortages, of course, have many causes besides theft. They include:

1) Errors in pricing and price changes.

2) Faulty stock work or mishandling in receiving, inspection, packing, and delivery.

3) Poor stock-keeping in reserve and floor stocks.

4) Sales check errors, special sales, promotions, and ringing sales on the wrong department key.

5) Clerical, accounts payable, sales audit, and statistical errors, etc.

6) Faulty end-of-period physical inventory (poor cut-off); record problems with invoices, merchandise transfers, charge-backs to the manufacturer, customer returns, and price change reports.

7) Buyer manipulation of markdowns (unrecorded markdowns).

Many times the causes of a high shortage are illusive. Shortage controllers themselves are often frustrated by their inability to find the sources of high-loss figures. Since there seems to be no other viable explanation, the tendency in such situations is to assume the losses are due to thefts. Many times, the real problem is that the buyer and shortage controller have not been able to get close enough to the floor operation to see what procedural breakdowns are actually causing the shortages.

By working every day in a problem department, the undercover agent trained in store systems and procedures can often locate the source of high shortages. If the shortages are being caused by stealing, the agent can uncover this fact; if by carelessness and errors, the agent can find out where control procedures have failed. Thus, he may discover that the buyer is manipulating markdowns, or he may find that numerous errors are being made in the pricing and remarking of goods. These and similar weaknesses in the operation can often be revealed. When a store has a high-shortage department that has resisted all normal approaches to bringing the shortages in line, the undercover agent becomes the next logical step to finding the needed answer.

Other Potential Benefits

In addition to locating the source of high-shortage figures, the undercover agent, when properly trained, can feed back a variety of information. He can help the store by reporting on problems in employee relations. Facts can also be developed regarding employee morale, supervisory competence, and employee and supervisory attitudes. Details may also be revealed concerning employees who are passing confidential information on to business competitors. Agents have uncovered executives falsifying company records, have found the source of production slowdowns, have solved vandalism and sabotage problems, and have identified other undesirable activities by individuals and groups.

Setting Up an Undercover Program

There are many steps to be taken and decisions to be made in setting up an undercover operation. As with honesty shoppers, one of the first decisions concerns the relative advantages of using an outside service versus establishing your own investigative department. Setting up an internal undercover program is not difficult. Some basic guidelines are all that you will require to put this valuable investigative resource to work within your company.

Outside Agency or Your Own Agents?

When a company decides to use undercover agents, it often hires an outside detective agency. If the agency is reliable and employs trained and competent people, this can be a wise decision, particularly when an agent is needed in a hurry. The outside service is also useful when management doesn't have the time to select or to work with its own undercover staff. But agency detectives will naturally be more costly than those employed by the store, as the agency does expect to make a profit.

As in all things, there are both outstanding and mediocre detective agencies, and all grades in between. Some agencies provide talented detectives, well trained and well qualified for the undercover job. Others put untrained and unqualified agents into the store who fail to produce needed information and often cause serious problems for the firm. Before hiring an outside service, management should investigate its competence by requesting and checking out some of its references.

Once the agency is selected, a member of top management should work closely with the organization. He should ask the agency executive for a detailed background report on the experience of the undercover agent proposed for the assignment, including what cases he's solved in the past, how long he has been with the agency, whether he's been screened for a police record, and what type of training he has received.

In dealing with the outside agency, the executive in charge should specify the information he wants and how and when he wants it presented. He should state clearly that he is not interested in reports on extraneous matters or minor infractions of rules, that he does not want reports on a daily or weekly basis, and that he only wants to hear from the agent when he has worthwhile information. He should also arrange to brief the agent personally on the background of the situation and the objectives of the investigation, and should see to it that the agent receives training in store procedures related to the assignment.

Outside agencies are useful when starting an undercover program, but, in the long run, the store should have its own undercover staff. At an early date, management should begin to develop its own department and phase out, except in extreme emergencies, the use of agents from outside agencies.

The advantages to using your own undercover agents are many. They are permanent employees of the company and thus develop company loyalty. The longer they work for you, the more accepted they become by other employees. Also, over a period of time, they learn the various control systems and procedures in the company and become familiar with management philosophy and company goals. Your own agents get to know a lot about department heads and employees throughout the company, and this knowledge allows them to give management more meaningful information when problem situations are uncovered. In turn, management gets to know its agents and to understand them as people—what motivates them, how to evaluate their reports, and how to work with them to improve the overall operation of the store.

The agent who is a permanent member of the store staff can be moved from one department to another (if the transfer can be made to appear logical to other employees). This often makes it easier to get an agent into a particular department without suspicion, and the employees in the new department will more readily accept him. The store also reduces the cost of the program since using its own staff is much less expensive than using agency detectives.

As one vice-president said: ''When we used outside agency detectives, it was not only more costly but too often unproductive. Sometimes it would take weeks or months for the agent to learn enough about our procedures and our people to provide us with the information we wanted. Now that we have our own undercover staff, we have experienced and knowledgeable people. They know our employees and our procedures, and they can quickly spot irregularities or pinpoint control system weaknesses because they know what they're looking for. On occasion, we still use an outside agency for a particular problem. We may require an agent fast, to hit a hot trouble spot, and we don't have one of our own agents that can be moved quickly to the problem department. In such a case, the agency gives us fast action which is a real service. But we find that, overall, our own staff is more effective and far less costly."

Select Agent Applicants Cautiously

Selecting the right people for your undercover staff is important. The individuals chosen must be keenly interested in this type of work and must be willing to perform whatever chores the job requires and whatever steps are necessary to carry out the investigation. In evaluating your candidates, it is advisable to check for the characteristics described below.

Good Character and Honesty. Be sure that the person you select has an unblemished record for personal integrity. Do a full background check before you employ him. This means a credit investigation, a neighborhood investigation by an outside agency, and a check for a police record. Have your local credit bureau provide a background report. Find out if the applicant is under any unusual financial pressures. Contact his former employers. As with any other job in your company, the good character and honesty of the applicant should be among your primary considerations.

You must keep in mind that there is always the risk that the agent will become dishonest and join the thieves. Experience shows that this has occurred in many cases. The person in an undercover job is often required to become intimately involved with criminals stealing from the store, and he may be tempted to join the thieves. Experience also shows that criminals often seek store security jobs, and for this reason the careful screening of all security people for a previous criminal record is vital. Often, as many as one in four security job applicants have previous criminal records.

Role-Playing Ability. Not every person is suited for undercover work. The best choice for a job of this type is a person who has shown a past interest in acting, who has always liked the theater, and who has performed in plays in high school, college, or a community theater group. Usually such individuals have the necessary creativity to find undercover work an exciting challenge.

Role-playing ability also calls for flexibility in the agent's personality. The agent must do everything possible to gain the confidence of his fellow employees. Sometimes this means that he has to give up some of his personal opinions and prejudices and has to share in the opinions and beliefs of the employees he is working with. For example, an inexperienced agent failed on a case because he couldn't give up his personal political beliefs. He was an ardent supporter of a liberal candidate for president, and the employees in his group supported a conservative. Opinions clashed and the agent destroyed any chance of winning the group's confidence.

The agent's taste in clothes and accessories may also have to be sacrificed in order to fit in with his background story for the job. The price, age, fit, and neatness of his clothing must be considered. Personal cleanliness may have to be sacrificed on certain assignments. His jewelry, watches, and other items of this nature must all be in accord with his assumed status level. If he brings tools to the assignment, they must be secondhand. The same holds for work clothes. All these adjustments are necessary at times in role playing.

If the agent finds he cannot play the role assigned, he should admit it readily. One undercover agent working on a suspected store executive was sent to a convention at an exclusive hotel, equipped with a suitable wardrobe and adequate bankroll. But after his first meal in the hotel's luxurious dining room, he phoned his boss and asked to be relieved of the assignment. He found he couldn't cope with the array of silverware on the table. Talking with other convention executives, he found they discussed matters which he knew nothing about. He was smart enough to see that he couldn't fit in with the other executives and wasn't properly equipped to handle the role called for by the assignment.

Analytical Ability. The agent will be constantly matching wits with dishonest employees, so a sharp mind is an important requirement. He needs mental ability to adapt quickly to emergencies, and he must have strong powers of logic and good reasoning ability—this means the talent to analyze information and to see how various bits and pieces fit together. Undercover investigations are often like assembling a jigsaw puzzle. Being able to figure out probabilities is part of the undercover job. Ask the applicant if he is adept at puzzles, plays chess, or enjoys bridge or poker. Seek something in his background that shows he has good analytical ability.

Fits in with the Work and People. The undercover agent needs to have some knowledge of the work situation where he will be assigned. If you plan to put him into the warehouse, he must know enough about warehouse work so he can take his place among the other workers. Unless the job is one requiring a novice, your agent will have to know enough about the skills required by the job to prevent arousing suspicion among the regular workers that he isn't one of them.

Workers in every department in a store have a particular language of their own. A person who steps into a job and doesn't use the language of the employees will be considered an outsider. Also, take note if the work group into which you are planning to put your agent has several people in it who speak a foreign language. If this is the case, it is important that your agent is able to understand and speak that foreign language fluently. Most people discuss their secret theft plans in their native tongue. Any agent placed in such a situation who doesn't know the language has a liability which is usually impossible to overcome.

Exercises Patience. A good agent is aggressive, and you want him to be aggressive; but be sure he also has the ability to endure frustration, because the job requires endless patience. Undercover work is like fishing. You catch the most fish with the right bait, a good fishing hole, and patience, particularly patience, so the fish gets a good grip on the hook before you pull it in.

Skilled undercover work requires patience on the part of both management and agent. A major employee theft ring may require six months to a year before the agent can work his way into the confidence of the culprits. When shortages indicate a major problem, by all means allow the undercover man sufficient time to gain the confidence of the suspected employees.

Shows Emotional Stability. Interview an agent carefully for indications that he is emotionally stable and has good self-control. The emotionally immature undercover agent can betray himself in many ways. He may, for example, give in to the temptation to boast to another employee about the work he is doing. He may be the type of person who simply can't keep a secret, especially in the evening hours after friendly conversation over a couple of martinis with another employee. Or he may give himself away by wearing something out of character, such as showing up for a stockboy's job wearing a diamond-studded wristwatch, which he can't help showing off. He can also give himself away by being overly aggressive or by asking too many personal questions too early in his association with the other employees.

Hire Through Normal Channels

Placing the agent on the job is a delicate operation. In some companies where the personnel manager also heads up the security operation, placement is easier because he can be taken into management's confidence. But if this is not the case, then security must be absolute, and the undercover agent must apply for the job and gain employment on his own. It is dangerous to have too many people aware of the agent's identity.

In the ideal situation, the agent should be hired without the personnel office knowing his real purposes. Don't notify the personnel manager that you want to "plant" a man in a suspected department unless there's simply no other way of doing it. Wait until there is an opening in the problem department and then send the agent into the employment office and have him apply for the specific job on his own. This should cause few problems if the store has high employee turnover. If it becomes necessary to take the personnel manager into your confidence in order to get the agent into the right spot, then at least caution him that *no one else* in the personnel department or in the company is to learn that the new employee is an undercover detective.

When you can, put the undercover agent in a job normally filled by a new and inexperienced employee. In this way, he doesn't have to have any particular retail experience or special skills. He'll be trained by his supervisor just as any other employee is trained. This makes it easier for him to fit into the work group.

Hire on a Contract Basis

Because of the nature of the work, even the agents hired as permanent members of your staff may have to be fired on a moment's notice if their cover is blown. To avoid any argument should such an unhappy situation arise, it is advisable to have the agent sign a contract spelling out the fact that he can be fired without prior notice. In stores which are unionized, this contract is extremely critical. After a period of time the agent would be required to join the union, and this would prevent his being fired even if his identity becomes known. Make the term of his contract for 60 to 90 days, but make it automatically renewable.

Don't set up a situation where you are forced to keep the agent as a permanent employee. This contract should be used whether the agent is your own or is hired through an outside detective agency.

How do you pay the agent? His regular wages, the same as those received by other workers in the department, should be paid in the same manner that other employees are paid. The additional money the agent receives can be given to him on a voucher, but usually it is better to pay him in cash. Submit a voucher through the bookkeeping department for some harmless item such as "advertising expenditure," so that no one in the accounting department is aware that an agent is on the payroll. If it is inconvenient for you to meet the agent to, give him the cash, then send a money order to his home. Whatever you do, keep the agent's extra salary off the payroll; don't let anyone in the book-keeping department know about him.

Develop a Substitute Identity

If the person you plan to use has previously been an undercover agent in other companies, then you are going to have to consider developing a substitute identity for him. This is particularly true when you use an agent from an outside detective service. Of course, when you're employing your own undercover agent and are selecting a person who hasn't previously done this type of work, it isn't necessary to build a new identity. This person will be a permanent store employee, and it's difficult to maintain a substitute role over a long period of time; therefore, it's better to let him use his own name and background.

Developing a substitute identity requires selecting a fictitious name, background, and personal history. Planning these carefully is important to assure both the agent's protection and the successful fulfill-ment of his job. The name selected should be similar to the agent's real name so that he will easily respond to it. It is usually advisable for him to keep his own first name or to adopt one like it so he won't be exposed by someone from outside the store unexpectedly greeting him by his right name with employees nearby. Keeping his own first name and providing a substitute last name is the best answer to this problem.

In selecting a background story, don't make it all pure fiction. Interweave fiction and fact, with a bit more fact than fiction. Select a personal history that includes cities the agent is intimately familiar with and schools that he has actually attended. Develop the complete story before he moves into the undercover assignment.

Before he begins his job, have the new investigator list every precaution he can think of to avoid betraying his identity. Then double check his analysis to assure yourself that nothing has been left undone or to chance. Even have him rehearse the part he will play on the job. Ask him questions he may be asked to be sure he answers easily and comfortably. Have him memorize every detail of his new background story. What is his name? Who were his parents? Where did he live as a child? What cities has he worked in? What schools did he attend? How did he happen to end up in this city? How did he happen to come to work for this company on this job?

Always brief him on the procedures and systems related to his assigned work area. Tell him everything you know about the problem and about the character and personality of the supervisor and other employees he'll be working with. Let him familiarize himself with their names and past experience. Copies of employment applications can be helpful here. It also helps if you can tell him about the various employees' hobbies, habits, and associates.

Arrange a Reporting Schedule

In most undercover situations, it takes considerable time for the "new employee" to gain the confidence of his fellow workers. Results will not be achieved overnight (although an alert agent will often observe significant incidents within a reasonable length of time). It is unwise, therefore, to require a daily report or even a periodic report from the undercover operator. If you place pressure on the agent for daily or weekly reports when he has nothing to say, he feels obligated to provide some type of information, and may, in desperation, make up stories which are not only misleading but dangerous if management acts on the information. The agent should be told to report *only* when something occurs that is worth reporting.

It should be made clear to the agent that management wants reports limited to the objectives of his assignment. The agent may work for many days or weeks without anything conclusive to contribute. Neither management nor the agent should feel obligated to fill in nonproductive days with a stream of reports on minor infractions of rules and other trivia. This avoids reams of meaningless paragraphs about employees guilty of sneaking a smoke on company time, of coming back from lunch late, or of making derogatory comments about their supervisors. Unless something extremely important occurs, he must restrict himself to reporting only findings relevant to his purpose.

Guard the Secrecy of Agent Reports

The agent must use extreme care in writing reports. They should never be written on the job. In one case, an agent went to a nearby post office on his lunch hour each day and wrote his report on a post office table, then dropped it in the mail. Employees soon became suspicious of his frequent trips to the post office. One of the gang of thieves followed him there one day, then waited behind a pillar and watched him writing. Before he had completed his report, the observer came over and slapped him on the back, grabbed the papers, and began reading them. A quick glance at the document confirmed the employee's suspicions, and the agent's effectiveness was instantly destroyed.

It's also advisable for the agent not to make any notes while on the job. If he feels he has to make a note, then he should write it when he cannot be observed doing so and in a manner that it will not be understood by anyone who might get hold of it. The note should be written on a scrap of paper, such as a matchbook cover, napkin, or cigarette wrapper. Under no circumstances should he carry or use a notebook.

If the report is to be mailed, the return address should *not* be the place where the agent is working or living. Instead, it should be a post office box or another address prearranged by management. The man hiring the agent should receive reports at his home address or at a post office box, never at the store. Discourage the agent from reporting in person to the boss. If an emergency arises, and it can't be avoided, the agent must take every precaution against being followed; and he should have a good story ready in case he unexpectedly meets one of his suspects.

If he uses a phone to report, then it should be a pay phone located away from the store, and his call should not be made during working hours. For such calls, the manager must have an outside private phone that is not handled by the company's switchboard. If urgency is not a factor, home phone contact is possible.

When the agent begins to work in collusion with dishonest employees, his situation becomes extremely delicate and complex.

Under the circumstances, it is sometimes advisable for management to arrange a time schedule for the agent to phone in his report. If any personal risk is involved, the lack of a report at the agreed-upon time signals management that something has gone seriously wrong and the agent needs immediate help.

Protect the Agent's Identity

Under no circumstances should you ever reveal the agent's true identity to the individual managing the operations where he's assigned. Ideally, the person employing the agent should be the only one who knows his true purpose. Granted it is not always possible to restrict this information, but management should make every effort to do so. Good agents have been repeatedly destroyed because of management's failure to observe this rule.

No matter how well-intentioned a department head may be, he has natural curiosity. Once he knows an employee is an undercover agent, he will watch him to see what he's doing. He may even question him privately from time to time to find out how he is progressing. Because of his attitude toward this employee, he will unconsciously arouse the suspicion of other workers.

Another problem is the manager who is defensive about his operation and his people. If he finds that an agent has been planted among his workers, he will do everything he can to prevent the detective from discovering dishonesty in his staff. The insecure manager will blow the agent's cover by pointing him out to his assistant and often to all the employees in the department.

If the agent's true identity as an undercover detective is discovered by the employees, this can lead to a serious morale problem, particularly when several employees are stealing. Thieves are easily frightened, and the discovery of a detective in their midst can cause panic and overreaction. In one company, when an agent was discovered working in the warehouse, all of the men working, including dock men and transfer truck drivers, responded by a deliberate slowdown. It was several days before management could get the operation back to normal.

In another store where an undercover agent was discovered by an employee, the group of dishonest employees agitated among the store staff calling the situation "an outrage." They succeeded in stirring up the other employees to the point where the entire staff angrily walked off the job. In a unionized store where management and union leaders are in constant conflict, the discovery of an undercover agent can be used by union leaders as an excuse to call a strike. Therefore, everything possible should be done to protect the identity of the detective and to insure he is properly briefed and trained for each new assignment.

Of course, an undercover agent doesn't have to be discovered. Stores have used hundreds of undercover detectives for years without the agents becoming known to employees. But this is only possible with well-selected and properly trained agents along with a management that recognizes the need for keeping the situation confidential. But do not ever underestimate the seriousness of discovery. A professional agent must be constantly alert. If he is betrayed, the results can be serious. He may be beaten or badly injured, even killed.

The agent's true identity should never be revealed, even after he has left the assignment. Here's a good rule to follow: *Never reveal the fact that you've used an agent.* This means the agent should never appear in court as a witness against the thieves. If the company plans to prosecute the offenders, then the agent can give the information needed to management so it can act to develop a case independently of the agent with its own witnesses from the store's regular security staff or from the management group. But keep the undercover detective out of the case. If an exposure of the agent is made, relations between management and employees will suffer. It may also place the agent in a position of physical jeopardy.

When a group theft operation is uncovered among employees, it often diverts suspicion to have the agent picked up and brought in for questioning along with the other malefactors. This may be particularly desirable if it appears that the physical safety of the agent might be at stake if he is discovered.

Once the agent has completed his mission, move him to another department where he can furnish new information. The undercover detective is a highly paid specialist, so keep assigning him as a troubleshooter to gain maximum return from his efforts.

Be Aware of Legal Restrictions

Both the company and the undercover agent must be completely familiar with all federal, state, and local laws relating to the use of undercover investigators with regard to union activities. In many states, there are laws that strictly prohibit the use of undercover agents to probe or investigate union activity among employees, and penalties for violations are severe. The law in New York State, for example, is typical of this legal restriction. It states:

"It is illegal to do unlawful acts to the person or property of anyone, or to incite, stir up, create or aid in the inciting of discontent or dissatisfaction among the employees of any person, firm, or corporation with the intention of having them strike.

"It is illegal to interfere or prevent lawful and peaceful picketing during strikes; to interefere with, to restrain, or coerce employees in the exercise of their right to form, join or assist any labor organization of their own choosing; to interfere or hinder the lawful or peaceful collective bargaining between employees and employers.

"It is illegal to pay, offer, or give any money gratuity, favor, consideration, or other things of value, directly or indirectly, to any person for any verbal or written report of the lawful activities of employees in an exercise of their right to self-organization, to form, join, or assist labor organizations and to bargain collectively through representatives of their own choosing.

"It is illegal to advertise for, recruit, furnish or replace, or offer to furnish or replace for hire or reward, within or without the state of New York any help or labor skilled or unskilled, or to furnish or offer to furnish armed guards, other than armed guards theretofore regularly employed for the protection of payrolls, property or premises, for service upon property which is being operated in anticipation of or during the course of existence of the strike, or furnish armed guards upon the highways for persons involved in labor disputes or furnish or offer to furnish to employers or their agents, any arms, munitions, tear gas implements, or any other weapons; or to send letters or literature to employees offering to eliminate labor unions or distribute or circulate any list of members of a labor organization or to advise any person of the membership of an individual in a labor organization for the express purpose of preventing those so listed or named from obtaining or retaining employment."

It is a good practice for management to keep the undercover agent focused on the problem of internal theft and to avoid any activities that might be construed as a violation of the laws surrounding union activities.

Management, in the past, has often overestimated the dangers of using undercover agents. A fog of secretiveness has long surrounded their use and from this has come some popular myths to the effect that using such detectives is tricky and dangerous. Nothing could be further from the truth. Setting up an effective net of undercover agents is no more difficult or dangerous than installing a staff of capable floor detectives. All that is needed is a little self-confidence and the few simple guidelines provided. A carefully planned, well-run undercover program is the most potent weapon management has to uncover internal theft activities.

PART **FOUR**

Interrogating the Suspect

7

PRINCIPLES OF INTERROGATION

Although the objectives are similar, interrogating the dishonest employee is far more difficult than interrogating the shoplifter.* In the shoplifting case, securing a confession is easy. You've witnessed the theft and the evidence is still in the thief's possession. But interrogating the dishonest employee often means proving innocence or guilt when the evidence is not at hand. In such situations, a confession can be difficult to obtain. Thus the interviewer must prepare more thoroughly for the employee interrogation. If he fails to do so or to understand the principles of questioning involved, the results can be disastrous. Take the case of one supermarket manager named Barry Thompson:

Leaning back in his chair, Barry Thompson stared at the report on his desk. Nancy, a young cashier-checker, sat across from him,

* (In *Security Control: External Theft,* the author discusses additional interrogation techniques useful in interviewing shoplifters and other outside larcenists.)

159

quietly straightening her skirt. Finally, Barry looked up and asked, "Did you give a special price to your sister when she came through the checkout line last Tuesday?"

There was a long silence as the girl leaned forward, her face showing shock and wide-eyed innocence. Then, in a hushed tone of voice that would have been a credit to a Broadway actress, she responded: "A special price? Why, that would be dishonest! I'd never do a thing like that."

"And you say you've never given your friend Mary Wilson any breaks on price either?"

The corners of Nancy's mouth tightened in anger. "Who says I did?"

Barry began to realize that his interview was not going to be as easy as he had planned. Obviously, he had not done well up to this point, and it seemed unlikely that the girl would admit her dishonesty despite the considerable information he had regarding her activities. Fortunately, he recognized his lack of proper preparation and had the good sense to withdraw when he saw the situation becoming untenable.

Nervously clearing his throat, he said: "Well, I just wanted to be sure. You know, Nancy, we have to be very careful when we ring up sales for our family or for our friends. If we make a mistake, other employees are apt to become suspicious; and you know how employees love to gossip. To avoid this problem in the future, I'd appreciate it if you would have someone else handle the purchases made by your family and personal friends. Then there won't be any danger of gossip among the staff that might be damaging to your reputation."

Nancy's voice sounded relieved as she said, "Oh, I'd be glad to do that."

Then, taking the offensive, he smiled and pushed his point even harder. "Now, you will be careful in the future, won't you?"

"Of course, Mr. Thompson. You know I'm very careful when I ring up sales. I wouldn't want anyone to think I was dishonest."

It was apparent that Nancy had taken charge of the interview as she firmly shoved back her chair, turned, and flounced out of the office, leaving her final words hanging in the air like a rattlesnake daring anyone to disturb them.

What had gone wrong? Barry Thompson's error arose from his lack of preparation for the interview. His mental fantasy of the interrogation prior to asking the young woman to his office gave him false confidence. In this fantasy, everything fell into place. Nancy not only confessed, but she involved other employees. After all, he was in complete charge of all the characters, the dialogue, and the action. Unfortunately, the fantasy world seldom resembles the world of reality.

The average store manager knows too little about the nature of employee interrogations. Many management personnel who are quite capable of interrogating shoplifters find that the same interrogation pattern doesn't work when applied to dishonest employees. Because many store managers are able to deal well with people, they incorrectly assume that employee interrogations involve the same skills as those applied in their day-to-day human relations. Store managers also tend to underestimate the risks involved in interrogating dishonest workers. Too often, they will try to bluff their way through such a situation, causing an emotional explosion and counter-accusations. The end result is a court case involving the store and the manager. When this occurs the company is often the loser, and the financial penalty can be substantial.

Because of the dangers inherent in this situation, many firms rely on specially trained interviewers to handle all interrogations. However, since counter-suits can arise from poorly conducted interrogations no matter who conducts them, it is important for any interviewer to be thoroughly familiar with the basic principles of interrogation.

Why Interrogate?

Before deciding whether to interview a subject, it's wise to review your goals in carrying out the interrogation. What information are you after? Is the primary purpose of your interrogation solely to gain a confession? Keep in mind that you should not be undertaking the interrogation unless you already have the facts and evidence needed to prove the person guilty of larceny in a court of law. Your reason for the interrogation should be to determine how the case may best be disposed of. Should the employee be fired, turned over to the police, given psychological help, or be made to pay restitution? You will also want to discover the employee's method of theft so that you can tighten your control systems or improve supervisory performance.

To search out the answers to such questions, your interrogation must uncover as much information as possible about why the person stole. Knowing what triggered the thefts can be extremely important in preventing similar incidents of dishonesty.

The following are some of the questions you will want answered in your interview:

1) Is the employee guilty or innocent?

2) What first gave him the idea of stealing?

3) About what date did his thefts start? Why did he start to steal? What was his motive?

4) How did he learn the method he used?

5) How frequently did he steal? How much cash or merchandise did he steal on the average each time?

6) Was he stealing alone or in collusion with other employees? Were people involved from outside the store?

7) What other methods of theft did he use besides the method that you uncovered?

8) What has he done with the stolen money or merchandise?

9) How much of it can be recovered?

10) Does he know of other employees who are stealing? Can he describe these incidents?

11) How does he think thefts like this could be prevented in the future?

12) What does he feel the store should do about his case now that he has been caught?

13) What is the employee's mental, social, and economic situation so as to determine the best way to dispose of the case?

The interview, therefore, has a double purpose. First, it must serve the store, not just by eliminating the dishonest employee and recovering its losses, but also by helping the store to improve its supervision and control procedures. Second, the interview should be directed toward helping the employee in trouble.

Preparing for the Interview

It is always surprising that a store manager with the analytical ability to lay out a receiving operation in a logical, step-by-step manner will approach an employee interrogation without any advance plan whatsoever. Similarly, security personnel often make the same mistake. To be successful, a step-by-step plan of progression is needed. The following are some of the most critical areas in which the interrogator must be prepared.

Can You Prove Larceny?

Before you take any steps toward interviewing a dishonest employee, ask yourself the important question: "Can I prove larceny?" The elements required in a larceny case are always the same. First, there must be a taking away of store merchandise or money of value; and second, the store must be able to prove that this was done *with intent to steal*. If you cannot prove in court that the money or goods taken by the dishonest employee were stolen from the store, then you do not have a legal larceny case.

While it is a simple matter for the undercover agent to gather sufficient facts to prove larceny in a merchandise theft case, clear-cut evidence regarding theft of cash on sales is often far more difficult to obtain. After all, even experienced honesty shoppers make mistakes, and the employee tested may be guilty of error rather than theft. There are many ways in which errors can occur, and many errors can *look* like thefts. For this reason, most stores give the employee the benefit of the doubt on the first violation. If the clerk *is* stealing, further theft violations will be easily obtained.

By getting at least two theft violations, you will guarantee that your case is sound, you will avoid the dangers of being charged with false arrest or defamation of character, and you won't accuse an innocent employee of dishonesty. In addition, admissions of guilt will come easier, and you can often get a more complete statement of the subject's past thefts, including the method and extent of his thefts and the activities of other dishonest employees.

There are two ways in which a shopping case can reach the point of interrogation. The first is called the *in-the-pocket theft*. In this type of cash theft, either the honesty shopper or her partner observes the employee pocket the cash from the sale. The money is not rung on the register and may be concealed on the employee's person, in the palm of his hand as he walks off the floor, or in a pocket or bag. In any event, the theft is obvious to the observer, and there is no doubt of the intent to steal. It is a solid larceny case.

At this point, one of the shoppers must keep the employee under continuous observation while the other contacts the store manager or shopping manager and reports the details of the theft. It is advisable to observe the employee for at least 30 minutes to allow him adequate opportunity to ring up the sale. Moving in on this type of situation too rapidly may jeopardize your case. Some judges have ruled that the person might have been "tempted" to steal, but the store did not allow him sufficient time to ring up the sale. It is also true that on some occasions a salesperson will put several customers' sales into his pocket and will later ring them all up at once. The clerk feels he is being more efficient by not taking the time to ring each sale separately.

A second way in which shopping cases reach the point of interview is when the honesty tests show a *series of unrecorded sales*. These are proven violations in which the shopping manager has audited the cash register tapes and found no record of the purchase. To have a solid case in this situation, it is best to have two or more of these violations.

In addition to checking the register tapes for the sale, the manager must check the clerk's sales receipts for that date to see if they balance or show an overage or shortage. Obviously, if they show an overage equal to or in excess of the amount paid by the shopper on the test purchase, the store cannot prove that cash was stolen. All the violation indicates is that the sale was not recorded in the correct amount or in the proper sequence. This is a policy violation or an error, but it is not proof of theft or *intent to steal*.

If you base your interrogation on the fact that the sale does not appear on the register tape and that the sales receipts for the day do not show an overage, you may find that this is not sufficient legal evidence of larceny. To prosecute a larceny case effectively, the store should have at least one witness to an actual cash theft. In addition, it helps if the stolen money is found hidden on the thief and if the store can prove by special markings or by a record of the serial numbers that this was the same money given to the clerk by the shopper.

Having previous shopping violations as evidence of earlier thefts is also helpful for another reason. Although these may not be used in the criminal prosecution of the employee, they can prove valuable when the court assigns a probation officer to investigate the case and to make a recommendation to the judge on sentencing. The probation officer, in such instances, usually visits the store manager or the security manager, and this evidence of previous thefts is entered into his report for consideration by the judge.

Can You Make Specific Charges?

The larceny charge in a criminal court must state the exact amount of money stolen. This can sometimes be a serious problem. For example, in one New York department store, a supervisor in the notions department was casually watching a salesclerk count her cash receipts for the day. He was a considerable distance away, and she was unaware that he was watching her. Suddenly, to his surprise, she took a handful of coins from the cash drawer and hurriedly stuffed them into her jacket pocket. It was done so quickly that the supervisor could hardly believe his eyes. He had known the woman for several years and was shocked to observe her dishonesty.

He thought about the problem overnight and decided he had better report it. So the next morning he went directly to the security manager's office and told him what he had seen. The security manager listened carefully to his story, made a few notes, and then had the supervisor accompany him to the selling floor to identify the salesclerk and to point out the location of her cash register.

Once this was accomplished, the security manager noticed that an air-conditioning duct ran along the wall above the counter where her register was placed. He immediately decided that an investigator could be "planted" in the duct to observe the clerk as she made up her cash at the end of the day. The manager thanked the supervisor for his help. He then went back to his office, called in two investigators, and gave them the details of the case.

About 15 minutes before store closing time that evening, Investigator "A" climbed a wall ladder located on a fire exit stairway, opened the trap door, and crawled into the air-conditioning duct. In a matter of minutes, he was in a concealed position directly over the cash register. At store closing time, the suspect opened the cash register and began to count her day's sales. As the investigator watched, the clerk suddenly stopped counting, looked quickly around, dipped her hand into the cash register drawer, and stuffed a handful of coins into her jacket pocket. She continued counting her receipts, made out her sales tally for the day, put the money into a cloth bag provided for that purpose, and closed the register drawer with the bank in it. She then removed her handbag from underneath the counter and left the department. The next evening, the second investigator took his place in the air-conditioning duct. Again the woman was observed stealing a handful of coins. Both investigators submitted their reports to the security manager.

The case appeared to be one involving clear-cut theft, but the security manager was cautious. He wanted to be sure he had enough evidence to prosecute if the clerk didn't confess. So he instructed Investigator "A" to observe the clerk again on the third evening. If she stole, he was to get down from his position of concealment and to hurry to the employee exit. When the woman came out of the building, he was told to apprehend her and to bring her back to the security office for interrogation. The manager also instructed a female detective on the staff to be available to search the suspect after she had been apprehended and to serve as a witness to the interrogation.

The next morning, the security manager came into the store expecting to find a signed confession waiting for him on his desk. Instead he found the investigator's report stating that although he had again observed the clerk stealing coins from the register, he had not been able to climb down from his hideaway in time to reach the exit door ahead of the suspect. As a result, he had not been able to apprehend her.

At this point, the security manager made a poor decision. He concluded that he had sufficient evidence to prove a case of larceny. So he phoned the department supervisor and told him to bring the clerk to his office for interrogation. On the face of it, the evidence certainly appeared to prove conclusively that the clerk was stealing cash from her day's receipts. But the interrogation did not go well. Under hours of the most adroit questioning, she stubbornly refused to admit that she had ever stolen so much as a penny from the store. Confronted with the signed statements of the investigators and the department supervisor that they had seen her pocket the money, she still refused to admit anything.

Now the security manager made his second poor decision. Frustrated and angry at his inability to get the clerk to confess in the face of what he believed to be overwhelming evidence, he finally decided to prosecute her. It was midafternoon on Friday before the police from the local precinct arrived at the store. At 4:30 P.M., the suspect was finally booked and charged with petty larceny. By the time the red tape was completed, there were no courts in session and no magistrates available, so the desk sergeant set bail at $500. Being unable to raise the money, the salesclerk was put in jail, where she remained until her preliminary hearing on Monday morning in Magistrate's Court.

The first witness was Investigator "A". He described in detail how the saleswoman had stopped counting her cash receipts, looked up and down the aisle, put her right hand into the register drawer, grabbed a "handful of coins," and put them into the right-hand pocket of the gray jacket she was wearing. At this point, the magistrate interrupted the investigator's narration. "You say that you observed this young lady take a handful of coins out of the cash register and put them into her jacket pocket, is that correct?" asked the magistrate. "Yes, sir," replied the investigator. "Exactly how much money is a 'handful of coins?' " he asked the witness. The investigator's face flushed in obvious embarrassment. The magistrate looked inquiringly at the investigator, waiting for a reply. Finally, the investigator blurted out, "I don't know, sir." The magistrate picked up his pen, made a few scribbled notations on the papers in front of him, looked up at the assistant district attorney, and said curtly, "Case dismissed!"

Although it was apparent enough to the security manager and to the investigators that this salesclerk had been stealing coins from the day's receipts, they could not legally prosecute the case *because they could not state a specific dollar amount she had stolen.*

Use a Last-Minute Checklist

It is wise for the interrogator to keep a checklist handy and to review it prior to beginning any employee interview. Here is a list of some of the questions you should ask yourself in preparing for the session:

1) Do I have on hand all the available facts, information, and evidence related to the case? Are there enough facts to warrant an interrogation in the first place? Is the evidence specific, detailed, and factual, or am I dealing only with suspicions, rumors, and gossip? If the employee denies stealing, am I able to provide proof to counter his claim of innocence? Do I have enough evidence to prove

his thefts in a court of law? (If the employee does not confess, you may have no choice but to prosecute.)

2) Do I know as much as possible about the employee prior to the interview? Have I pulled the suspect's employment card and reviewed it carefully? Are there any time gaps in his employment record? If so, do I want to question the suspect about this during the interrogation? Who are his references? Are any of them employees of the store? (These names will be important if you later question the suspect about collusive thefts or whether he has knowledge about other dishonest employees.) Did his former employers give him a good recommendation? Have I telephoned them to ask a few questions? (You may very well uncover information of value to your coming interrogation.)

3) After reading the report by the store detective or honesty shopper relating to the case, did I take the time to arrange a personal interview with the detective or the shopper so that I can learn firsthand any further details that may not appear in the report? Do I have a clear picture in my mind of exactly what is supposed to have occurred? Am I completely familiar with the entire situation surrounding the reported theft? What time of day was it? Does the detective remember what the suspect was wearing at the time? Where was the detective standing? What aspect of the situation first drew his attention? (These and many other questions will suggest themselves as you discuss the incident with the security person who made the investigation.)

4) If the reported theft involves manipulation of company records, am I sure that I completely understand what this manipulation consists of, what document was altered, how it was altered, when, and by whom? Was it written over? Was it erased? Etc. Do I have available on my desk every single one of the documents in question before the interrogation starts? In addition to the store detective, have I interviewed the personnel involved in the transaction from related areas, such as the accounting department, the

cashier's office, or anyone who might have additional information related to the embezzlement?

5) Have I checked the actual documents against the detective and honesty shopping reports? If I'm dealing in a fraudulent refund case, have I checked the amount on each of the forged refunds to be sure it corresponds to the amount stated in the detective's report? In the case of the honesty shopping test, have I examined the day's cash receipts to be sure the figure does not show an overage against the register for that day? In addition, have I checked the shopping violations reported by the shopper against the actual cash register tape for that date? Am I reassured that the sale was not rung up either in its proper spot on the tape or later, say three or four sales down? (Everyone makes errors from time to time, even detectives and honesty shoppers, so it's wise to try and catch these errors before you do the interrogation.) If I want to interrogate an employee on the basis of a single honesty shopping theft because the employee has the stolen money hidden on his person, am I sure: a) that the money has been properly marked and recorded, and b) that I know exactly where on the suspect's person the money has been concealed?

6) If the reported theft is made by a person who is not a member of the store security staff, have I questioned this employee very carefully to be sure he actually saw and reported exactly what happened? Have I carefully separated the employee's factual observations from his suppositions? Is there any ulterior motive the employee might have for making such a report? (Today most employees do not come forward with information about other employees who are stealing; therefore, it is wise for the manager not to jump to conclusions when an average employee brings in such evidence.) Do I have some method of cross-checking the validity of his evidence? (Books could be written about the tragedies in which a psychologically disturbed employee destroyed the reputation of a co-worker.) Have I gotten a written, dated,

signed, and witnessed statement, preferably in the handwriting of the person who is making the accusation? Does
this statement contain sufficient evidence to justify interrogating the suspect? If not, should I have the honesty
shoppers test the suspect or the security department
observe the suspect entering and leaving the building? If
it is a particularly serious accusation, should I first move
an undercover operator into the department to work closely
with the suspect?

You may want to add some additional points to your checklist,
but, by and large, these points are essential. Keep in mind that each
employee interrogation has a theft situation behind it which involves
facts and information. Your job before starting the interview is to get
as many of these details in your possession as the time and situation
will allow. Don't rush the investigation. You can usually delay the interview until you have completed whatever research is necessary. The
employee will be working for you, and he will therefore be available;
so take the time to select the best time of day, the best situation, and
the optimum set of surrounding elements involved in the encounter.
Take care of all the details before you confront the suspect.

Coach Your Witnesses

Equally important in preparing your interrogation is the need to
coach any members of your staff who are going to help you during
the period of questioning. They should know in advance what is
expected of them. For instance, if you plan to use a witness to confront
the suspect, you should prepare this person and have him available at
the time of the interview. It is embarrassing to reach a critical point
in the interrogation when you want to call in the witness and then discover to your dismay that he is across the street having a cup of coffee.
In some situations, you may want to use personnel from the accounting
department to bring psychological pressure to bear on the suspect.
Perhaps you will want a cashier to walk in carrying in the sales receipts
tallies and the cash register tapes for those dates related to the honesty
shopping reports. If so, this person should be coached so he will know
in advance what you expect of him. Instruct such people not to talk
directly to the subject. Only one person should do the questioning. Any
conversation between the witness and the suspect will destroy the inter-

rogator's effectiveness because it will ruin his rapport with the person he is interviewing. In other words, at no time should the witness ever talk directly to the subject. If the suspect questions him or tries to engage him in conversation, then it is up to the interviewer to keep control of the situation. You can do this either by asking the subject to refrain from addressing questions to the other person or you can take over and answer the question directly. Whatever the approach, you must keep control of the interrogation. In addition, when you're going to have a person identify the subject, tell him in advance how to respond to your questions. Do you want him to nod his head, to answer yes or no, or to make a complete statement such as, "Yes, this is the man I saw take the money and put it in his coat."

It is often wise to have a witness to the interrogation, but be sure the witness sits behind the subject so that any movement or facial expression he makes will be hidden from the person being interrogated. Explain to the person sitting in on the interview that you want to keep the questioning strictly between the subject and yourself. Give this witness a pad and pencil so that if he feels a question has been missed by the interrogator, or if he has facts of value to add to the interrogator's line of questioning, he can jot this information down on the pad. He can then quietly fold the sheet, with as little distracting noise as possible, and lay it on the desk in front of the interrogator. When a logical pause comes in the questioning, the interviewer can open the paper and read the note. He may then decide to use the information or not, as he chooses.

By instructing the witness not to interrupt the questioning, the interrogator is better able to hold the full attention of the suspect. Using the written note approach has two advantages. First, it heightens the pressure on the suspect since he doesn't know what is in the note; and secondly, it allows the witness to suggest a new line of questioning, to refute a statement made by the subject, or to add other valuable information helpful to the interrogation.

A final point to remember is that only management personnel who are directly involved in the investigation, or people who have information to contribute to the investigation, should be present during an employee interview. If the interrogator allows other personnel to listen in on the conversation through an intercom or permits them to be present during the interrogation, this can later lead to charges against the store of slander and defamation of character.

Prepare Yourself Emotionally

Most store managers care about people; therefore they find employee interrogations a difficult experience. They may even know the employee personally and be emotionally upset over the discovery that he is dishonest. Perhaps by listening to a store manager as he reviews his own feelings in such an interview, we can develop a better understanding of the problems that the interrogator must face and the mistakes he may make in this type of situation. This is the way one supermarket manager described his feelings:

"I have all of the facts of the case before me on the desk. The honesty shopping reports, register tapes, the whole bit. I've gone over them carefully to make sure there aren't any errors. Once I'm satisfied I have all the facts, I call the department manager and ask him to send the employee to my office. Now I sit back and wait. This period is nerve-racking. I straighten up my desk a dozen times; I drum my fingers nervously on the edge of the blotter; I twist paper clips and throw them broken into the waste basket. After what seems like an eternity, the person arrives.

"I look down at the desk because, in a sense, I'm embarrassed and I find it difficult to look her in the eyes. Somehow I feel as though I'm the one who's in the wrong because I know what I'm going to have to say to her in the next few minutes. Up until the moment she walks into my office, I have been very angry about her thefts. I have been angry about her. But now as I see her before me, she suddenly seems a defenseless young lady, a person I've known and liked for a long time. My anger drains from me, and I realize that my hostility is really a result of my own disappointment and frustration. I had high hopes for this girl. Now, as she sits across the desk, she doesn't look tough; she doesn't look like a criminal. In fact, she looks just the way she has always looked to me, a pleasant, smiling young woman who has always had a kind word for her customers and for her fellow employees. I've always thought of her as a delightful person, and she's been one of the top producers and the best cashiers I've ever employed.

"I think to myself: 'If only she would look rough and hard, if only she would come in angry and hostile, perhaps then I wouldn't feel so guilty.' But she doesn't do any of these things. Instead she looks pale; the blood is drained from her cheeks, and she's obviously nervous. She twists her handkerchief, and she's apprehensive and frightened.

"Before this employee entered my office, I had built up a picture in my mind of an arch criminal, an enemy of society, a person who should be thrown behind prison bars. But now as I look at her, it suddenly hits me that this isn't the situation at all. She is just another human being who has been unable to resist the temptation to steal and now has trapped herself and tangled her life because of a moment of weakness.

"For a moment I stare at her, but I'm not really looking at her. Then, suddenly, I'm angry at myself because I'm soft and because I want to avoid the whole unpleasant discussion that lies ahead. I want to get her out of my office and out of my mind as fast as possible. My voice is gruff, and I ask her bluntly, 'Why have you been stealing cash from the register?' And even as I listen, my words are harsh and grate in my ears.

"This approach, of course, is disastrous. It's no way to begin an interview. I realize this the moment the words escape my lips. But it's too late to withdraw them. In this case, the girl reacts by breaking down and crying softly. She sobs her denials through her handkerchief, and it's difficult for me to deal with anyone who cries. But she could have reacted in exactly the opposite fashion; she could have suddenly become angry and self-righteous; she could have sat bolt upright in her chair and angrily denied the charges. Either response would have destroyed the effectiveness of the interrogation.

"I realize at once that I have allowed my own emotions to interfere and that I have lost control of the interview situation. I have successfully defeated any possibility of a constructive and civilized conversation between us. I muffed the interview for one simple reason: I didn't know how to begin."

It's understandable when a store manager gets angry prior to an employee interview. He may be angry at himself because employee thefts are frustrating. He may feel it's a reflection on his managerial ability. He can also be angry because he feels he has been betrayed by a person he liked and trusted. Anger can also result simply from the feeling of nervousness which most of us have when we anticipate the unpleasantness of a dishonest employee interview.

If you are the type of person who is quick to anger, one suggestion does help. Increase the supply of oxygen in your blood. This has a calming effect. To do this, before you invite the subject to your office, pause a few seconds and take four or five very deep breaths. You'll be surprised how this will relax you. In addition, try to center your thinking on the employee. Instead of wondering how you are going to look and sound, start to ask yourself questions about the other person.

Ask yourself what could have led this employee into this situation, what his problems are, what type of person he really is, and so on. Involve yourself completely in trying to learn as much as you can about the other person. This will take your mind off yourself and make it easier for you to communicate without feeling nervous and uneasy.

Recognizing the causes of poor openings will help you to develop a more constructive approach. Here are some of the more common pitfalls to guard against:

1) Nervousness created by the natural stress of the situation.

2) A desire to rush through the interview in order to get the unpleasantness over with as soon as possible.

3) A lack of self-confidence in your ability to handle the interrogation.

4) Insufficient facts, evidence, and proof to substantiate the charges of theft.

5) Poor timing because you are not at your peak of emotional, physical, or intellectual condition. You may have a bad cold or some other ailment. Or you may have scheduled the interrogation at a time when you're being pressured by other serious problems in your operation.

6) Emotional concern about the situation and sympathy for the employee or feelings of anger or betrayal by a person that you trusted.

Explore Your Personal Philosophy

Before you interrogate a dishonest employee, you owe it to yourself and to the person you intend to question to explore your own personal philosophy and sense of responsibility toward your fellow human beings. Failure to do so can result in a type of ruthless or thoughtless interrogation that can lead to a lifetime of emotional scars. An attack on another human being can be costly. The person you are going to question is like yourself; he has the same fears, nightmares, complexes, and delicate inner personality adjustments. When handled gently and intelligently, the interview can be therapeutic and constructive. Handled carelessly or with sadistic and destructive force, it can cause permanent harm to the employee's personality.

Before interrogating, stop and weigh your objectives carefully. Evaluate them against your moral responsibility to this other human being and to yourself, then try your best to achieve these objectives with the least amount of damage to both your personality and his. To do so, the interrogator must know and apply the principle of empathy; that is "the willingness and ability to enter mentally into the feelings and perspective of the person you are questioning, to see and to understand the world from his viewpoint." Empathy does not mean sympathy. You need not *approve* his view; you need only try to *understand* it. The interviewer's job is to assume, insofar as he is able, the internal *frame of reference* of the subject. He tries to see the world as the subject sees it and to perceive the subject as the subject sees himself. The interviewer becomes a counselor and participates with the subject in the feelings to which he gives expression. He tries to feel them—not just to observe them—and to absorb himself completely in the interview.

In the emotional security of the empathy relationship, the subject experiences a feeling of safety. He finds that the attitudes he expresses are accepted as well as understood. This gives him the needed confidence to explore his deeper feelings, and he can perceive for the first time the antisocial meaning of his behavior. He comes to understand why he has acted the way he has and how he must readjust his behavior if he is to free himself from guilt. He discovers disturbing inconsistencies between his image of himself and what he actually is. But as he does so, the accepting attitude of the interviewer helps him deal with this painful experience and helps him discover the better qualities in his own nature.

This ability to understand how others see things is not a natural talent. It is a learned skill and requires the most intense, continuous, and active attention to the feelings of the person being interviewed. The interviewer who tries to interrogate by a formula that is not backed by a personal philosophy is doomed to failure. There are some who see the interrogation as an opportunity to get some things off their chest, to get into the pulpit like an old-time minister and give a sermon on morality or the horrors of today's rebellious youth. Others may have a streak of sadism in their nature and may enjoy punishing and frightening the employee. They see him as an object to be dissected, diagnosed, analyzed, and manipulated. They express their sadistic tendencies while rationalizing their approach as the only means they can use to gain a confession.

But they are mistaken. Stress, unlike empathy, causes new psychological problems to develop where present ones already exist. It increases the dangers of a major traumatic experience. Empathy on the other hand, leaves the door open for the future rehabilitation of the criminal. It often results in a first step toward improved personal adjustment.

Using fear tactics to cause a subject to confess may lead to a panic reaction which can paralyze the person's ability to respond to your questions. Some people are so sensitive to fear or have such limited mental endurance that, when placed under this type of pressure, they are unable to respond even if they want to; and complete inhibition occurs. The thief is likely to encounter this type of mental block because, in many cases, the very fact that he has stolen indicates a serious psychological problem. Your aggressive attack may destroy any hope of future adjustment and may have a permanently negative effect on his personality. This is a type of damage which none of us wants to risk.

Sometimes, as a result of these excessive emotional pressures, the subject responds by becoming completely submissive, as though he were in a hypnotic trance. It is here that many interrogations go wrong, because the questions asked by the interrogator often indicate the answers he would like to hear. In this completely submissive condition, the subject has only one desire, and that is to please his questioner; so he fabricates fanciful and false information.

It is interesting that many interrogators who prefer to use stress, threats, name calling, and violence assume that they are able to achieve meaningful interview results. Studies show that people, even under stress, demonstrate an amazing capacity for self-protection. They do not easily lose hold of their critical judgment, and, instead of confessing, they become evasive to avoid the pressures. They lie and reject the demands of the interrogator who attempts this approach. It is also interesting how the aggression of the interrogator can turn against him and can cause direct and immediate retaliation by the subject, either verbally or physically. Thus, fear tactics prove unsuccessful in securing meaningful results.

To be an effective interviewer, empathy must be genuinely consistent with your own particular attitudes toward people. Ask yourself: "How do I look upon other people? Do I see each person as having worth and dignity in his own right? If I do hold this view at the verbal level, to what extent do I practice it at the behavioral level? Do I tend to treat individuals as persons of worth, or do I subtly demean them by my attitudes and behavior? Is my philosophy one in which respect for the individual is uppermost? Although I certainly condemn a person's bad judgment in committing a crime, do I respect his capacity and his right to self-direction; or do I basically believe his life would be better if guided by my ideas? Do I have a need and a desire to dominate others, or am I willing to let people choose their own values? Do my actions reflect that I would be happiest with those people who permit me to select their values, standards, and goals for them?'' The interviewer owes it both to himself and to the employee to know his honest feelings with regard to these questions before undertaking an interrogation.

Escorting the Suspect to the Office

When the decision has been made to interrogate the employee, considerable care should be taken in how this person is brought to the office that will be used for the interview. If the cash theft is quite blatant, for example, if the employee has folded and placed the shopper's money in the heel of his shoe, then there is little need to be cautious in making the apprehension. A store security person or a department supervisor can be dispatched to escort the employee to the manager's office or to the security director's office for interrogation. It is presumed, of course, that the suspect has been kept under constant observation by an honesty shopper from the moment of the theft until the detective or supervisor arrived to escort the suspect to the store or headquarters interview office. If there has been any break in the continuity of the observation, then the case is severely weakened.

But the average case does not involve such an obvious theft; therefore, it is advisable not to send a detective to escort the employee to the office. Although the evidence may strongly suggest dishonesty, questioning may bring out the fact that there are extenuating circumstances. What at first seemed positive proof of guilt may turn out to have a logical explanation which can be verified by reliable witnesses. Naturally, this invalidates the larceny charges.

If a store detective or a uniformed guard escorts a suspect to the interviewer's office by forcibly taking the subject's arm, this may cause serious repercussions. First, it can develop extreme fear on the part of the subject, which may make the entire interrogation considerably more difficult than it would have been if the subject arrived in a more casual fashion. Second, in certain cases it may cause the suspect to panic and bolt from the store, requiring additional work to locate him and to bring him back for an interview. Third, it may allow the suspect time to prepare a defense against the questions that will be asked, and the interrogator will lose the element of surprise. And finally, it will be injurious because of the anger of the other employees at the way the employee was treated.

Based on experience, it is better for the employee to be handled with courtesy and consideration. He should go to the office voluntarily, believing that it's just a matter of business, a discussion about some procedure or a review of some special assignment. Even though he may have some slight suspicion that the store has finally caught on to his thefts, he can't be sure. Therefore, he will usually put this disturbing fear out of his mind. The result is that he does not anticipate the interrogation and does not have the opportunity to begin building a defense. Nor does he have reason to set up a barrier of hostility and anger. This will enable the interviewer to establish rapport with the subject, which is needed if a full confession is to be obtained. In other words, it is best all around if you can handle the apprehension of your suspect so it appears to be a casual walk to the boss's office on the basis of an invitation.

In some situations it will be appropriate for the manager himself to act as the escort, but it is usually best if the department supervisor escorts the suspect to the office for questioning. Before he does, however, he should be told exactly what the situation involves and should be cautioned not to allow the suspect to leave him even temporarily to go to the washroom or to his locker. If the suspect is a woman, he should ask her to bring her handbag with her. She may have some of the shopper's marked money still in her possession. The supervisor should be advised not to betray to the subject the purpose of the interview but to keep him as calm and unconcerned as possible, staying alert to any possibility that he might throw away merchandise or money on the way to the office.

The supervisor should also use good judgment. For example, he should not take the employee's arm or cause any scene in the store which might make it look like an arrest. His conversation with him as he walks to the office should be casual. If the employee asks him what the boss wants to see him about, he should either say that he doesn't know or that it has to do with systems and procedures. The important point is to keep the suspect off guard, so that he does not realize the actual purpose of the interview.

Although the supervisor is escorting the employee to the office, it is sometimes advisable to have a store detective follow from a distance to observe if any merchandise or other evidence is discarded by the suspect along the way. The detective is also helpful to have on hand if the suspect insists that he must go to the restroom before going to the office. This may be an excuse to discard incriminating evidence. Once alone in the restroom, the suspect may flush away torn up sales checks and cash register receipts, or he may discard stolen merchandise.

The supervisor can often prevent this problem by assuring the suspect that the interview will be brief because the boss has a full schedule. He can urge that the visit to the restroom be delayed since the boss is waiting. If the person still insists on going to the washroom, the supervisor will have to acquiesce. He should, however, immediately assign one of his people to follow the employee. If the suspect then attempts to discard or destroy any evidence, the person following can take steps to prevent this. Usually this type of situation calls for an actual arrest, and the employee is brought to the interview office on the arm of the observer. Once the detective and the suspect arrive at the interview office, the detective should take the interviewer aside and acquaint him with the details of what has happened on the way. Any recovered evidence should be turned over to the interviewer.

Questioning Behind Closed Doors

When the employee arrives in the office, the interviewer must be certain that there is no indication that the individual is being unlawfully treated in any manner. Recently, a cosmetics department manager was spotted stuffing several bottles of store merchandise into her handbag. The manager was convinced that she was a link in a larger theft chain, and so he and two other executives questioned her in the manager's office for several hours. The interrogation was done behind closed doors.

Early in the ordeal, the employee admitted she had stolen perfume. She was clearly frightened by what was going on but would not implicate any other employee or outside conspirator. The manager finally asked her to go home and return the next day. She left the store and never returned. Several months later, much to the surprise and shock of the manager, the store was hit with a massive damage suit for "false imprisonment."

In court, the former employee made the following claim: 1) "I was questioned behind closed doors, and I was told that I would be prosecuted for theft if I did not disclose the other people involved with me in stealing. I was so frightened that I stayed in the manager's office. I was afraid to leave. 2) If I had not been intimidated by him, I would have left the office; and I feel this is the equivalent to keeping me in the office by force. 3) As a result of this action, I suffered a consequent nervous breakdown and was unable to work or to carry on my usual household duties."

The store responded with its own version. It claimed she was not kept in the office by force, but she was free to leave at any time; and further that she never asked to leave nor made any attempt to get up and leave the office. Instead, as both the manager and his assistant reported she sat in the office and answered questions quite freely and voluntarily. Her nervousness was obvious, but it was of her own making and not that of the store's.

The case was dismissed. The judge said there was no evidence that the employee was forced to remain in the office. Even when threatened with prosecution, she was still free to get up and leave at any time. Although the judge held in favor of the store, questioning the employee behind closed doors is always treading on dangerous ground because juries are notoriously sympathetic to the underdog, particularly if a large corporation seems to be picking on some minor employee. The dishonest employee appears to be a victim of a heartless, impersonal management.

To protect your store from liability, it is advisable that when you reach the point of asking about the actual thefts, the interviewer should tell the employee that further discussion of this problem is on a voluntary basis and that the employee should feel free to end the discussion and leave at any time. You can close the door in the office during the interview for the sake of privacy, but *do not lock the door*. If you actually lock the door, this can well be construed in court as imprisonment. A large Chicago store had to pay a substantial amount of money to an employee questioned in an office where the door was locked during the interrogation.

In addition, try to avoid giving the impression to the employee that he cannot leave until he answers all your questions. Don't resort to such comments as, "Now, just answer one more question, *and then I'll let you go.*" The very statement "and then I'll let you go" strongly suggests that the employee is being held against his will either by fear or by force.

One further point, whenever possible try to arrange to have all dishonest employee interrogations conducted during store work hours. Of course, this is not always possible. Sometimes an employee is apprehended at the end of the day. If an after-hours interrogation is unavoidable, be sure you have a second person in the room so that you are well protected against any later charges of abuse, improper advances, or misconduct. If the employee being questioned is a woman, be sure a female staff member is present to witness the interview.

Taping the Interrogation

Tape record all employee interrogations. This can prevent future charges and counter-charges based on poor memory or deliberate falsehoods. The recording can also be important if the subject makes a verbal confession and later refuses to sign a written statement. It also shields the interrogator from future charges of abusive tactics or of threats and promises to induce the suspect to confess to the crime. Even in the best-prepared case, there are occasions in which the employee hires a lawyer and tells a completely fictitious story about being abused physically or mentally by the interrogator. He tells his lawyer that the interviewer threatened him and forced him into making a false confession. Usually lawyers do some investigating before serving a complaint against the company. Once he listens to the actual tape of the interview, the lawyer will usually drop the prosecution.

The recording also serves to keep the interrogator in check and to prevent excesses on his part. In the heat of interrogation, he may use improper language and threats, or he may succumb to the temptation to make promises in order to obtain a confession. Any statement obtained from a malefactor in which the interrogator resorted to threats or promises is, of course, useless, because the statement was obtained under duress. The tape recording of the interview proves that no threats or promises were made to the subject.

The employee shopping case is particularly sensitive in this respect. The employee who steals cash on sales is frequently one of the top producers in the department. Because of his superior performance, he is usually well liked and admired not only by fellow employees but by his supervisors as well. When management moves in and accuses him of stealing, it is often difficult for the people who work with him to believe he could be guilty. In turn, he may refuse to admit his dishonesty and may appeal to the department head, the buyer, or even the merchandiser for help. Often, they are quick to believe his story of being mistreated and abused. The factual evidence of the shopping tests and the tape recording of the entire interview can clarify the situation, reassure other members of management, and refute the lies of the employee. It puts the case back into a factual perspective.

Should the recording be done openly or secretly? The answer depends on management philosophy. Although one might assume that the presence of the tape recorder would inhibit the suspect, this is usually not the case. Some security specialists, however, do prefer to make these recordings secretly. But a secret recording of the interrogation may jeopardize future uses of the tape. For example, a secret recording is not suitable for playing to a subject's attorney who is questioning the techniques used in the interrogation. Also, when the suspect knows that his admissions are on tape, he is less apt to seek legal redress against the store. In the long run, the best policy is to make the recording openly and with the full knowledge of the employee.

It is also possible to reserve use of the recorder to the end of the interrogation. After the subject has confessed and written a statement, you can have him read the final confession aloud and record it at that time. Following this reading, you might want to ask one or two questions related to the interrogation, particularly as to whether the statement is being made without any threats or promises of any kind or whether it is a complete and accurate statement of his theft activities.

There are many benefits from using a tape recorder. Whenever a subject volunteers to a house search or agrees to a polygraph test, this agreement should be recorded. Whenever you interrogate a woman suspect, record the names of the people who are in the room and state the fact that a qualified female witness is present during the interrogation. Having such a witness in the room whenever you interrogate a woman suspect may seem to be an obvious point, but it's surprising how many interrogators have failed to realize the importance of this rule. In some cases, they have later faced legal charges of making improper advances toward the suspect.

Finding a suitable tape recorder today is easy. Many machines on the market will do an excellent job. Choose a machine that is reliable. Don't buy a cheap machine that will break down under prolonged use. Most interviewers, no matter how experienced, tend to be nervous during an interrogation; and this means considerable fumbling when loading a reel-to-reel recorder. The cassette type is preferable as it easily snaps in and out of the machine. Cassettes come in lengths of 60, 90, and 120 minutes. Keep in mind that if you're spending more than two hours interrogating an employee, you may be courting disaster. No employee should be detained an unreasonable length of time, and two hours is certainly the maximum for even the most complex employee interrogations.

Choose a battery-operated tape recorder, if possible. This machine is the most flexible and doesn't have to be set up in advance of the interview; nor does it have an extension cord to trip over or require a nearby wall outlet plug. The batteries, of course, should be checked periodically; and it is advisable to use alkaline batteries because of their longer life.

In selecting a microphone, it is probably better to select one which has an off-and-on switch controlling both the microphone and the tape recorder. A voice-activated microphone can be used with such recorders to conserve tape, but these devices tend to cut off one or two words at the beginning of the sentence as the activation circuits take hold. In addition, when you later review the tape, you have no way of judging the length of the pauses between the questions and answers. Such pauses can be highly significant.

Several manufacturers also offer automatic volume recording controls which enable the recorder to adjust automatically for both far and near sounds, and the recording volume does not have to be set by the operator. Any sound from a whisper to a shout is automatically modulated by this device so that a clear and crisp reproduction results.

These tape recordings offer a valuable training device for the interrogator. Not only is the tape recording a permanent and reusable record of the session, but it also provides the coloring and emotion of the words as they are spoken. It shows where the subject hesitated, stuttered, or repeated previous statements, and it shows the length of a pause, particularly when a critical question was asked of the subject. It can reveal the mood and the attitude of both participants.

Sometimes you will find in replaying the recording that your suspect attempted to confess on several occasions, but you were so carried away by the sound of your own voice and by your line of questioning that you completely ignored his attempts to do so. By developing a library of successful and unsuccessful interrogations, you can soon develop and improve your techniques. Such a library is also useful for training your assistant or other key personnel so that they can remove some of the burden of interrogation from your shoulders.

In reviewing a particular recording of an interrogation, search out the words or phrases that triggered the admissions by the subject. Not only does this review show you what questions were successful in motivating the subject to confess, but it also reveals the questions you failed to ask in the less-successful interviews. Listening to the tape also shows where you rambled and wandered off into irrelevant materials or failed to focus on the key point vital to every successful interrogation. Sometimes a review of the recording reveals important points overlooked during the interrogation that contained clues requiring further investigation. If the interrogator must at some future date appear in court as a witness in the case, he can easily refresh his memory by running through the tape.

Beginning the Interview

Unless you know the employee personally, begin your interview by establishing the employee's identity. You can ask a question such as, "You are Mike Wilson, a part-time stockclerk, is that right?" If you don't know Mike Wilson personally, let me assure you that identification is important. Occasionally, the interrogator discovers too late that he has accused the wrong employee of dishonesty. This can be a serious mistake.

Once the employee's identity is verified, start the discussion with some small talk, some questions about the employee's home, family, and activities on the job. A good source of such questions is the subject's employee application form. You may say, for example: "I see that you used to work at the J. C. Adams Company. What type of products do they manufacture? What work did you do there?" Or you may notice a list of his hobbies, and you may say: "I see that one of your hobbies is photography. What sort of subjects do you like to photograph? What kind of camera do you use?" Ask questions about his school life, his interests, what books he likes to read. Try to avoid questions that can be answered by a simple yes or no. Questions that begin with the words "How" or "Why" are often good because they encourage an explanation by the subject. Obviously, to put the subject at ease, try to avoid any questions which might arouse an emotional reaction. Stay away from personal questions regarding the employee's marriage, health, or anything which might be emotionally upsetting or might stimulate an undesirable response.

From the start of the interview, no matter what the age or status of the subject, use his or her first name. A person's first name has been used by his friends throughout his lifetime. By using it you psychologically represent an interested and concerned friend in the unconscious mind of the subject. Addressing the subject in a formal fashion, particularly at the start of the interview, becomes a barrier to easy communication.

Use a "you" approach. The purpose, remember, is to try to get him to talk about himself. He is a lonely, frightened, puzzled, and disturbed person. People, of course, are drawn closer to people with similar ideals and similar opinions. So when it is possible to agree with him, do so. This will help you win his confidence. People are like mirrors, and they reflect other people's attitudes and interests. If you are genuinely and honestly interested in this person and you show this, he will respond in a favorable way.

After the nonthreatening questions, introduce more emotional ones. Ask about his wife, his personal problems, his financial pressures. Talk to him a bit about his relationship with his children. But stay away from questions directly related to the crime. Probe for emotional problems that may have upset his personality. Explore his social relationships, his economic situation. These may help to explain why he stole. His explanations may also help later when you want to offer him face-saving reasons so he can tell you about his thefts.

What if the subject asks, "What is this all about?" or interrupts the interviewer and says, "This is all very interesting, but why did you want to talk to me?" The interviewer may be tempted to move immediately into his questions about the subject's theft activities, but he should not give in to this impulse. Instead, he should put him off by saying, "We'll get around to that in a moment, but first I'd like to talk a little bit more about you." He should then return to the discussion and continue his efforts to establish a meaningful personal dialogue between himself and the employee. He should follow his planned strategy and not allow the employee to panic him into a premature introduction of the problem of the subject's theft activities. If he allows the subject to change his plan, then the employee will have taken over control of the interrogation. This is obviously undesirable.

Approaching the Feedback Stage

Perhaps you have now talked 10 minutes or so to get him to a point where the subject appears to feel free to confide in you about his personal problems and his feelings. At this point, you are well into the empathy interview. He has confidence in you, and you are becoming sincerely interested in him. You are now ready to approach the more critical part of the empathy relationship. If he is willing to talk about his innermost thoughts, you can encourage him to reveal himself even further. This is done by a technique called *nondirectional counseling*. Through your feedback of his feelings, you enable the subject to keep talking on emotionally disturbing subjects.

For instance, he may reveal himself by showing a deep inner feeling, and then he may suddenly stop talking. He has reached an emotional block. To help him continue, you respond by summarizing the last feeling he expressed just before he stopped talking. "You feel that when your wife left, you couldn't go on and you got depressed." This reflection of his feelings allows him to continue, and he says: "Yes, that's right. Mary and I loved each other, and I couldn't understand why she would leave home." By reflecting his feelings, you remove the psychological block in the road of communication between you.

One dishonest employee described her thoughts at the feedback stage:

"As I talked, I would amost at times feel as though I were out of this world. Sometimes I would hardly know what I was saying, as though I were talking to myself, talking out my thoughts. It seemed to me that the boss was trying to let me see myself, really see myself for the first time. It was a very difficult and dangerous period for me, and he was helping me to realize what I thought and what I felt.

"Sometimes he would help me see the significance of what I had said or sometimes he would say something like, 'I wonder if this is what you mean. . .,' and I was conscious of a desire to get what I had said clarified, not so much for him, but to make it clearer for myself.

"Sometimes he would interrupt me during pauses, and I know he did this because he felt that pauses made me nervous and self-conscious. However, at the time, I often wished he would let me talk without interruption and let the pauses go. He must have sensed this, because after a while he let the pauses go whatever length of time was necessary. During these long pauses I had time to work hard on untangling my thoughts, and I began to see my situation, to understand my feelings. Although nothing was said, I knew by the boss's attitude that he was working right along with me. He wasn't restless, and he didn't act angry with me. He simply sat patiently and helped me to discover what I had done and why."

This feedback principle is important in the empathy interview. You should practice it until it becomes an easy response.

Approaching the Topic of the Crime

As you continue your interview, you must decide how much time and effort is required to establish rapport and then how much feedback is necessary before the subject is completely convinced of your genuine interest in him. Then you are ready to take the interview into the area of the crime itself.

Moving from the preliminary discussion of noncritical elements to the subject of the particular crime should be done carefully. In interrogating a cashier, for example, your first questions may be phrased quite generally, along such lines as: "We have noticed some problems lately concerning the failure of certain of our cash registers to balance properly at the end of the day. You have recently had a series of cash shortages, and I've been wondering if perhaps you have some explanation for this."

In answer to this question, the employee usually does not have any explanation. Then you can move into more specific questions. "I noticed that your register drawer showed shortages three times last week. For instance, on Tuesday your drawer was short $7.50; on Wednesday, $15.00; and on Friday, $4.72." Here you may pause for a moment and then ask, "I've been wondering if you could provide some explanation for these losses?"

Based on the suspect's reply, you can then start to move in closer by asking specific questions about how she handles the register. Does she, for example, ring up each sale in the correct amount and in the proper sequence as she was instructed during her training? Invariably she insists that she does. This is a good question, because it defeats any later attempts to try to justify a shopping violation by explaining that she sometimes accumulates customer sales and rings them as a single amount. This explanation would, of course, make it very difficult to prove the shopping violation.

Now you might ask, "Do you give a sales receipt to the customer on every sale?" Again, the subject will usually say quite confidently that she does. At this point she has gone out on a limb because she has stated categorically that she follows store procedures related to the handling of sales. The interviewer may say at this time: "Well, in view of the fact that you ring each sale in its proper sequence and in the correct amount and you always give a register receipt to every customer, I'm wondering if you can explain what happened Monday. You failed to ring a $3.59 sale and didn't give a register receipt to the customer."

The subject may defend herself by saying, "Oh, Monday we got terribly busy. Vivian was off sick, and I must have made an error. I certainly intended to ring the sale in the correct amount, but, of course, it's possible I didn't. Everyone makes errors. Perhaps the customer simply threw the receipt on the floor and didn't take it with her. That often happens, you know."

The interviewer may now say, "Assuming you were busy and didn't have the time to ring up the sale, I imagine you would put the money in the register anyway." He pauses here to allow the subject to commit herself. Usually she will seize his suggestion and say something to the effect, "Yes, that must have been what happened." "That means," says the interviewer, "your register cash receipts for that day should have shown an overage, is that right?"

The employee may now begin to fidget a little because she sees she has been backed into a corner. She may say: "Well, yes, I suppose you're right. It should show up as an overage at the end of the day." At this point, the manager silently takes the register tape and carefully goes over it with his pencil. As the employee watches, he then picks up a tally envelope with the amount totaled on the register tape. Finally, he turns to the employee and says: "It's an odd fact, based on your story, that your register was not over on that day. As a matter of fact, the records show your sales receipts are actually short $14.00 for Monday. How do you account for this discrepancy? If you put the money in and didn't ring the sale as you said, then you should be over by that amount, isn't that correct?'' Then, to emphasize his point, the interviewer can show her the cash register tape and tally envelope.

The thief is now in a tough spot, and yet she has not been directly accused of stealing. The interviewer has used a friendly open manner, has kept his language at conversational level, and has taken a questioning approach. He has suggested that an error of some type has occurred and that she undoubtedly will provide a simple explanation that will clear up the matter. At no point has he accused her of stealing, threatened her, called her a liar, or become abusive. Also, he has not shown any anger or hostility.

At this stage in the questioning, the employee may deny she is stealing. You should smooth this over by pointing out that you haven't suggested she steals. Repeat that you are only concerned with discovering the cause of the irregularity. As the employee tries to explain away the so-called ''error,'' the interviewer, using logical and common-sense arguments, finds holes in her explanations. By asking questions, he picks away at her defenses until she has none left. The only possible explanation is that she took the money.

Securing the Confession

One of the most important elements in securing the confession is the use of suggestion. From a psychological standpoint, suggestion is a process of communication aimed at bringing about the acceptance of an idea or a belief by the subject. To do so, the suggestion should be logical and should offer sound reasoning as to why the suspect would benefit by giving you the information you desire. For example, if you are going to present a suggestion such as, ''I'm sure you want to straighten this out and get it off your conscience,'' then you should also explain why it is important for the subject to get it off her conscience, that she will feel relieved and will rid herself of her sense of guilt.

If a good relationship has developed between you and the subject, then she will usually accept suggestions on impulse; she has a desire to please you and wants to give you the information you seek. You suggest that she may wish to get everything off her chest. You point out that there is sufficient evidence to go to court and prosecute her if necessary, but you want to give her a chance to examine the situation. You are seeking answers as to whether her behavior is a symptom of a psychological problem or some hidden pressure on her personality. You want to help her face the situation and find some constructive value in the interview.

Your words are reassuring: "Undoubtedly you are upset now because this is a difficult situation you are in, but I can promise you that in a few days, after the initial shock of this interview wears off, you will begin to feel better than you've felt in a long time. Your present burdens, your anxieties, and your feelings of guilt will fade. This healthier life is what we are seeking to accomplish in this questioning, but to gain this I need your cooperation." This idea, implanted in the future tense, allows time for achievement and is therefore accepted as a reasonable and logical suggestion.

Whatever the problems that triggered her thefts, whatever the causes, they can be woven into statements by the interviewer to suggest that if the subject is cooperative, she will gain fresh insight into the inconsistencies between her undesirable behavior and her better nature. As a result of this new knowledge about herself, she will find a change in her life for the better. She will be relieved of the pressure of fear and torment that has haunted her ever since she began stealing. This is not an idle suggestion. Some dishonest employees have come back later to tell the interviewer that being caught was one of the best things that ever happened to them, because they now have a new life free of the burdens of fear and guilt. The suggestions made during the interview have, in fact, come to pass.

To heighten the degree of suggestibility in the subject, you must remove as much fear as possible from the interview relationship. Granted, this is a difficult thing to do. The employee has a fear of the unknown, a fear of punishment, and a fear of embarrassment. She visualizes all sorts of terrible things that may happen to her. But, in spite of these problems, a real attempt should be made on the part of the interviewer to show that he respects the employee as a person of dignity and value. You should do everything possible to remove the feeling of threat and to make the relationship as safe as possible for the employee. Try to get the person into a relaxed and calm state of mind. Provide a comfortable chair and see that nothing is irritating and upsetting. Avoid having the room excessively hot or cold; eliminate drafts and bright lights, or anything else which will dispel the calmness of the setting.

In using the principles of suggestion to gain the confession, one situation to avoid is called the *Law of Reversed Effect*. The Law of Reversed Effect functions when someone is under too much pressure. She may be thinking to herself: "I want to tell him about this. I want to very much. But I can't!" Like a person with insomnia, the harder she tries to sleep the more wide awake she becomes. The more the subject *tries* to cooperate with the interrogator, the less she is able to reveal herself. This Law of Reversed Effect must be considered when you phrase your suggestions. For example, if you say to the subject, "You are going to tell me all about this," and you speak too loudly, are too dominant, or too authoritarian, you may apply enough pressure to activate the Law of Reversed Effect. Your words must be softer and your suggestions more indirect. Don't command. Instead say, "Perhaps, working together, we can review what got you into this mess and find out how it started."

Using suggestion also involves the *Law of Dominant Effect*. At any given time there is available in the mind only a certain amount of energy. This is marshaled to activate the strongest emotional feeling that is present. So to achieve the best results, your suggestions should be attached to a positive emotion, a strong positive emotion that has the energy capacity to trigger the type of reaction you want. By working with positive emotions such as pleasure or relief of pain, you don't run the risks involved in using dangerous, volatile negative emotions, such as fear, anger, anxiety, or worry.

The usual approach is to combine your questions with a positive mental picture, a description, or a story. But you can also contrast negative pictures with the positive ones to show by comparison why the positive picture is the more desirable one. For example, you may create a picture of the subject being taken to the police station, fingerprinted, thrown into a cell, and left to sleep in the jail overnight. Then compare this with pictures of the employee walking out of the office, free, ready for a fresh start. She has made the right decision. She has come to terms with herself, walking home a free woman, able to enjoy her evening perhaps for the first time in months or even years, for the first night getting a sound uninterrupted sleep, waking up rested and happy, ready to take on the world.

Because the subject is only capable of handling one idea at a time, the fewer ideas you present, the easier it will be to obtain acceptance. Clarity is of the utmost importance. There must be perfect understanding on her part if you expect her to carry out any of your suggestions.

Tell her exactly what you want to know. Make it straight and simple. Her reasoning powers will not be at their best because of the fears that accompany the interrogation.

Also, be alert to those people who are *negatively suggestible*. You can test for this at the start of the interview by saying to the employee, something like, "You can place your handbag on the desk." Interestingly enough, most subjects will immediately lean forward and put their handbag on the desk, but a few will say, "No, thank you, I prefer to keep it in my lap." These people may be negatively suggestible. Keep this in mind throughout the interrogation. Quite often you can gain acceptance by asking questions in a negative fashion. For example, you may say, "You probably would prefer not to review the method of stealing you used." It is really astonishing to see how responsive the negatively suggestible person is to such statements. "Certainly I want to tell you about it, why wouldn't I? I've nothing to hide." And so on. On the other hand, the same type person, if you had tried a positive suggestion, would have said: "I took the money and you've caught me. Why discuss how I did it." Knowing whether a person is positively or negatively suggestible is important when you formulate your suggestions.

When making a suggestion, the wording should be carefully thought out to secure ready acceptance. Try to avoid poison words such as "steal," "theft," "crook," "crime," "larceny," "malefactor," and so on. Avoid stimulating a hostile response. Also be careful about bluffing. You cannot create a good relationship with bluffing. This will destroy your credibility and weaken your relationship. You may find it's impossible to re-establish the type of rapport necessary to get the person to give you the information you want.

The combination of suggestion and the employee's own feelings and knowledge of her guilt will usually bring on her final confession. There comes a moment in the interview when her feelings of guilt and a recognition that she has been found out lead her to break down suddenly, just like a house of cards in a draft of wind. In the beginning, she will not make a full confession. But what you are seeking is a single admission of guilt; and, once this is obtained, then further questioning will usually develop the other information you need.

At first, she may say that this was the only time she ever stole. But you can point out the fact that almost no one is ever discovered the first time she steals. You can even suggest to her that you have a folder on your desk containing a series of shopping reports which all indicate considerable previous theft activities. The question now is whether she wants to cooperate and tell you the full story to show that she is basically an honest person who has merely made a mistake, or whether she prefers to play the role of a criminal who lies and cheats and tries to put up defenses typical of the criminal mind.

To get a complete picture of the thief's activities, you must make confession easy. To do this, you offer opportunities for the subject to save face. Ask her questions related to why she stole. By giving her an opportunity to explain why she stole, you also make it easier for her to tell you the whole story. At no point during the interview should you indicate either by your facial expressions or by your words that you feel she is a bad person; rather take the viewpoint that she is a good person who has used bad judgment.

Explain that you believe she is basically a fine person, but one who has simply made a serious error in judgment. Reassert that your primary purpose in talking to her before taking any type of action is to give her a chance to explain why she was dishonest and to work with her to set the record straight. You can also add that you're sure she has a reason for the thefts. You may even suggest some possible explanations: "Did you have hospital bills that came unexpectedly? Did your husband lose his job? Did you need money to buy clothing and things for the children? Are you supporting a sick relative, or do you have to take care of aging parents?" Offer rational explanations that can help her save face in this difficult situation.

Usually, after a period of time, the employee will provide the details; but if the employee doesn't wish to cooperate, you can suggest it will be necessary for you to turn the matter over to the authorities. Notice that you avoid saying the word "police." A mild threat is more effective than a strong one. She will interpret the word "authorities" in her own manner, but you will have avoided an overthreatening situation which may paralyze her ability to respond. You're working through her imagination by using suggestion.

One point should be emphasized. This interrogation may be only one of the many problems you have to handle on this particular day; but for the person sitting across the desk from you facing the charge of theft, it is probably the most traumatic experience of her entire life; and it may very well be a turning point. The moment you become involved in the situation, you must assume responsibility to see that your interrogation does not result in personal penalties in excess of those justified by the crime.

Conducting the Prestige Interview

Up until this point, we have seen how the interrogator places himself in the role of a co-worker who has asked the employee to help solve a mutual problem. He works on the same level with the employee, untangling the theft situation. Another approach to the empathy interview, which some interviewers prefer, is to play the role of a "professional" person who is dealing clinically with the dishonest employee. They are like doctors talking to their patients about their symptoms, about their possible causes and cures, and about what can be done to alleviate the problem troubling the "patient."

The person who takes on the role of the "professional" achieves his prestige position by several means. One way is to obtain the proper personal appearance and the proper appearance of his office. He, himself, must dress and act with dignity. He could not succeed in this approach by putting his feet up on the desk or by taking off his coat and rolling up his sleeves. Nor could he create the right image by trying to conduct the interview in sloppy, rundown surroundings. He must use an office that is dignified, neat, and impressive.

It is important that the prestige interrogation takes place in a prestigious atmosphere. The interrogator must not, for example, make a "house call" on the subject, because he will lose the status effect of his office. On the other hand, the person who uses the co-worker empathy approach can often do a very successful empathy interview on neutral ground, such as in a conference room or even in the living room of the employee. Because he is assuming a cooperative role and is treating the employee as an equal, the location of the interrogation plays a minor part in its success. This is not true of the prestige-empathy interview, where the status effect of an impressive office is needed.

In the prestige-empathy interview, familiarity must be avoided. Of course, this is not true in the co-worker type of interview in which familiarity is of primary importance in the success of the interrogation. Familiarity does not enhance prestige; in fact, it tends to destroy it. And prestige is the factor which the interrogator of this type is depending upon in order to establish his empathy relationship. Of course, the prestige-empathy interview does not imply an attitude of being uncooperative or distant, not by any means. The attitude of a good doctor is neither of these. Maintaining prestige is one thing, but attitude is another; and the interviewer's attitude is quite similar to that of the person who approaches the subject as a "co-worker" with a problem that must be shared by someone who understands.

In both methods of empathy interview, the early stages consist of an attempt to get the employee relaxed and mentally passive. This will aid in concentrating his attention on what is being said and in reducing his feelings of being threatened. You are unwise, for example, if you instruct him to "pay attention to your words," or say "now, listen to me," or "now, I want you to pay close attention to me," and so on. This has a tendency to cause the mental blocking out of your words, even though it seems as if it should cause the person to give you better attention.

The fact of the matter is that as a person relaxes and becomes mentally calm, he will concentrate his attention automatically on the words that you are saying. In this state, he will listen even if told not to pay attention to what you are saying. Being calm, he hears everything you say. It registers on his mind because his mind is passive. Therefore, *avoid conscious commands.*

In the prestige interview, the interrogator, from the very first moment, attempts to induce in the mind of the employee the impression that he has most of the information concerning his actions. Unlike the co-worker technique where the interviewer often appears to be just as doubtful and questioning as the employee, in the prestige type of relationship the interviewer must exhibit an air of complete confidence in himself. He must suggest that he has full knowledge of the entire situation and of the subject. To do so, he often inserts comments on such personal bits of information as the school the subject attended, what grade he got in English, the name of his school principal, and other details to suggest he knows all about the employee.

When the effects of authority and prestige have convinced the dishonest employee that the interrogator knows all about him, suggestion then enters into their relationship, just as it does in the co-worker approach. The difference here, of course, is that suggestions work because prestige has given the subject complete faith in the interrogator; and at no point must the interviewer show any cracks in his armor or any weaknesses in knowledge. This means it is imperative that he must never bluff. A bluff is extremely risky. If it fails, it can destroy all of the confidence-and-belief relationship he has built up. It may even cause extreme anger and hostility on the part of the employee, because he feels his trust has been betrayed. The interviewer must present only detailed, factual bits of information which are not in any way exaggerated or open to question.

One point that the prestige interviewer has to be careful about is not to move into critical questioning before he has established the doctor-patient relationship. Sooner or later, of course, he is going to have to move into questions which are emotionally loaded because they concern the crime. If the person responds negatively to the first question or two, then it is quite important that the interviewer take a few steps backward and return the conversation to safer ground. He should also give some sort of explanation as to why the subject failed to respond properly to the question. This justification is far more important than it is in the co-worker method of interview, because an early failure, if it is not properly explained and coupled with assurances, may destroy the prestige which the interrogator has been carefully building in the mind of the subject. The prestige interviewer suggests that he has handled many similar cases, and the problems simply can't be neglected. He suggests that many dishonest employees have placed themselves in his hands (just as the doctor says to his patient), and they have often found he was able to help them.

In the prestige approach, the interviewer should not say, "Now I will *try* to get you to tell me about what happened on the day that you stole the cartons of cigarettes." Nor should he say, "I will *try* to help you." His statements must be positive: "I *will* help you." He has to exude confidence. There is not the slightest doubt that their discussion will be successful, that the employee will respond to his questions, and that he will discuss the problems that are bothering him.

In the empathy interview, quite often it helps to describe to the subject how you believe he feels in this situation. At some point where the emotional pressures begin to mount up and it's quite obvious you are getting higher emotional responses, it is sometimes useful to talk a little bit about how he feels, to show that you understand. Let him know that you have some conception of what he is going through, that you do understand his feelings of nervousness, his fears, and his tensions.

Always allow a little time for your suggestions to take effect. It may be a minute or two before he can fully react. In addition, it is helpful to put your suggestions into the *future tense*, to allow him time to see that your suggestions are taking effect. If you say, "You are no longer tense and frightened," when in fact he is still tense and frightened, he won't believe any other suggestions you give him. Therefore, for a suggestion to be effective, it must be predicted or put into a future tense, but not as far off as in the cooperative interview. You can say, "In a few minutes you will feel more relaxed and calm." This gives the subject time to adapt to your suggestions. As they take effect, you will develop a strong relationship and the subject will become more and more suggestible. Soon your suggestions will cause a reaction to occur within moments of their being offered. Everything you suggest will happen—because the subject believes it will happen. You have convinced him, and he has already seen that the feelings you predicted have come true.

When the prestige interviewer feels he has established strong rapport and finds that the subject is responding and has a desire to talk, then he can begin to use his prestige relationship and can change his suggestions from the future tense to the present. He begins to tell the subject that, "He is now going to explore this aspect of the crime" or "He is now going to tell him about what happened last Friday when he took the sweater," and so on. He begins to express his questions in a more direct manner. If these first attempts to state his questions in a more positive tone prove successful, then he can often move over into almost direct commands.

The employee may be told to explain what happened on Friday with regard to the thefts of cash from the register. Or he may be instructed to detail exactly how he stole the slacks from the stockroom, and so on. But these commands must not be spoken in an angry fashion. The interviewer should not be abrupt or brusque. He should take care not to make his orders sound too emphatic, but he can state them in a positive manner.

Each person you interview is different; most good interviewers study their subject as they talk with him. They try to size him up as a person, try to see what his particular personality pattern is and whether he responds best to more positive statements or needs more reassurance and indirect questioning. Very few dishonest employees in the empathy situation respond well to a loud voice. Loud tones border on stress. The sound hitting the eardrums causes a physiological stress impact on the body and the nervous system. Therefore, subjects seldom respond well to questions phrased in loud tones, and good interrogators in the empathy field tend to use a low and even monotonous tone of voice, only occasionally emphasizing individual words.

In some cases, it is well to speak rather rapidly. The mind has a great capacity to gather in words. We speak at about 125 words a minute, but the mind can listen at rates as high as 400 words a minute. Sometimes a good empathy interviewer will speak fairly rapidly to prevent the subject's mind from wandering. Occasionally, he will also drop in a question that requires a detailed answer by the subject. This insures he is maintaining contact with his mind.

As you get further into the interview, your tempo can pick up and you can become a bit more emphatic. Perhaps the most vital feature of all is that your suggestions should be repeated. Repetition is critical to success. Your statements should be reiterated again and again. Each single idea or each group of ideas, questions, statements, explanations, and suggestions should be repeated several times.

Usually, there are a number of thoughts that you want to impart to the subject as suggestions in order to achieve your interview objectives. These will occur as clusters throughout the interview. One of the early clusters will be around the need to persuade the employee to confess. Then another cluster will occur around the question of when he started stealing, another around the question of what triggered his thefts. A cluster of questions will occur with regard to how frequently he stole, and so on. In arranging the questions or suggestions, it is advisable to put minor points first, more important ones next, and those of greatest consequence last. The suggestions of a lesser nature prepare the employee for those of greater importance. You repeat each of them individually, and then you repeat the entire group, ending, of course, with the question or suggestion of the greatest consequence for that particular cluster.

In both the authoritative and cooperative type of empathy interview, the interviewer establishes rapport. The only difference in the interviews will be in the relationship of the employee to the interrogator. In one, the employee regards the interviewer as a person of prestige who will protect him or cure him. In the other, the employee looks on the interviewer as a close personal friend. In both cases, there will be feelings of dependency and insecurity. There will also be underlying fear, resentment, and hostility. But even the most unskilled interviewer, if he approaches this type of interview with a sincere interest in the subject, cannot help but gain a tremendous amount of information about the crime and about the person he is interviewing. In addition, he will be providing relief and constructive therapeutic benefits for the employee, changes that can result in a new, happier, and more useful life for the person caught up in the tragedy of dishonesty.

Establishing Restitution

Upon securing a confession and the details of the thefts, the next step before terminating the dishonest employee is to secure the information needed to arrive at a fair total in deciding the matter of restitution. First, determine the pattern of this person's thefts. In the shopping case, the subject will have been tested by the shoppers on several occasions. This gives you some indication of the maximum and minimum amount the employee was stealing and how frequently. Obviously, if the shoppers test the employee three times during a week, and on every occasion the employee steals, this means his total thefts will be high. If only one theft occurs in three shopping tests, naturally the total thefts will be less. The shoppers should vary the amounts of money used for the test to see how much the employee will steal on a single sale.

By knowing the pattern of thefts, the interrogator can then determine their extent in a general way. For example, let's assume a salesclerk is shopped on four different days. On Monday, he steals $12.50; on Wednesday, $9.05; on Thursday, $15.50; and on the next Monday, $9.07. Since some of his thefts are over $10.00, it seems reasonable to assume that he has been stealing an average of at least $10.00 each time a customer offers him the opportunity with an even-money purchase. He may actually be stealing more than this, but the $10.00 figure appears to be a fair one; and this is what you're seeking in establishing restitution, a fair and equitable settlement.

In interviewing this suspect, do not start by stating the amount of his individual thefts nor the daily average you believe he has stolen. Keep that information in reserve. The first fact to establish is *when* he started stealing, so you can determine how many weeks, months, or years his activities have been going on. This is a vital point. Thefts are usually triggered by some problem or by some psychological drive. Although most people can't remember how much they've stolen, they do remember the first time they stole. The fear, the excitement, or the shock to their nervous system causes the first theft to leave a strong imprint on the mind. Although the second theft can't be recalled, the first theft is usually crystal clear. That starting date is the fact the interviewer wants to establish.

Next, the interviewer wants to determine the full amount of the subject's thefts. If the average number of thefts per week and the average amount of each theft can be worked out, based on the shopper's factual evidence, a realistic estimate as to the total thefts can be calculated. In determining a restitution agreement, don't attempt to get a maximum amount and don't seek an unrealistic or excessive figure. Restitution is not intended to be a form of punishment, but an attempt to recover the money stolen by the employee. Even if you do a careful job of interrogation and work intelligently with the employee, you should not expect to recover all of the stolen money; but you should be able to get back a reasonable amount of it. This makes the effort well worthwhile. By seeking a fair and conservative figure, you avoid the danger of committing some act of aggression which can later be interpreted as extortion or blackmail. Any restitution on the basis of threats or promises is highly dangerous and should always be avoided.

Let's take a recent case and see how this is done. Mary, a checker-cashier in an Atlanta supermarket, was caught stealing cash on sales. The honesty shoppers spotted her pocketing a sale for $9.67. As the store had two previous theft violations on her, she was brought in and questioned closely about *why* she started stealing.

"It began," said Mary, "when my husband was injured. It was near the end of last November, and he was working in a salvage yard when the large overhead crane slipped and clipped his back. The blow cracked two vertebrae, and he ended up in the hospital. The salvage company wouldn't pay his bills; they claimed it was his fault because he was careless. They also stopped his salary. We had only my check to take care of the food and the rent. With three children, it simply wasn't enough; and when Christmas arrived, the pressure became unbearable. Kids don't understand when you don't have money for Christmas presents. We didn't even have enough money to pay our food bills, so I charged the presents and I've been trying to pay them off as best I can."

The interviewer sympathetically continued to question Mary and learned that she had first taken cash from the register during the second week in November, when she needed cash for a prescription. He also learned that the most Mary remembered stealing at any one time was $15.00. She told him that she usually took about $6.00 or $7.00 from the register about three or four times a week. By using the date of her husband's injury as a starting point, the interviewer determined that Mary had been stealing for 32 weeks before she was finally caught. Based on an average weekly theft of $24.00, this brought her total thefts to about $768. Because the interrogator had taken the time to develop the amount of the admitted thefts in a logical manner, the employee willingly accepted the amount as a fair and conservative estimate of her thefts. She also volunteered to repay that amount to the store.

It could, of course, be argued that this amount doesn't represent Mary's real thefts, that, in fact, she may have stolen considerably more. This is always a possibility. But a restitution figure based on some kind of logical analysis of the situation, particularly when it is accepted by the dishonest employee, is a far better way to determine a settlement figure than to pull the figure out of thin air or to make up an estimate that has no foundation in factual evidence.

When restitution cannot be established on the basis of shopping tests, a second approach is to build a picture of the thief's expenditures and compare it against his income. In this instance, begin with questions such as: "What does it cost you to live? What do you spend your money for?" Then ask a series of specific questions about expenditures by the employee and build a detailed picture of the subject's spending habits. For example, you can ask: "How much is your rent? How much do you pay each month in car payments? Do you belong to a Christmas Club? How much do you put into it? How much money do you bank every week? Do you have loan payments each month? What stores do you have charge accounts in? What sort of monthly payments do you have to make on them? How much do you spend for entertainment? How often do you go to the movies? How frequently do you eat out? When did you buy that watch you are wearing? How much did it cost? What does your wife earn?" It takes patience to dig out this information, but the thief usually lives above his income; and if you take the time to do it right, in a courteous and friendly fashion, you can develop a reasonably complete list of his expenditures. In the end, you'll find they far exceed his income.

Try to pin his expenditures down to a monthly or weekly amount. In other words, how much is he spending each month or week over his income? This amount is then bracketed in that period of time he admitted stealing from the store. The date he began stealing is still necessary. Sometimes you can help him set that date by determining when he had a large expenditure. Perhaps he bought a new car, or a new house, or his wife had a baby. You may learn that he had a serious family calamity that may have required additional money for medical bills or to make up the loss of income from the fact that his wife was out of work. This, of course, is one of the tragedies in many dishonest employee cases. Many times, normally honest people turn to theft only because they don't know how else to resolve the unexpected pressing financial problems which hang so heavily over their lives.

The heart of this approach, therefore, is to establish the amount of the thief's expenditures, then compare them with the amount of known income. The elements involved are: 1) known expenditures, 2) known income, 3) length of time he admits stealing. But—and this is important—be sure that you get agreement each step of the way; then, finally, be sure that you get his complete agreement on the total estimated theft figure. The interview is only successful if he agrees that this figure is an accurate picture of his thefts.

One other method for determining the amount of his thefts is by using the polygraph (lie detector). This can be useful if the thief really knows the extent of his activities. But most dishonest employees don't have any real idea of the total amount of their thefts. Usually, some type of questioning has to precede the polygraph test before results ar valid. You should question him on his expenditures before he takc the test, otherwise the test will not show the true extent of his theft. He can only respond to what he remembers, and his guilt may caus him to minimize the extent of his dishonest activities in his mind. Th polygraph can only show the thefts he believes he committed. Anothei word of caution here: the person must be a sensitive reactor to the polygraph. That means he must have a strong sense of fear. If he is psychotic and has little fear, then it will be difficult, if not impossible, to get a reliable polygraph reading.

The polygraph test can work. In one store, for example, a porter at first admitted stealing $4,000; but later after he had gone home and thought about it, he came back to the store and told the manager he had been pressured into saying he'd stolen $4,000 worth of merchandise. He said he'd lied to get out of the store and stay out of jail. He now claimed his total thefts were no more than $200. Naturally, the manager was concerned, not only because he believed the thefts were greater than $200, but because of the wide difference between the original confession and his new claim. So he persuaded the porter to take a lie detector test. The test results showed the porter believed his thefts to be over $12,000. That was the amount finally agreed upon for repayment.

It cannot be emphasized enough that whenever restitution is considered in an employee case (or in a shoplifting case), the interviewer must always lean over backwards to make sure that this is not a coercive situation. The dishonest employee must feel the amount is as accurate and fair as possible, and any agreement to repay the store must be entered into voluntarily, without any promises or threats by the interviewer. It is a mistake to obtain restitution under duress. It is also advisable to keep in mind that once the store accepts even one dollar in restitution, it loses all rights to prosecute the employee on criminal charges. As soon as any money has been accepted as repayment, the larceny is changed; it now becomes a debt.

Restitution can be collected on a monthly payment basis if the employee has signed a promissory note. If the employee defaults on his agreement to repay the store after he has been terminated, then you can take him to court with a civil suit and recover the full amount of the note. In civil court, the store is not obliged to tell the court what the debt represents. The fact that the subject has signed a promissory note agreeing to pay a certain amount of money owed to the store is in itself sufficient for the store to take legal action for a judgment to collect the money in a civil lawsuit.

Preparing the Confession and Case History

After the questioning is completed and the employee has admitted his thefts, detailed his methods of stealing, and agreed on restitution, it is time to take a written statement. This should be an informal statement. It can be written by the employee on a yellow, lined pad. Usually the story of his activities is dictated to the employee by the interviewer, getting agreement from the employee on each sentence before it is finalized in the statement. He gets the specific, detailed facts from the honesty shopping reports, the detective's reports, or other sources of factual information about the subject's thefts. These are enlarged upon by including the statements the employee has made during the interrogation. Hopefully, the interrogator has kept notes during the interview and is now able to organize the material into a document that details when the thefts started, why they started, and the specific incidents of dishonesty. The statement should cover the method of theft and the amount of money or value of merchandise stolen. Usually the statement starts like this:

"I, Mary Wilson, working as a checker-cashier in the Square D Supermarket, have been stealing from my register for the past 32 weeks. I first began stealing when my husband was injured by a crane in the salvage yard where he worked in November of last year. This accident led to a financial burden on me because the company that he worked for refused to pay his bills and stopped his salary. With Christmas coming, I also felt I needed money to buy presents for my children.

"My husband's injury occurred at the end of November, and I recall quite distinctly that the first time I stole money on a sale was on a Friday afternoon a week afterwards. I was getting desperate for money to pay some immediate bills. The amount of the sale was $10.50 The customer gave me the even amount of money for the sale, and I put her money on the register shelf and bagged the merchandise. After she left I put this $10.50 into my register along with the money from the next sale, but I didn't ring it up. Later, in the afternoon, when I left the floor on my relief, I took a $10.00 bill from the register, folded it, and put it into my shoe. In the ladies' room, I transferred the money to my pocketbook." The statement then goes on to detail other specific thefts.

"The most money that I remember stealing at any one time was $15.00 On the average, I would steal about $6.00 to $7.00 from the register three or four times a week. To the best of my knowledge, my thefts have continued off and on since the second week of November until the present date of August 15th. Based on an average weekly theft of $24.00, I believe that it is a fair statement that my thefts from the store amounted to at least $768.

"I used the money for payment of doctor's bills, prescriptions, toys for my children, food, and household necessities. I am sincerely sorry for what I have done, and I wish to repay this amount to the store. I make this statement voluntarily without any threats or promises of any kind."

Once a statement is taken, the interviewer and at least one other person should act as witnesses. But before the statement is witnessed, the interviewer should have the employee read the statement aloud and then ask him if he understands everything that is in it. If there are any changes in the statement, have him make the corrections with his pen and put his initials beside the correction. Before signing the statement, he should also write, "I have read this statement, and it is true to the best of my knowledge." After he writes this, he should sign his name and address. If there are several pages to the statement, the employee should sign each page. Then the interviewer and another person who has listened to the statement should sign it as witnesses. In addition to the statement, a promissory note should be signed by the employee.

When possible, both the promissory note and the statement should be notarized.

At this point, the interrogation has been completed and an assistant may take over. He asks the employee to empty his pockets onto the desk, and he examines their contents. If the employee is a woman, her handbag should be emptied. Any weapons or anything that might be used by the employee to injure himself should be removed. The employee is told that these belongings will be returned later and is given a receipt for the items. In going through his personal effects, the person doing the search should look for pawn tickets, locker keys, or any other items which might indicate a storage site for stolen merchandise. If such articles are discovered, the subject should be questioned about them. The employee is also asked to take his money out of his pocket or wallet and to count it out. Both the assistant and the employee should agree as to the amount of cash on his person. This amount is recorded on the case history form.

Use a standard case history form, such as the one shown in Figure 5. The case history form should have the full name of the subject, the employee's home address, and the persons with whom he resides (husband and wife, father and mother, etc.). If the employee is a woman and she is married, then her maiden name should be noted. Also include his apartment number, home phone number, age, date of birth, birthplace, whether he is a citizen, ages of his children, and a full physical description. This means any scars on the hands, arms, or face, any distinctive points, such as glasses, limp, etc. Write down the identification numbers shown on the driver's license and social security card. If he has charge accounts, record these numbers as well. Also list previous addresses at which he has resided. A space should be provided for listing the exact cash on his person at the time of the interrogation, and a square should be left open for the name of the person who did the search.

The time the employee came to your office and left should be noted. If the decision is to prosecute, then both the time the police were notified and the time they arrived should be stated. The name of the person conducting the interrogation should be included on the case history form. If the thefts were observed, then that observer's name should be inserted. The place and time first observed would apply if this is a merchandise theft case witnessed by store detectives. For a shopping case, the details of the shopping violations will appear on the shoppers' reports attached to the case history. The local stores protective

Name of Subject (please print)		Date Issued	File No.
Home Address		Nee	Reference
City	State	Alias	

Resides with (Name)	Relationship	Apt. No.	Home Phone
Employed by		Occupation	
Address of employer		How Long?	
City	State	Salary	Bus. Tel. No.

Age	Date of Birth	Birthplace	Citizen	Lineage or Extraction

Sex	Color	Height	Weight	Build	Hair	Eyes	Complexion	Marital Status	No. of Children

Further Description

Identification

Previous Address

Personal History - Names, Addresses and Business Connections of Family and Friends

Cash on Person	Searched by	Came to Office (about)	Police Notified	Left Office	Interviewed by
Place and time first observed			Reason given for act		
Observed by	Witness		Previous Record		Checked by
Subject approached (place and time)			Charge Acct. No.		
Name and Shield No. of Police Officer			Purchases made by subject		

(over)

Figure 5. Case history form

association or the police should be contacted to see if the dishonest employee has a previous arrest record. The form should include the name of the person who does this telephone check with the police. If it is a merchandise theft, record the place and time of arrest. If the police come to the store, then the name and the shield number of the arresting officer should be recorded. The case history should show the subject's dates of employment in the store and the position held. If any purchases were made by the subject on the day of the apprehension, these should be noted and whether there were sales receipts or not.

On the back of the case history, space should be provided for a summary narration by the interrogator or by the arresting detective detailing the theft which led to the apprehension. For the honesty shopping case, the only fact that would have to be noted is, "The subject was interviewed as a result of honesty shopping tests which are attached." For the merchandise theft, however, the detective who observed the subject gives details about the theft. "I saw subject remove merchandise from behind the counter and stuff it into her handbag. . . .," etc. This section of the report detailing the theft should be signed by the detective.

The case history form should not be filed with the confession statement. Keep the confession statement in an office that has a locked strongbox and the case history form in another location in a locked file cabinet. If a tape recording has been made of the interview, this should be kept in a third location. Separating the records gives protection against two dangers: 1) The records cannot be easily stolen and destroyed, which would leave the store in a vulnerable position in terms of a lawsuit by the employee. 2) It protects against the danger of blackmail of the employee. Supervisory personnel have been known to obtain such records and use them to blackmail the dishonest employee by threatening to reveal them to his family. To avoid this possibility, security specialists recommend that such records be kept in at least two or three separate locations.

It is also advisable that all cases be placed in a cross-index file by name and by type of case; for example, "employee theft," "refund operation," "shoplifter," "burglar," etc. Assign each case a reference number, and then file the case by number. This method of filing cases originated with the Federal Bureau of Investigation and is used by them because of its efficiency.

Once the search has been completed and the case history statement has been taken, further questioning may be required to learn more about an excessive amount of cash found on the culprit or why he's carrying pawn tickets or a locker key. It may also be desirable to ask the employee to sign a release for a house search to recover stolen merchandise, or you may want to escort the employee to his locker to see what it contains. There is sometimes a considerable amount of "clean-up" work that has to be done before a final disposition of the case is made.

Before deciding on how the case should be concluded, the interrogator should sit down again with the employee and further explore the private life of the malefactor. He should also pay particular attention to the employee's present mental condition. Reassure yourself that his emotional state is stable, otherwise it may be unwise to let the employee go home alone. If the employee seems to be emotionally upset or afraid to go home, then it would be better to have a member of the staff escort the subject or have a member of his family come for him. Security files are filled with stories of tragedies concerning emotionally disturbed employees who were allowed to leave the premises alone. In some cases, young people have run away from home, and in others, certain individuals have been so emotionally disoriented or depressed that they have injured themselves or even attempted suicide.

When the interview is finally over and the employee has left, the person who did the interview should write a detailed statement about the case. He should briefly review the method of theft, why the employee started stealing, when the stealing began, and any other information pertinent to the case. This summarized review should be done immediately after the employee has left, while all the facts are still fresh in the interviewer's mind. It may prove to be extremely important if any court action should result at some later date. The interrogator may have to testify in court for the store as a defense witness. The summary report he writes after the case cannot be introduced as evidence in court, but it will refresh his mind prior to going on the witness stand.

This need to refresh your mind can't be overemphasized. Counter-lawsuits against the store may not occur for six months or more after the interrogation, and memory fades rapidly. Studies of memory show we lose at least 50 percent of the details of such an interview within three days. By the end of six months, most details are forgotten unless there is a report of the case available to reread.

One might ask why you need to write such a report since you

already have the thief's confession and the shopping reports as evidence of the employee's dishonesty. The answer is that in a summary report of the whole incident by the interviewer, he can put down the many details of the case along with his own personal opinions and reactions to the subject. He does not have to stay within the limits of a formal, factual report. The facts, as such, are coldly presented in the confession, case history, and the shopping violation reports. But often it is the interviewer's own emotional reactions, his personal judgments and thoughts, his interpretation of the situation which will later revive a clear picture in his mind of the entire case. What he saw, heard, and felt will recall the material needed for later court testimony.

If the subject has proved cooperative, quite often you've learned valuable information about thefts by other employees. In fact, you may now be able to clean out a whole nest of thieves as a result of his confession. When the employee has revealed information about thefts by other employees, a separate statement should be taken in narrative form on a writing pad of exactly what the person being interviewed knows about the thefts by these other employees. Include as much detail as possible in the statement: the name and the payroll number of the person observed stealing, facts about the actual incident or theft, a list of the merchandise stolen, the dates or approximate dates of the thefts, the method used to steal, and all the other possible specific information he can remember. If several employees are involved, take a separate statement on each one. Have these individual statements signed, witnessed, and sworn to before a notary public.

A decision must then be made as to whether to move in immediately on these other dishonest employees or to wait and develop other factual material to strengthen proof of their dishonesty. If the information furnished by the subject appears to be factual and is sufficiently detailed, it is quite possible to move in at once and interrogate these suspects. A point to keep in mind, however, is that if this is your decision, make your move before the employee who made the statement has left your office. Take him into another office and have him wait there while you interrogate each of the people he has implicated. If you let the present thief leave and plan to interrogate the other suspects the next day, don't be surprised if your informer has gone to them and confessed that he has told management about their thefts. The result is that they either won't report for work, or, if they do, you'll find them well-prepared to fight the charges. Your chances of getting an admission will be slim. This can lead to complications and difficulties, such as lawsuits for false arrest, and so on.

In court, the accusing statement made by your known dishonest employee won't be useful. The defense lawyer will claim these accusations were made under duress, and the employee himself may repudiate his statement in court. So, if the evidence is solid, move in fast. If, on the other hand, the employee's statement is vague or obviously speculative, even though it may have some basis in fact, it is better to wait. Arrange to have the suspect tested by honesty shoppers or move in an undercover agent. Do whatever is needed to develop factual evidence of dishonesty.

Discharging on Violations

Getting a theft confession often depends upon the experience of the interrogator and upon the psychological attitudes of the person being questioned. Occasionally, in spite of the most damning evidence, a stubborn thief will insist that he "doesn't know what happened." He will state repeatedly, for instance, that he has always rung up every sale and, further, that he has never taken a penny from the store. Facts in the form of register tapes, sales receipts, tallies, etc. appear to have no effect whatsoever on this story.

When the interrogator runs up against this type of barrier, he should make a reasonable effort to show how the facts contradict the assertions by the employee. But if he is still unable to gain an admission after a reasonable interrogation effort, then he must point out that the employee has nevertheless violated store policy by failing to ring up the sale accurately and in proper sequence. Usually the employee is relieved to be given this way out of the situation, so he invariably agrees to this fact, though he persists in denying that he ever stole a penny from the store. Such a suspect cannot be discharged for dishonesty since there is no witness to the cash theft, and the interrogator cannot get an admission of guilt.

In order to avoid any repercussions from this type of situation, it is wise for the store to have a written policy to the effect that *every employee is responsible for ringing up each sale accurately, individually, and in proper sequence.* This policy should also state clearly that any failure to follow this rule is cause for immediate dismissal. To insure that the suspect knows about this policy, it is advisable to have every employee sign a printed slip at the time of employment which says: "I understand that I am required to ring up each of the sales individually, accurately, and in proper sequence. I also understand that failure to do so may lead to my dismissal." The applicant should be asked to read this slip aloud to the employment interviewer. It should then be signed in his presence and counter-signed by the employment interviewer as a witness. The slip should be stapled to the employment card. With this signed statement, the dishonest employee who does not admit his thefts can be fired for a violation of store policy.

The employee who admits to a policy violation should then be asked to prepare a written statement admitting the situation. The employee's statement, like the confession statement, can be written on a yellow pad preferably by the suspect, although the interviewer may help him phrase the document. The paper should be dated, and then the employee should write out a detailed account of the theft incidents. For example, he may describe the specific sales made by the shoppers and the fact he has examined the register tapes and has not found any record of them. The statement should also contain all the details of the sale as they appear on the shopping violation report, including the date and time of the purchase, specific merchandise that the shopper selected and bought, and the money tendered to the clerk for each shopping test showing a violation. It should say that the employee has examined the cash register tapes for these dates and that the sales do not appear on the tapes. The interviewer should also show the suspect the sales receipt tallies for that date to prove there is no overage. This fact should be included in the employee's statement.

After he has completed the document, the employee should conclude it by saying that he recognizes that these sales should have appeared on the register tape, that he has no explanation for his failure to ring these sales in the correct amount or in proper sequence, and that he realizes he has violated store policy. At the end of the statement, he should write, "I make this statement voluntarily and without any promise or threats of any kind. I realize that what I have done is wrong and that I have violated store policies by failing to ring up all of my sales accurately and in proper sequence, and I further understand that my failure to do so is cause for dismissal." The employee should then sign his full name, payroll number, department number, and home address. He should also sign each page of the statement.

When all of this is completed, the interviewer should sign the statement as a witness and should then bring in his assistant or a department supervisor and have the employee read the full statement aloud. Then the interviewer should ask the employee, "Do you understand everything you have read?" After the employee agrees, he should ask a second question, "To the best of your knowledge is everything in this statement true?" After the employee agrees, the witness then signs the statement.

Handling Case Records

After the employee has been terminated through the normal termination process, the employment card of the suspect should be marked "do not reemploy" and should have a coded reference to the case history and confession forms which will be filed in separate locations. At no point should the personnel office have any of the records connected with the case. If the personnel office requires a reason for termination, let it be noted as "discharged for violation of store policies." No other information should be given. In response to a request for a reference, the personnel department should limit its reply to the employee's dates of employment and to the fact that he was discharged for a violation of store rules, without additional details.

If the store manager receives a request for a reference check, he must be particularly careful not to reveal any of the details concerning the discharge. He may, if he wishes, state that the employee was discharged for a violation of store rules, but he should *not* reveal the nature of the violation, stating that company policy requires such matters to be kept confidential. Under no circumstances should anyone say the employee was discharged for dishonesty. This would be most unwise, as the store has no factual proof that he stole cash.

The store manager who receives a phone request from a friend will have to exercise extreme caution in anything that he says concerning the case. The temptation will be strong to confide all the details of the situation. Naturally, he will want to protect his business acquaintance from taking on a dishonest employee, but it would be most unwise for him to give in to this impulse. The consequences can be devastating.

One situation occurred in a large supermarket chain operating in Southern California. The store manager had a checker-cashier who was stealing cash on sales. When interrogated, she refused to admit that she had ever stolen any money from the store. She did agree, however, that she had, on occasion, accumulated items and rung them up as a single transaction. On the basis of this admission, she was terminated for a violation of store policy. A week after she was discharged from the store, the store manager received a phone call from a business friend of his inquiring about this particular cashier. The friend said that he contacted the company's personnel office, and they had indicated that she had been discharged for a violation of store policy. Although he wouldn't give any further details, the personnel head did say the employee had a good record as a cashier and that her annual appraisals over the past three years had rated her "outstanding." Since he was in need of a capable cashier, he thought he would just check with him to find out exactly what had happened.

The store manager responded in a very human fashion to his friend's request. He wanted to protect him from taking on an employee who probably would "steal him blind," so he told his caller that the woman had been dismissed for a violation of store policy because she failed to ring up her sales accurately and in proper sequence. But he went much further. Bluntly, he stated that she had been stealing cash on sales for some time. Then, apparently still frustrated by the cashier's refusal to confess her thefts, he went on to say that the former employee was both a "liar" and a "thief."

His friend thanked him profusely for the information, promised to keep it confidential and, of course, didn't hire the woman. Unfortunately, the store manager learned the hard way that confidences can sometimes be misplaced. His friend not only told the woman that he wouldn't hire her, but he told her that he had talked to her former boss and repeated exactly what he had told him.

Unfortunately for the store manager and his company, the woman hired a lawyer who went into the store and confronted the manager. At this point, he made his second mistake. He not only admitted that he had said these things to his friend, but further elaborated on his belief that the cashier was not only a thief but also a "prostitute," a "no-good tramp," and other excessive statements that further exposed his lack of judgment.

The end result was a civil suit for $100,000 naming the supermarket chain and the manager as defendants. Charges included "false detention," and "defamation of character." The company's legal department made an investigation of the case and discreetly settled it out of court for $20,000. The end result was that the manager lost his job and was labeled by the industry as incompetent. The loose tongue of this store manager who wanted to ''help'' his friend gave the dishonest employee more money than she had stolen from the company.

Disposing of the Theft Case

Every year, thousands of store management people face the problem of what to do with a trusted, highly competent, long-term employee who is caught taking store merchandise or money. The manager is not only shocked to discover that the employee is stealing, but he recognizes that the thefts are really unlike the normal character of the person involved. Should this employee be turned out into the street like any other thief? Or does his fine work record and his long-term employment entitle him to further consideration? Shouldn't he be given a second chance?

The answer is *no*! No matter what you think the mitigating circumstances are, no matter how sorry you feel for the employee, no matter whether you feel the store—or even yourself—may be partly at fault, no matter what, discharge him!

There will be people who will argue that you may go out and hire another person off the street who will steal even more from you. They will also point out that perhaps the person who is really truly sorry for what he has done will make a more loyal employee than a stranger and that you can deal better with an employee when you know his weaknesses. In the case of a minor theft, some may think that it is of no consequence and that the store owes this employee and his family more consideration than just a summary dismissal. It is also costly to discharge and replace any employee, particularly an experienced one.

But all of these arguments are unimportant in view of the evidence that such a person will steal again. He may sincerely repent. In fact, he will usually say, ''I just don't know why I did it; I didn't need any of these things.'' And that very truth—that he does not know why he stole—is evidence of the underlying danger of keeping him on the job.

Like most dishonest people, he is a disturbed person who has found crime a satisfying substitute for certain aspirations or needs. He may honestly believe he will never steal again. But the cards are stacked against him and the store that rehires him, because he will usually steal again. Moreover, he will steal far more the second time than he did the first. The store not only risks losses from such a person's thefts, but also risks the contamination of otherwise honest employees. Often, the formerly honest employee who notices that you have put a dishonest person back to work becomes angry at the store and in an attempt at revenge starts to steal.

The Federal Bureau of Investigation has made a study of criminals released by the courts and prisons to determine what percentage continued their lives of crime. Its *Uniform Crime Report* for 1970 shows that of the larcenists released in 1965, 62 percent were rearrested within the four years following their release. Sixty-seven percent of the forgery offenders were rearrested for new violations within the four-year follow-up period.

One frequent temptation is always to assume that the teenage offender, being immature, has made a normal type of mistake when first caught stealing and is therefore a fairly good risk at the point of employment. The F.B.I. studies refute this conclusion. The younger the age group, the higher the repeating rate. This has been documented many times. For example, of the persons released in 1965, 74 percent of those under 20 years of age were rearrested within the next four years. Some 71 percent of those arrested at the ages 20 to 24 were rearrested. Keep in mind that these figures represent a minimum return to theft, since most larcenies are undetected.

Can there ever be an exception to this rule? Suppose you have a person of unusual ability, a person with some length of service in the company, or a person who makes a significant contribution to the business, is there any situation in which you could retain such a person after he is caught stealing? The answer is *yes*. But it can only be done if the dishonest employee faces up to the fact that his stealing is a symptom of a serious personality problem and voluntarily goes to a competent psychologist for treatment. If, after treatment, the psychologist will vouch for the employee and if strong supervision is provided, the employee may then return safely to his job. During the period of treatment, however, the employee who has been caught stealing must be suspended from store employment. With this single exception, management should recognize that every employee theft is a sign of a personality disorder which will lead to a continuing series of thefts if the employee is retained. Therefore, it has no choice but to discharge the first-time offender.

In disposing of the theft case, the store has a choice of terminating such an employee on the basis of dishonesty, of closing him out on the basis of a violation of store policy, or of prosecuting him for larceny. Whatever the decision, the action should be based on the attitudes and policies of the company as to where *responsibility* lies when an employee steals. Does it lie entirely with the thief? Or does management have a responsibility to *prevent the employee from being placed in a position of undue temptation*?

Sometimes the store sets up a situation which becomes an invitation to steal. For example, in one case a store held a sale of expensive wallets which were displayed at a counter at least 40 feet away from the cash register where the sales had to be rung up. The saleswoman at this counter started the day by walking down the full length of the aisle to the cash register on each sale. But as her counter became mobbed with impatient customers, it soon became apparent that this was inefficient and annoying to those who were trying to get waited on.

To speed up service, the woman began to accumulate three and four sales at one time before ringing them up on the register. Her only desire was to help management. The sale continued over a three-day period. On the second day of the sale, the woman came into the store wearing a suit which had jacket pockets. She found that by using the pockets, she could accumulate far more sales than she could carry in her hand back to the register. She could then ring them up as she had the opportunity. Unfortunately, at the end of the second day, she discovered when she arrived home that she had failed to ring $12.00 which was still in her jacket pocket.

She had no intention of stealing this money, but she was afraid to bring the money back to the store in case someone might see her returning it and suspect the worst. She would be accused of theft and discharged. On the following day when she came into work no one said anything to her about the money, and it soon became apparent that the store's accounting controls over cash register receipts were inadequate. So, on the third day she deliberately allowed some money to stay in her jacket pocket, and she took it home with her.

After the wallet sale was over, this clerk still continued to wear a suit with pockets, and she began to steal cash on sales in earnest, pocketing the money from one sale while waiting on another customer. It wasn't long before the honesty shoppers spotted her and she was apprehended. Questioning brought out the background of the case, and it was apparent to management that it had at least indirectly caused this employee to be placed in a position of undue temptation to steal.

Admittedly, no procedure for handling cash or merchandise can be foolproof, but the company must provide adequate supervision. Are money-handling control procedures adequate? Are the procedures enforced? Has the supervisor discharged his responsibility to the employee? Such questions can help determine store policy as related to the disposition of the dishonest employee case.

Summing Up Interrogation Procedures

1) Develop a personal philosophy which allows you to respect the person being interrogated as another human being with the right to human dignity. Even though you don't by any means approve of his criminal behavior, you can still respect him as a person of value.

2) Develop a confidence-and-belief relationship with the subject. This can only be done if the interviewer has a genuine interest in the person he is questioning and only if his own philosophy respects the rights and dignity of the individual.

3) Keep a neutral attitude toward the subject. Try to see matters from his point of view and try to understand his feelings. You can be warm and considerate, but your genuine interest and concern for the subject does not mean lapsing into sympathy. Seek to understand the viewpoint of the subject and attempt to see life from his frame of reference.

4) In the beginning, ask neutral questions which don't have emotional connotations. Develop rapport between you and the employee.

5) The good interviewer is subject-centered. Learn to be a good listener. Lean forward and show your concern and interest in the subject. But remember your interest must be sincere. People are not puppets to be manipulated. Apply the Golden Rule. Ask yourself, "How would I want to be treated if I were sitting on the other side of the desk?"

6) Move smoothly and carefully from neutral and non-emotional questions to questions that may have emotional connotations. Avoid questions that are too threatening for the subject to deal with. Be alert to recognize the symptoms of stress and shift to less threatening questions. Try to avoid all threats to the individual. Probe very gently at first and, if necessary, retreat frequently until you can see the relationship is strong enough so you can move on to more emotional questions. You are seeking honest and sincere responses free of fear. Convey to the subject that he is safe in this interrogation situation even though the nature of the questioning would normally be a frightening and threatening ordeal.

7) Next, shift from the emotional test questions related to the crime. Start "after the fact." Don't become involved in any discussions as to whether the subject did or did not commit the crime. Assume that the facts speak for themselves. The subject did, after all, steal the money or the merchandise. If you don't have proof of this, then you should not interrogate him. Center your questions on *why* the person committed the crime and *how* the crime was committed.

8) Use the feedback or nondirectional interview technique to remove emotional blocks and to help the subject examine the causes and results of his antisocial activities. Help him face the unpleasant situation in which he finds himself.

9) Try to get your first admission of guilt by indirection. Discuss why the crime was committed and offer face-saving suggestions to allow the subject to rationalize his actions. Successful interrogation is a creative skill, and learning to use empathy will require some trial and error. But, after you have attempted it a few times, you will find that it is a viable method that accomplishes your objectives.

8

THE EMPATHY METHOD: A SAMPLE CASE

To show the empathy method in action, here are excerpts from an actual case in which a young woman was questioned regarding the writing of fraudulent cash refunds. Interrogations sometimes take a considerable period of time; but, in this instance, rapport took only a few minutes and the first admission of guilt occurred 10 minutes later. At the end of half an hour, the case was fully developed. A summarized version of this interview appears below.

Having been asked to come to the office to discuss a business matter, the young lady entered the room and was cordially requested to sit down. The interrogator's goals were first to establish identification and then to build rapport. His initial questions were purposely neutral and avoided any emotional and touchy subjects that might make the interview more threatening.

Q. "Let's see, you are May Livingston, is that right?"
A. "Yes."

219

Q. "And you live at 417 Courtland Street?"

A. "Yes."

Q. "How long have you been working for us, May?"

A. "I started to work here nine years ago."

Q. "Where did you first work when you came into the store?"

A. "You mean in what department? Well, I started as a clerk on the returned goods desk. That's when we had the old system of returned goods desks. We don't have those any more."

Q. "Yes, I remember. Which floor did you work on?"

A. "I was on the third floor, better dresses."

Q. "Where did you go after that?"

A. "Well, I was on the service desk for about a year and a half, and then they made me a department manager. I worked mostly on the main floor—gloves and handbags."

Q. "Tell me, May, how did you originally happen to apply for work in our store?"

A. "I don't really recall how it all started. I always liked the store. I think a friend of mine suggested I apply for a job. I was looking for work; so one day when I was walking by, I decided to go up to the employment office and apply."

Q. "Did you work anywhere else before you came here?"

A. "No, not really, except on my summer vacations. I did some camp counseling. One Christmas I worked in a small neighborhood store."

Q. "Where did you go to school?"

A. "Over at Weston."

Q. "I see. How old were you when you started working here then?"

A. "I was 18."

Q. "That was right after you got out of high school?"

A. "Yes."

Q. "Do you live with your family? Are you married?"

A. "No, I'm not married. I live with my mother."

(Note that this last question concerning marriage and family is an initial test to see if the subject is at a point where she can tolerate emotionally loaded questions. There is an immediate return to neutral questions. This is like testing the ground in front of you to see if it is solid or quicksand. You take only one step at a time, and you keep one foot on firm land each time you make a test step.)

Q. "How long were you a department manager?"

A. "A year—almost two years really."

Q. "Did you always work on the first floor, or did they shift you around the building?"

A. "No, I stayed pretty much on the street floor."

Q. "You say you are living with your mother now? How old is she?"

(This is again testing with an emotional question to see if she is reaching a good point of toleration. It is a gradual shifting to the emotional aspect of the interview.)

A. "My mother is 59 years old. There's just the two of us since my father died."

Q. "When did that happen?"

A. "A year ago. He died just four days before Christmas. He was going downstairs into the basement and he fell. The doctor said he had a heart attack. We might have been able to save him, but we didn't hear him fall. I don't know how long he lay at the foot of the cellar stairs before Mom found him. But then it was too late."

(Notice that we have now really hit upon an emotional aspect of the young woman's life. The memory of her father's death is undoubtedly extremely upsetting, but the employee has been able to control her emotions sufficiently to answer the question in a calm manner. This suggests that her relationship with the interviewer is growing into one of confidence and belief, which is the objective.)

Q. "That must have been a very unhappy period for you."

A. "It was a great shock to all of us. It took me a long time to get over it. Even today there are periods when I feel extremely lonely and depressed without him. We were very close."

Q. "What did your Dad do for a living?"

A. "He was a postman. He only had a few more years before he would have retired."

Q. "Are you an only child?"

A. "No, I have three sisters and two brothers. I'm the second youngest. They've all left home except me."

(This gives a sample of how the interrogator moves from neutral questions into more emotional ones and encourages the subject to talk about her personal life and the more meaningful events which have happened in the recent past. In the complete interview, there is considerably more material along these same lines before the interviewer shifts over to a discussion of her income and expenditures—a first step toward discussing her thefts.)

Q. "How do you arrange your relationship at home with your mother? Do you pay her for your board and room?"

A. "Yes, I pay her $35.00 a week. Sometimes I buy extras too, you know, like sheets for the beds or new curtains for the living room. Mom likes plants, so I often buy her an azalea or some other plant."

Q. "How much do you earn here on the job?"

A. "My salary at present is $125 a week."

Q. "What's your take-home pay?"

A. "Most weeks around $94.00 after deductions."

Q. "And you give your mother $35.00 of this? Do you ever have other expenses like doctor's bills or anything like that?"

A. "Sometimes I also help my mother pay for her medicine. She has to have cortisone every day for her arthritis. It gets terribly expensive, so I often help out with her prescription bills."

(The interviewer is seeking information which will help to explain her need for the additional money she's been stealing.)

Q. "None of your brothers or sisters lives at home with you?"

A. "My youngest brother comes home sometimes for a week or so, but my other brother is in the Navy."

Q. "Does he help with the bills at home?"

A. "No, not very often. He's kind of careless with his money and spends a lot on himself. He throws Mom a $10.00 bill now and then, but overall he doesn't give her much."

Q. "What about the rest of the family? Do they help out?"

A. "Oh no, they're all married, and they all live away from here."

Q. "That means you have a lot of responsibility then, because you are handling the job of taking care of your mother almost all by yourself, is that right?"

A. "Yes, I guess you could say so."

Q. "How well do you get along with your mother?"

(Here we have another sensitive question. To determine exactly how much confidence she has in the interview relationship, the interviewer has to see whether her calm exterior is a facade or a true reflection of her feelings.)

A. "Fine, we get along real well."

(In her case, the question did not turn out to be an emotional one.)

Q. "You are probably getting old enough to think about getting married, aren't you? Do you have a steady boyfriend?"

A. "I . . . I did . . . but I don't get along too well with fellows . . ."

(Obviously we have now hit an area of emotional disturbance.)

Q. "Why, what happened?"

A. "May I please ask what all this discussion is about?"

(This is a perfectly normal response which sometimes occurs much earlier in the interview. The interviewer attempts to avoid answering this question.)

Q. "Well, as a matter of fact, I wanted to talk with you a little bit to learn something about you before we get into some business matters that I want to discuss. Were you engaged to someone and you had a falling out? Is that why you say that you sometimes have problems getting along with fellows?"

A. (slightly angry) "No."

Q. "But you did have a fellow that you went steady with, isn't that right? And I suppose you found it just didn't work out?"

A. "He wasn't my type. Everything looked great in the beginning. But then something went wrong, and . . . well . . . we just broke up, that's all."

Q. "But you are still fond of him?"

A. "No, not any more."

Q. "How long ago did you break up?"

A. "Last April."

Q. "Is that the first time you had an experience like that?"

A. "No."

(The young woman has now revealed an important emotional problem.)

Q. "You have had other similar situations previously?"

A. "Yes."

Q. "Sometimes things like that can make you very unhappy."

(This remark by the interrogator lays the groundwork so she can later explain and justify her thefts. It is becoming clear that she may have stolen to compensate for feelings of depression.)

A. "I was very upset about it this last time. We were engaged to be married. When he broke it off, I went through a nervous breakdown. I had to go to a doctor. He told me to leave town for a few weeks, so I went down to the shore and rented a cottage. But all that did was to make me feel more lonely and sad.''

(It now becomes apparent that the interviewer has struck a very responsive emotional chord. He has uncovered a deep psychological disturbance in the subject's background which could have led to her dishonesty.)

Q. ''Did you go home then?''

A. ''No, I stayed at the cottage as the doctor had ordered me to do. After some rest and quiet, things began to straighten themselves out. Finally, I thought I was over it, so I went back home. At home, I was calm for a while, but I couldn't eat. I lost a lot of weight—25 pounds. Just the thought of food upset me; I can't explain it.''

Q. ''You look all right now.''

A. ''Oh, I feel much better. Of course, I'm still real nervous, but I'm eating better. I get depressed sometimes. I try to put on a good front when I'm at work. I do my job all right, don't I?''

(Notice here that the young woman is trying not only to explain away the nervousness she feels under the pressure of the interview, but also to show that the periods of depression have not yet been resolved. She is still wrestling with her frustrations. She has not learned how to overcome them or to deal with them, and they have not substantially lessened.)

Q. ''So, you got sick. You found that you couldn't sleep well; you cried a lot.''

A. ''Yes, and I still have days when I can't eat. I sometimes can't keep anything down.''

Q. ''Have you told the doctor?''

A. ''Yes, I've told him I couldn't eat. He gave me some pills. He said it was mostly my nerves.''

Q. ''Tranquilizers?''

A. ''Yes, to relax you.''

(At this point, the interviewer senses that his probing questions are becoming disturbing to the subject. He wants her to regain her calmer frame of mind. His next step is to begin using the material she has offered him to help her explain what's been happening in her life and how this may have led to her stealing.)

Q. ''You know, May, sometimes when people go through experiences such as those you have had that make them very unhappy and depressed, this changes them. They may even do things which they would not ordinarily do, things that are not typical of their own standards of right and wrong. Now the reason that I have been talking at length with you is to discover, if I can, what exactly is troubling you. I am trying to understand you. In that way I think that you and I can work out a solution to a serious problem that we both face.

"You are like most people. All of us at some time or other find ourselves in an unhappy situation. Things occur to each of us which are in themselves tragic, like the death of your father; and things can depress us, like the breaking up of your engagement to that young man you had hoped to marry. Oddly enough, people, being the way they are, sometimes try to overcome these feelings of emotional disturbance and depression by doing things which are inconsistent with their character. The point to keep in mind is that your problem is not unique; it can happen to any one of us.

"Before you even realize what's happened, you suddenly find yourself in deep water. Your whole personality changes. It's like getting scarlet fever; you don't know you have it until you wake up one morning and see the blotches on your face. Then you are shocked; but it's too late to prevent it, because the disease has already taken over. Now, the important thing is to work on a cure."

A. "A cure?"

Q. "Yes. When you find yourself in a situation like this, the important thing is to get to the root of the problem—to try to see if you can figure out a way of overcoming your frustrations that won't be harmful to someone else.

"I think that now, from what you've told me, I have some understanding of why you have become involved in activities that are not typical of your character. You used bad judgment, of course, and I am unhappy about the things you have been doing. But these things have been done, and we can't undo them. So now our problem is to try to figure out together what we can do to improve matters and to help you.

"As you know, the company, and I, personally, are interested in every person who works here. I am particularly interested in a person like you. You and all of the other people who work here are what makes a store successful. It's my job to counsel with you and to help you with your problems both on the job or off. That's the way responsible human beings feel about one another. You know I'm not just talking; this is how I really feel."

A. (very soft) "Yes."

(Now the interrogation has moved into the first reference to the fact that this young woman has committed a crime. Indirectly, she is being forced to face up to the facts that have led to this interview. But this is done gradually so she can accept the situation and face it. The interviewer does not want her to panic, nor does he want the situation to appear threatening. He wants her to be able to deal intelligently with what has happened.

(At this point, he opens his desk drawer and calmly takes out one of the forged refunds that she had written. He puts it on the desk in front of him and stares at it thoughtfully. Nothing is said for a long time. She sits and watches him. He knows that when she saw the refund she immediately comprehended the entire situation. Finally, after she's had enough time to absorb the emotional shock of this action, he continues the conversation.)

Q. "I noticed you wrote a refund last week and forged the signature of your supervisor. You also forged the signature of the person who is supposed to have returned the merchandise to stock. You and I both know this is wrong. I'm sure that now that you've had time to think about it, you're sorry that you did it. You're not the type of person who ordinarily does this kind of thing. Like all of us, I assume there are times when you simply can't stand the pressures on you. Money pressures or emotional pressures can be hard to handle, and sometimes they cause us to go off the track. The result is that we do something like this which we are later ashamed of and wish we hadn't done. But we can't pretend this incident never happened. I would like to do so, as much as you, but it can't be done.

"What you did was dishonest. If I took it before a judge, he would call you a criminal. But I don't think you are a criminal. Having talked to you and having explored with you some of your personal problems, I know that you are basically a fine person. You take care of your mother and her home; you're tied down with serious responsibilities. I admire you for this. It is obvious that you normally have high personal standards.

"The big problem is that you've made a mistake. Now you must show your true character and face the situation. I want you to help me untangle this problem. I want to know how it happened, why you did it. Perhaps once I know these facts we can work out a constructive solution which will benefit you and help the store.

"There is a great difference between a real criminal and a basically honest person who has made a mistake. When a criminal is discovered, he makes every effort to get out of what he has done; he lies, he denies everything. This shows his inherent dishonesty. On the other hand, a normally honest person who realizes his mistake makes every effort to straighten matters out and to repair the damage.

"I know that's what you're going to do in this case. Let's see if we can work out a solution to this problem together. Suppose you begin by telling me why you started doing this type of thing. Why did you decide to write a fraudulent refund?"

A. "I don't know why; it's not like me. I've never done anything like it before in my life. I never stole anything even as a child. But the refund? I don't know why I did it. I didn't need the money; it wasn't that. It just seemed so easy, perhaps that was it."

(Now the interview has reached the "point of confession." The employee has made her first admission of guilt. The case is now a solid one legally. Notice that although she has not been directly accused of stealing, she has had the situation presented to her and she has admitted her forgery. Many thieves don't have any real idea of the personality pressures which have led them into the theft situation. May is typical in this respect.)

Q. "I understand what you are trying to say."

A. "I simply don't know why I did it."

(May puts her head in her hands at this point, and the interviewer gives her a few moments to compose herself.)

Q. "Do you think it is possible that you might have done this because you felt depressed? Do you suppose that writing these refunds and cashing them to get money in some way compensated for your feelings of sadness about the death of your father, about the breakup of your engagement?"

(The interviewer offers her a logical analysis of the frustrations which have led her into this situation. He has also provided her with a face-saving excuse which will allow her to explain her actions without the stress and emotional pressure that would result from anger or accusations on the part of the interviewer. The present approach avoids danger to her personality.)

A. "That may be the reason; I can't say for sure. I simply don't know, but it could be true. Perhaps when I got terribly depressed I wrote the refund to cheer myself up."

Q. "Where did you originally get the idea for writing forged refunds? Was it something you thought of by yourself? How did you learn about it?"

A. "I just thought it up myself. I wrote customer credits every day; and then one day I realized that nobody ever checks on them, so why shouldn't I do the same thing for myself and put the money in my pocket?"

Q. "What did you do with the money when you got it?"

A. "I spent it—some of it on clothes, some of it I gave to Mom for things we needed around the house. The money didn't mean anything to me. I couldn't really tell you what I did with most of it."

Q. "Then you didn't save it?"

A. "No."

Q. "What else did you do with it?"

A. "That's all I can remember. I don't really know what happened to all of it."

Q. "Well, perhaps you used it for other things. Do you have any hobbies?"

A. "No."

Q. "Do you read a lot of books?"

A. "Oh yes. I buy a lot of books."

Q. "Perhaps you used some of this money to buy books?"

A. "Yes, I guess I did use quite a bit of it to buy books. In fact, I used to go down to the bookstore on my lunch hour and buy books."

(There is now a period of discussion about the type of books that she purchased, and then some questions about her feelings toward her brothers and sisters. The questioning then returns to the matter of the thefts.)

Q. "Do you remember the first time you wrote a fraudulent refund?"

A. (long pause) "Maybe a month ago . . . I think . . . no . . . it was at least two months."

(Notice that she is trying to figure out how much the interviewer knows, and she wants to minimize her thefts, if possible. Most people have difficulty admitting the full extent of their actions. The interviewer recognizes that she is making a genuine attempt to face the reality of her situation, and he must try to help her through this difficult period of self-analysis.)

Q. "Well, now, that's surprising. I would like to believe what you say, but I think perhaps it is difficult for you to admit the actual length of time you have been doing this.''

(Notice how he does not refer to her actions as ''stealing'' or as a ''crime.'' Wherever possible he tries to avoid these threatening words. She knows she has stolen, and he helps her avoid the unnecessary pain of direct confrontation which has no value to the interview and may only upset her.)

Q. ''My folder here has the records on your case. Studies by the auditors show that your activities go back a lot longer than two months. I can understand that perhaps you can't remember how long they have been going on because it is emotionally disturbing to recall. But, on the other hand, if we are to straighten out this problem—and I know this is what you want to do—you're going to have to face the full extent of your activities. It's the only way you can find peace of mind for yourself. I have to know the full story if I am to help you to readjust your life and make a fresh start.''

A. ''I am trying to remember when I began. I simply can't.''

Q. ''I am sorry to hear you say that, because that makes the matter quite serious. You see, the first time anyone does anything like this there is a strong guilt reaction, particularly when it's a person who is normally honest. This leaves a lasting impression in the mind because it is so frightening. Therefore, if you are the type of person I believe you are, you should have felt extremely guilty and frightened the first time you wrote a bad credit. Now, if you say you can't remember that first time, then that's a very bad sign. It suggests you have been dishonest many times before, and that is something that I don't want to believe. I want to help you and I can help you, but only if you tell me the entire truth. Now, shall we start over again? Do you want to try again and see if you can tell me when it started?''

(The interviewer has made every effort not to let her get entrenched behind her lies. He has tried to throw her lifelines to make it easy for her to get out of the hole she is digging for herself. If he had directly contradicted her statement and accused her of lying, chances are she would have stubbornly resisted his questions. The interrogation would then have bogged down into a meaningless argument. When this occurs, neither person wins. More important, the facts are seldom uncovered.)

A. (after a long pause) ''Well, I do remember the first time. I have to admit that now. It started two years ago.''

Q. "Now, this first time it happened, do you remember the details?"

(At this point, catharsis begins, and the subject at first hesitantly and then gradually with more strength and more sureness begins to unfold her tale. She details the whole incident of the first time that she wrote a fraudulent refund. She tells about the fears and about the thoughts she had as she wrote the refund and as she signed the forged name. She recalls how her hand shook and how she couldn't sleep that night. Now she continues to remember a number of incidents. Yet, even with her best intentions, she cannot recall all of her thefts. But from the incidents that she can recall, it isn't difficult to get a fairly accurate picture of her thefts.)

Q. "Now, on this first day, you just wrote the refund out, is that right?"

A. "Yes."

Q. "Did you do it to get the money to buy something specific? Perhaps there were a couple of new books you wanted to buy?"

A. "No, I don't remember taking money for any specific purpose."

(Usually a desire for merchandise is not the motivating factor in a subject's thefts. Rather, it's a need to satisfy an emotional drive or to overcome frustration.)

Q. "Would you say there is any relationship between these credits and your periods of feeling depressed?"

A. (hesitantly) "There might be."

(She replies cautiously because this is again getting into emotionally upsetting territory.)

Q. "Now let me ask you another question, and I am sorry to be so personal, but I am trying to help you. Did anything else depress you besides the death of your father and the breakup with your boyfriends?"

A. "Well, sometimes when I think about my father, I get very depressed?"

Q. "Did you and your mother used to talk over your problems with your father?"

A. "No."

Q. "What depressed you about your father? Was he strict?"

A. "Yes. He was hard to get along with. I loved him, but he

was very old-fashioned, always suspicious. He accused me of things I never did.''

Q. ''How was he strict?''

A. ''He didn't want any of my friends to come to our house. He never would allow me to go out with boyfriends. I had to sneak out on dates. I had to lie and say I was going to the movies with a girlfriend. Then I had to be home at night at a certain time. Things like that. I often had to lie to him.''

Q. ''So after he died, you felt guilty when you went out with fellows.''

A. ''Yes. I often felt he was somewhere near me, invisible—but watching me.''

Q. ''How far back do you remember his being strict to the point that it bothered you?''

A. ''All though my school years, as long as I can remember.''

Q. ''Were you allowed to go to school dances and parties and things like that?''

A. ''No, not usually. Sometimes Mom would stick up for me and talk him into letting me go. But after all the fighting at home, I didn't have a good time.''

Q. ''You felt guilty?''

A. ''I knew my father would disapprove, and I knew that he'd be waiting for me to come home. He'd be sitting in the living room, angry. I was afraid of him, and he made me feel guilty, like I'd betrayed him.''

Q. ''Why did he act that way?''

A. ''I don't know.''

Q. ''Well, you tried to love him, but you found your relationship with him painful, didn't you?''

A. (in a sudden explosion of anger) *''I hated him.''*

(At this critical point, empathy has been established by the interviewer. The subject has suddenly revealed the focal point of her emotional disturbance. It is important to compare this violent statement with her earlier comments about how much she loved and missed her father. There is now further discussion as to why she disliked him, his treatment of her and her mother. She reveals her mother's instability, her extreme nervousness, and the fact that she was easily upset. Her close ties with her mother made her father's hostility, anger, and authoritarian manner difficult for her to accept. His problem traits became emphasized to the point where they seemed out of proportion, and she was unable to deal with her emotions toward him in a rational manner. After exploring the subject and her problem with the young men she dated, the interviewer again returns to her dishonest activities.)

Q. "Our problem now, May, is to try to find out, if we can, the extent of your activities. We both know you've been doing this sort of a thing a long time. We sent out test letters to check on the names and addresses on your refunds and quite a few came back not known at the address. In addition, we have studied the handwriting on your refunds, so I have quite a few here that appear to be forgeries."

(The interviewer takes a stack of refunds out of the drawer and puts them on the desk in front of her. She does not look at them or seem to be interested in them at the moment.)

Q. "One of our problems is going to be figuring out, if we can, how much money is involved in your activities, and, of course, we want to know why you did this so we can see what can be done to straighten this matter out. How often would you write one of these refunds?"

A. "Maybe twice a week."

Q. "Some weeks it might be three times, perhaps?"

A. "Yes, it could be three times."

Q. "When you were on the service desk and started doing this, did you get the idea from somebody else? Did you see someone else do it first?"

A. "Well, I guess I heard about it being done by other people, that's why I thought about doing it."

Q. "Were there any periods when you wrote more than three or four refunds a week?"

A. "No, I don't think so."

Q. "What about before Christmas? That's when you needed money for gifts for your mother and for your boyfriend."

A. "Maybe then."

Q. "I noticed that most of these refunds were around $18.00 to $25.00. Is that about what you usually wrote them for, or did you write some for a higher amount?"

A. "I don't remember, but I don't think I wrote any that were higher."

Q. "What was the most that you remember writing, the highest amount?"

A. "Let me see." (pause) "I wrote one once for $47.00; that was the most."

Q. "What was the least?"

A. (a long pause) "Oh, about $2.00."

Q. "Most of them, however, were around $5.00, $18.00 or $25.00? That's what I see in these I have here. Would you say that they are typical of the amount you usually wrote?"

A. (pause—wrings her handkerchief in her fingers and looks at the floor) "I suppose that's about the amount that I wrote on the average, yes."

Q. "Well, what do you suppose you did with all that money. When you stop and think about it, it was a lot of money, wasn't it? Oh, not a tremendous amount, but week after week, it really amounts to quite a bit. What happened to the money? Do you have much of it now?"

A. "No, I don't think I have any now. Maybe $50.00 in the bank, that's all."

Q. "I see, and what did you do with the money? Did you buy gifts for your boyfriend?"

A. "Well, I loaned him some money once."

Q. "That was right after you first came here and started working on the service desk, right?"

A. "Yes."

Q. "How much did you loan him?"

A. "About $350."

Q. "Did he ever pay it back to you?"

A. "He paid back some, about $20.00, not much really."

(The occurrence of the loan helps to verify the length of time the subject has been stealing and indicates that the amount of thefts was substantial even when she began her stealing. This is not something that has developed only in recent weeks. The amount of her refund thefts were probably high from the start.)

Q. "Did you ever pay for any dates with your boyfriend when he was short of cash?"

A. "Well, sometimes, not often."

Q. "What else happened to the money?"

(The girl is again obviously struggling with her memory, and like many dishonest employees, she simply finds it a blank. She spent it, but where? On what?)

A "I just spent it I guess, I simply can't remember."

Q. "Try! We have to figure out where you spent it."

A. "I just bought things, that's all. Clothes, books, presents for my boyfriend, cufflinks, you name it! I bought him new shoes once, and a pair of slacks, I remember that."

Q. "Did you ever give gifts to your mother?"

A. "Oh yes, many times. I bought her a rocking chair one time."

Q. "What sort of things did you buy for her besides the chair?"

A. "Oh, I bought her a robe once and some jewelry, a dress, things like that."

Q. "You felt that your father neglected your mother, and that the least that you could do was to try and make it up to her by giving her some things?"

A. "Yes, that was how I felt."

(Further discussion proved to be unproductive in establishing many individually large expenditures of money. There were several loans made to her boyfriend in addition to the one she originally admitted, and there were many gifts for her mother, including a shadow box and a piece of furniture for the dining room. Further expenditures were revealed in money spent on entertainment, the payment of house bills for heat and lights, and so on. Finally, the question of the total amount of her thefts is brought directly into the interrogation.)

Q. "Can you think of any other way that you spent the money?"

A. "No, that's about it as far as I can remember."

Q. "Then how much money do you think you took all together? Now, before you answer, I know it is a hard thing to figure out. I'll let you tell me first what you think it is. If your estimate isn't close, then perhaps based on what I already know from the study and the investigation we made of your refunds we can figure out what the real amount is."

A. (long pause—much twisting of the handkerchief) "I just don't have any idea . . . I don't know . . . I just can't add it all up."

Q. "Well just try to make a guess."

A. "Do you think it is as much as $2,200?"

(The interviewer moves the folder back and starts to go through the refunds, moving his head slightly in a negative fashion. Then he closes the folder and pushes it to the center of the desk.)

Q. "It's a lot more than that I'm afraid."

A. "Then you'll just have to tell me, because I can't even begin to estimate how much it is."

Q. "Well, just think back. You say you have been doing this three or four times a week, right? The average refund we said was between $15.00 and $25.00; let's say roughly $18.00 as an average. We know how long you've been doing this, how many times each week."

A. "Do you think it's as much as $4,000?"

Q. "You will have to think again, May. Don't think about the money that you can remember spending. Think about the money that you took."

A. "Then you figure it out for me. Tell me how much you think it is."

(The interrogator takes a yellow pad out of the desk and starts to do some figuring on it, taking the average figure of $18.00 a week and working backwards based on three times a week over the period of time that she admitted. The total is logical and conservative.)

Q. "From my figures, May, it looks to me as though it is a little over $9,000."

(May is obviously shocked as are most dishonest employees when the magnitude of their thefts suddenly confronts them. The shock is genuine because they simply don't recall spending that much money. The fact that there is so little left makes it difficult for them to really believe they have taken such a large amount.)

A. "I just . . . I just can't believe it. I just didn't think it could be possibly that much."

Q. "Well, we have discussed in some detail quite a few of the things you did with the money, and we talked about how often you took the money and how much you took each time. That's right, isn't it?"

A. "Yes."

Q. "To be perfectly honest, May, I imagine this is probably less than you actually took. But I want to be fair with you. Even if the total amount actually is one or two thousand dollars more than this, I am not really concerned about that as much as I am at your arriving at an honest appraisal of the situation. I want you to have some understanding of what is involved in all of these weeks and months that you had been writing these credits. I have taken an average figure, and I have not added the extra money that you took at Christmas for gifts.''

A. (long pause) ''I don't have any of the money left.''

Q. ''You didn't save any, that I know. It's hard to see how you could spend so much money, isn't it? Except that it's spent over a period of time.''

A. ''I don't know why I did it. I simply don't.''

(At this point she suddenly breaks down. She puts her head in her hands. The interrogator waits patiently for her to pull herself together.)

Q. ''Well, May, it is easy to see how you could spend it all. You got paid yesterday, right?''

A. ''Yes.''

Q. ''What did you do with the money you got paid yesterday?''

A. ''Well, I put $45.00 down on my charge account.''

Q. ''I see. How much do you owe on your charge account right now?''

A. ''I owe $210, something like that.''

Q. ''How much would you ordinarily buy on your charge account in a month? I don't mean during Christmas or Easter, but during the rest of the year?''

A. ''Maybe $150 worth of merchandise.''

Q. ''It would be higher in some months, however, wouldn't it?''

A. ''Yes, sometimes it goes up as high as $350 or $400.''

Q. ''What sort of things do you buy on your charge account? Say last month?''

A. ''I bought a set of luggage. You see I am going on vacation next week. A girlfriend and I are planning to go to Bermuda, so I needed some luggage.''

Q. ''How much did you spend for the luggage?''

A. ''It came to $270. I bought it on my contract account.''

Q. ''I see.''

(At this point the interviewer continues to detail the cost of items that she has purchased: the amount she spent on her mother's robe, the gifts she gave her brothers and sisters and her mother for Christmas, the items she gave her boyfriend. She also spent a considerable amount of money on her clothes, on an expensive high fidelity music system, a color television set, and a new car. In the end it was not difficult for her to realize that she had actually stolen over $9,000.)

Although the entire interrogation is not represented here, the questions and answers do show the method of empathy interviewing. They show how the interviewer establishes rapport with the subject, how he gradually moves his questions into emotionally sensitive areas, withdrawing when he sees that the questions are becoming too difficult for the subject to handle. It also shows how he eases into an indirect discussion of the crime and obtains a confession without any direct accusations.

In addition, the interview shows how the interrogator builds the case toward a logical and realistic amount of restitution by establishing when the thefts started, their frequency, and the average amount stolen each time. He backs this up by a cross-check against how the stolen money has been spent. As a result, when the interview is completed, the subject is in full accord as to the figure agreed upon for restitution.

Finally, a written statement is taken down, dictated for the most part by the interviewer, but using the phrases and the explanations as expressed by the subject. It is written in her own handwriting, and she, of course, is allowed to alter it, to make it a valid statement of her theft activities.

Once the statement is completed and notarized, May is moved to another office and some lunch is brought in for her. After an hour is taken to relax and recover from the emotional tension of the morning interview, there is some further discussion as to May's method of repayment. A promissory note is signed and the subject agrees to repay the total amount on the basis of $15.00 a week. A member of her family is telephoned and asked to come to the store and take her home. When he arrives, the case is briefly explained to him with May present. After some further discussion, he assumes responsibility for her and the case is concluded.

PART FIVE

Creating a Controlled
Working Environment

9

GENERAL CONTROLS

Until a few years ago, there was no accepted explanation for the causes of theft. Every specialist had his own pet theory. Some believed that certain people are born to be bad; others claimed that dishonest individuals are simply incapable of telling right from wrong. There were those who held that social and economic environments were the cause of theft; while still others said that people steal to get something for nothing, or because their parents were too lax, or because their parents were too strict. Some theorists just adhered to the old cliché, "It's caused by the general breakdown of morality in our times."

Each expert had his own opinion, and the experts rarely agreed. In many instances, there was some truth in their theories, but specific examples could always be cited that proved exceptions to the rule. Invariably, there were too many loopholes in the theory to apply it across the board. Finally, in 1939, scientists at Yale University conducted a study into this question entitled "Frustration and Aggression," by Dollard, Doob, Miller, Mower, and Sears. They examined the role of frustration in the socialization of the individual and in the characteristic aggressiveness of criminals. The result of their research was a unifying theory for the criminal act.

The essence of the Yale findings was that an act of theft is precipitated by the coming together of three factors in the life of the potential thief. Thus a theft situation may be visualized as a triangle, with each side representing one of the three critical elements: 1) aggression, 2) frustration, and 3) low anticipation of being caught. The obvious answer to the control of theft, therefore, is the destruction of the triangle through the elimination of any one of these three critical factors.

Aggression and Frustration

Management has long viewed natural aggressiveness as a desirable quality in its employees. We want aggressive people on our staff, employees with strong drive, who are physically active and who have large reserves of energy. We choose aggressive employees and are unlikely to agree to sacrifice this valuable trait. But natural ambition and energy is far different from the undesirable and hostile form of aggression that leads to theft. It is this form of aggression that comprises the first side of the triangle.

To eliminate this theft factor, we must often deal with its source. Frequently, these undesirable feelings are found to be the direct result of frustration, the second side of the triangle. Unfortunately, we can do little about some forms of frustration, such as a physical handicap, difficulties at home, or health and money problems. But others are unnecessary, because they are caused by elements within our control, elements which arise in our store setting.

Often when people steal in a department, the cause of their frustration can be traced to the supervisor's failure to relate properly to his employees on a personal basis. He may be too authoritarian, causing them to steal as a transfer of their feelings of hostility against him and the store. Or he may provoke theft because of his lack of consideration in dealing with his employees.

One case involving tactlessness on the part of management was directly responsible for triggering a theft. The young lady involved had been hired by a store as a Christmas extra but was considered so competent that she was retained as a permanent employee. She assumed that having survived the Christmas layoffs, she would remain with the store indefinitely. However, unknown to her, top management had decided to cut back on personnel.

On a Wednesday morning, the department supervisor casually walked up to the young woman, stopped for a second, and said, "Oh, by the way, Jeanette, you will be closed out as of Friday night." He gave no further explanation and walked away. Appropriate procedure would have been to call her into his office, explain that the staff was being cut, and offer some hope for future re-employment. In this case, his lack of consideration caused her to undergo an emotional reaction. She brooded about his rudeness and the unfairness of her discharge.

The next day, she came in wearing a skirt with pockets and began to steal money on every even-money sale. Ironically, the shoppers happened to be testing salespeople in her department that day. A knowledgeable shopper spotted her skirt with pockets, tested her, and saw her steal the cash. The shoppers then made three more test purchases. In her blind anger, she pocketed all three of the sales.

A polygraph test later showed that this young person had been scrupulously honest prior to this incident. The combination of events and the method in which she was fired caused her to experience psychological pressures to which she responded by stealing. Her case is a classic example of how an inconsiderate supervisor can trigger a theft response by creating serious frustrations in an employee.

Unrealistic company policies can also lead to frustration. One company, a chain of 27 supermarkets, learned this lesson the hard way. Being concerned about the frequency of cash register shortages, the company controller persuaded management to institute a policy stating that any cashier showing a shortage of more than 25 cents in her daily receipts would have to repay it out of her next payroll check. In two or three months, almost all the registers balanced daily. Six months later, the improved cash register figures were so impressive that a steak dinner was given in the controller's honor.

But, at the end of the year, management was astounded to discover that inventory shortages had doubled. An outside security consultant was quickly called in, and he soon discovered that almost every employee working on the cash registers was stealing. He ultimately traced this situation to the unrealistic store policy.

What might have happened was as follows: Helen Brown, a cashier, unwittingly punches the wrong key on a sale and is short $6.00 at the end of the day. The next morning, the manager stops by and notifies her that this shortage will have to come out of her pay. What is the clerk's reaction?

Helen is angry. She knows that she didn't steal the money. She even wonders if she actually made an error. Perhaps the head cashier or someone in management took the money. Why should she be held responsible and have to repay the shortage out of her hard-earned pay check? Helen spends a good deal of time brooding about this problem, trying to figure out a way to get her money back.

It doesn't take long before other cashiers in the store also make errors and are forced to pay penalties. Eventually, they exchange information and devise techniques to recover the money they feel was unfairly taken from them. Their view is likely to be: "Two can play at this game. If management feels I'm dishonest, then I might as well be dishonest." Unfortunately, once the cashier starts out to recover her money, she invariably ends up stealing additional cash from the register.

Studies have shown that even capable people punching keys on a register will make unconscious errors. Penalizing such people through a rigid policy of accountability may therefore cause a theft reaction. In one such investigation, an unrealistic repayment policy led to theft by nearly every cashier in the chain's 42 stores. The result was a near disaster. Management realized that the company could not continue to operate if it fired all of its dishonest cashiers, but it didn't know exactly how to go about rehabilitating these workers. The company tried to bring things in line for a period of months, but losses continued to be so substantial that there was a wholesale firing of staff both at the management and cashier levels. Only after releasing numerous employees and hiring new ones was the company able to bring its shortages under some measure of control.

Because frustration triggers dishonesty, the supervisor needs to know how to reduce employee frustration. One step is to establish a solid foundation of positive attitudes which he not only feels but communicates to his employees. This means he should be trained in good human relations skills and in how to counsel with employees to help them overcome their feelings of discontent. By applying these techniques, he can help his staff gain insight and find solutions to their problems. In addition, the supervisor needs to recognize the importance of a disciplined and reasonable work climate in the employee's life. Lack of direction, lack of leadership, and the failure to exercise proper controls can make every employee feel emotionally insecure and unsafe. Nevertheless, even the highly neurotic person *can* remain a worthwhile, honest employee, providing supervisors understand how frustration triggers theft.

Low Anticipation of Being Caught

The third side of the theft triangle, low anticipation of being caught, is the opportunity required to enable the aggressive and frustrated person to steal. "Anticipation" is the key word here. Fear of being caught is the greatest single deterrent to crime.

In many cases, the failure to enforce company policies provides the opportunity for large-scale thefts. These thefts carry with them few feelings of guilt, since the store obviously cares little about its money or merchandise. The employee easily deduces this fact from the general negligence, carelessness, and indifference of store management in enforcing control systems and procedures, and from the general attitude of disregard for the protection of company assets.

Management attitudes or lack of awareness are very often the providers of opportunity to the dishonest employee. In some stores, management is unaware of how much dishonest activity is taking place in its operation or of the dangers of not keeping internal thefts under control. The manager, being honest himself, finds it difficult to believe that employees steal. He tends to see only the good qualities in his staff, which is usually an excellent, healthy attitude. But the result is that even when there are obvious indications of dishonesty, he tends to rationalize the employee's actions and to persist in believing he is honest.

Some managers set up an atmosphere conducive to theft because they feel that it is unnecessary to be watchful for signs of dishonesty. They labor under the naive misconception that if there are dishonest employees in their operation, they will be reported by other employees. This hope is not substantiated by experience. Usually, the employee who discovers a co-worker stealing will say to himself: "What Harry does is his own business. I'm hired as a salesperson, not as a detective." He feels no guilt or responsibility in ignoring the situation. In some cases, where he dislikes his department supervisor or others in store management, he may even feel a certain satisfaction that someone is getting even with the store.

A final blind spot is caused by a manager who does not pay enough attention to what his people are actually doing on the job. The manager must really look at his staff. He cannot walk through his operation day-dreaming or preoccupied with other matters. He should know his control systems thoroughly and be careful to investigate every transaction he authorizes to insure that he is not being set up as a patsy for a dishonest employee. This means that he must be alert to all the clues to dishonesty and must question anything an employee does that appears irregular. Whenever an irregularity occurs, a vigorous follow-up investigation should be immediately undertaken. If store employees know that any violation of policy will be challenged and that any irregularity will be investigated, they will soon realize that they are working in a disciplined environment. They will reason that if they were caught when they violated company rules, they will surely be caught if they steal.

Training and supervision play important roles in reducing employee theft. Store management has a responsibility, first, to be sure the employee is well trained. Second, the store must provide competent supervision. This means alert, sympathetic managers who set a personal example of honesty and do not allow employees to violate company rules. Finally, the store should conduct periodic audits and reviews of every control system and procedure to assure management that the controls are operating as intended. Enforcement of store systems and procedures is a major supervisory responsibility, and store effectiveness in this regard should be regularly examined and rated.

The next time you receive your copy of the inventory shortage figures and find that they are high in a certain department, recognize that the solution to these shortages is to get at the causes of the problem—and most shortage problems have several causes. The basic factors are unhealthy levels of aggression, usually rising from excessive frustration, combined with a working environment where the employee has little fear of being caught, because of a lack of discipline, a lack of supervisory enforcement of controls, or a lack of adequate procedures. Eliminating any side of the theft triangle will help in creating a controlled working environment and in setting up policies and working conditions which encourage honesty.

The Value of Controls

Strong systems and controls can prevent many theft losses. They can reveal the fact that employee thefts are occurring and may often lead to uncovering the culprit. In addition to protecting store cash and inventory, they are one of the best means for protecting your store's greatest asset—its people.

Losses cannot be computed purely in terms of dollars. As Virgil W. Peterson, managing director of the Chicago Crime Commission, has pointed out: "In many instances—perhaps the majority—an individual would not have turned dishonest had reasonable precautionary methods been exercised. To take steps that will successfully prevent this dishonesty is to save many lives from ruin."

The control of the business enterprise is largely achieved through the administration of its managers. If each manager successfully carries out his responsibilities, the firm will function properly and prosper. If he does not, the selling of quality products or services at competitive prices will be impossible, for internal thefts will cause a constant financial drain on the company.

To achieve a satisfactory measure of control, each manager must be able to do an adequate job of planning, organizing, and applying the techniques of the controls embodied in this section. The following is a discussion of areas in the retail operation that are frequently exploited by dishonest individuals, especially in department and discount stores. Front-end controls for supermarkets and other stores with checkout operations are covered in the next chapter. Important control systems and procedures are discussed for each area in an effort to provide management with the tools necessary to create a working environment that will intelligently limit the opportunities for theft.

Receiving Area Procedures

Some stores, unfortunately, do not really understand the full significance of having adequate control procedures for the receiving area and back room. This area is a vital control point, because every single item of merchandise that enters the store must pass through it. Once the dishonest employees begin to exploit this area, they have access to every type of store merchandise—and in carton quantities. Management is usually too busy out front to give the area proper attention, and outsiders as well as employees often have free access to the merchandise it contains.

Any program of shortage control should begin with an analysis of the security of your receiving operation. In one case, management had a hunch that something was wrong but couldn't put its finger on it, so an undercover detective was assigned to the receiving dock. The detective had been on the job about two days when he sensed that Mike, the receiving boss, seemed troubled. He paced more nervously than usual and was somewhat more irritable in his commands to the men. Mike was standing by the tailgate of a large, battered green truck. Everything looked natural at first. He was apparently just watching a driver unload some large cartons of linens. Mike's face was clearly visible to the detective, and he noticed a curious intensity in his eyes as he stared at the cartons coming off the truck.

Then, an odd thing happened. Without raising his head, Mike's eyes came into contact with the eyes of the driver. In an instant, the look vanished, and the scene was the same as before. Yet the detective was sure there had been a flicker of recognition between them. Grabbing a hand truck loaded with cartons, he moved to a position where he could get a better view. He was close enough now to see Mike's hand tremble ever so slightly as he signed the driver's invoice. That one glance and the slight trembling of Mike's hand was all he had to go on, but it was enough.

After he signed the invoice, Mike turned and walked briskly away to the far end of the dock where he started talking to another driver. His back was turned to the green truck. The detective watched as the driver carefully folded his invoice and slipped it into his jacket pocket. Then the trucker turned his back to the dock and started walking toward a nearby flat of cartons containing typewriters and tape recorders. The driver slid a rolling jack under the flat and slowly eased it to the tailgate of his green truck. Mike still had had his back to him.

It was hard to understand why no one noticed so obvious a theft. But the fact is that no one saw it because no one wanted to see it. With a thump, the flat rumbled onto the truck. In a moment, the empty jack was back on the dock, and the driver climbed into the cab of his vehicle. The detective moved quickly. He dashed across the dock, flung the trucker's door open, and placed him under arrest. In this case, the store was lucky. Similar incidents occur daily in stores across the country and go undetected.

The next time you visit your receiving area, stand for a moment and watch your employees unpack and mark your goods. Consider this: merchandise represents 60 to 70 percent of your business investment. Several times each year your entire stock passes through your receiving opeation. Ask yourself one question: "In terms of these facts, is my merchandise being adequately guarded?"

Many stores have already recognized the risks inherent in this area, and some have decided to take action to improve their receiving controls. One important step has been to change the traditional idea of store organization and to put responsibility for receiving under the control division. Even at best, receiving is a difficult department to operate. Three store divisions have an interest and responsibility here: operations, control, and merchandising. Receiving is, of course, in business to serve the merchandiser. After all, the first job of every store is to sell merchandise. Therefore, its primary aim has always been to move incoming goods through the receiving and marking process as rapidly as possible and onto the selling floor.

A second aim, however, has now become equally important. This is the protection of merchandise and invoices during receiving operations. The security function of receiving is rapidly becoming recognized as an important job. The receiving manager's aim is to bring the two prime functions of movement and control into harmonious balance.

Both external and internal thieves threaten the receiving area. Truckers making deliveries may steal cartons of merchandise off the store dock. Dishonest employees may engage in large-scale thefts, encouraged by the fact that thefts from this area are not easily detected. The constant movement of goods in and out of this location makes it difficult for the store to protect merchandise.

One of the most serious types of internal theft in receiving is, of course, embezzlement. Through manipulation and falsification of records, dishonest employees succeed in converting merchandise or money to their own uses. A good system of paperwork control over receiving merchandise can prevent embezzlement, especially when it involves the manipulation of purchase journals and accounts payable records.

Your first step in strengthening your operation is to analyze your present control systems and procedures in the receiving area. There is no such thing as maintaining the "status quo" in operating a department as complex as receiving. The operation is either being constantly improved, or it is deteriorating.

To keep a control system operating properly, it must be checked periodically by management. One of the first steps you can take is to reread the manual which you used as a guide when setting up your present receiving controls. Review each step of your original receiving plan. Ask yourself where it needs strengthening, and change it if it does; then go out to the dock, to the checkers and markers, and bring your operation back into line. Finally, mark a date on your calendar to review the operation again during the next few weeks.

In checking your controls, pay particular attention to the physical protection of the receiving room. This area should be locked whenever there is no supervisor in attendance. Many stores have their receiving personnel take the same lunch hour. During this time, the area is deserted. If receiving and marking rooms are not locked during the lunch hour when everyone has left, then you have set up a potential theft situation. Sooner or later, a dishonest employee will discover this weakness and will return to these areas to steal while everyone is at lunch.

Checking and marking areas should also be locked at night. The key should be carefully controlled. Sometimes it's advisable to put a strip of invisible cellophane tape across the bottom of the receiving door where it cannot be noticed. Do this in the evening when it's locked, and then examine it the first thing in the morning before the room is opened. This way you can tell if anyone on the night crew has opened the door during the night.

Someone may ask: "Why do we need to lock the receiving room? After all, our stockrooms are left open, and merchandise is available all over the store!" The reason the receiving area is more vulnerable than the average stockroom is because theft in the receiving area is less likely to be detected. Therefore, if you want to cut shortages, you must provide adequate physical protection for receiving merchandise.

Another important control element is to insist upon good housekeeping. A clean, well-organized back room cuts thefts. When the room is allowed to become a giant trash pile, thefts are encouraged because loss of cartons goes unnoticed. Even the psychology of keeping the room neat acts in management's favor because it implies that management *cares* about its merchandise. Conversely, when the room is disorderly, it suggests management does *not* care; and it invites the dishonest employee to help himself. He does.

One rule should be strictly enforced—no employee, whether a receiving room employee or anyone else, should be allowed to exit across the rear dock at any time, including the lunch hour, relief, or when leaving at the end of the day. This rule *must* be adhered to, and any violation should be severely dealt with. No employee should be allowed to make trips between the receiving room and his car "to get my sandwiches," "to check to see if I turned off my lights," "to move my car to the shady side of the building," and so on. These trips may become blinds for concealing merchandise thefts. To avoid the problem from the start, don't allow anyone to leave the store at any time across the rear dock!

Other suggestions to prevent receiving area thefts are as follows:

1) Do not allow buyers and salespeople to take goods out of the receiving room before the merchandise is processed. If they must, they should sign a control record listing the items in detail.

2) Employees working in the receiving room should not be permitted to bring personal packages or large handbags into the area. These provide the means for concealing stolen merchandise.

3) At the end of the day, after the receiving door is locked, check the back dock area for any merchandise that may have been left purposely on the dock or slid out underneath the door.

4) Check case counts and make a random spot check of item counts.

5) Do not allow the receiving checker to be interrupted at any time while goods are being received and checked. If he must leave the job, have another employee available to prevent possible stealing.

6) Permit no one but proper receiving personnel to have pos-

session of invoices, all of which should bear the receiving manager's signature.

7) Supervise the handling of stales, empty bottles, and other return goods.

8) Do not permit outside resource delivery drivers to have access to the store, to stockrooms, or to the inside area of the receiving operation.

9) Place all delivered merchandise in an unobstructed space sufficient for complete and unbroken assembly and checking of orders.

10) Discourage delivery at times which are not convenient for the supervision and the checking required.

11) Do not have the receiving room cleaned at night. This is a poor practice because it opens the way to systematic thefts by night porters.

Good supervision and adequate physical security are important to strong receiving room controls, but, by far, the greatest need in any store is a good receiving system. This should *not* mean red tape! A well-designed receiving system doesn't hinder the receiving operation; it actually moves merchandise through faster because it simplifies work.

Your control system must protect not only the goods, but also the paperwork records your store needs to maintain accurate inventories and to pay resources. One such system used by many retailers is called "Key-Rec." Designed by Jack Moss, a former receiving manager at Lazarus in Columbus, Ohio, this control system keeps track of all received merchandise through each step of checking, marking, and accounts payable, thereby preventing and detecting thefts along the merchandise pipeline. A strong receiving system, such as this, also prevents employee dishonesty because of the built-in psychological effect of strict controls.

A good receiving system should be designed to allow you to:

1) Write up incoming shipments at the proper time, when they enter the back door of your store.

2) Unpack your merchandise with safety, whether there is an invoice or not.

3) Control price marking so that tickets and invoices will reflect correct retails and other valuable information necessary to proper inventory control.

4) Make certain that for every shipment received and put into stock, an invoice is charged to the department's stock within the same accounting period.

5) Guarantee that there will be no duplicate payment of the invoice, and assure prompt passing of invoices to obtain anticipation and discount.

6) Give prompt and accurate inventory figures.

7) Tie in with your buyer's unit stock control so he can reorder wisely.

8) Assure follow-up of merchandise shortly upon arrival.

9) Provide a corroborative record that enables the store's auditors to check the validity of paid invoices.

10) Provide internal control over the purchase order, receiving, unpacking, checking, marking, distribution, and inventory of merchandise.

Insist that your receiving operation has good supervision, adequate physical protection, and sensible and effective control systems and procedures. Good receiving controls can avoid shortage disasters and increase your profits.

Branch Transfer Checks

Stores should keep a separate inventory record for their branches. If the store fails to make accurate branch transfers and fails to consolidate branch invoices and shipments with its records in the accounting department, this can badly distort inventory figures and conceal major loss situations. In fact, losses may appear to be occurring in a branch store when they are actually occurring in the parent store, and vice versa. This causes investigation problems.

At least once a month, an audit analysis should be made of branch transfers. You should check to see if the transfer merchandise is being properly recorded and if the transfer control system is being operated as planned. If you desire a quick answer on the effectiveness of your receiving controls at the branches, remove several garments from a rack going out to a branch store on transfer. This should be done before the rack reaches the transfer checkout point. Will the four or five garments you removed be noticed and reported missing by the person checking the transfer goods? Is a unit count being made at both ends of the branch transfer operation? If neither end catches the error, you will know that a reeducation program is immediately in order.

Truck Sealing Tests

Many stores today use an expensive padlock and railroad seal to protect goods moved in trucks between stores and warehouse. To check the effectiveness of your particular sealing system, you should occasionally remove the normal seal after the truck is en route and replace it with a substitute seal. If the person who checks the seal at the receiving end does not report the variation in the seal number, then you will know that your control system is not being operated as planned and you can take appropriate corrective action. Presentation of the correct seal number to the branch store receiving checker is often a dramatic method of education. It reminds him to do a more conscientious job of overseeing this important control.

Employee Package Controls

Looking at her frightened face, you couldn't help feeling sorry for her. She was a salesclerk in the cosmetics department, and if it hadn't been for a "tip" from a long-time employee, she would never have been caught. The interrogator grimly turned the paper bag upside down. Several jars of night cream and two boxes of perfume tumbled onto the top of his desk. "Is this what you were taking out of the building?" he asked.

Silently, she nodded.

"But what would you want with them?" he questioned.

"I don't know," she responded. "I don't know!"

He picked up the register stub she had used when trying to walk past the guard at the employee exit door. "And you used this receipt?"

Again, she nodded.

"But it's only for 53 cents," he persisted. "Where did you get it?"

"I . . . I . . . bought something," she stammered.

"What did you buy?" he asked. "Each of these items is worth $5.00 or more."

She started rummaging in her handbag. Finally she found what she was looking for and brought it out. It was a small pendant on a thin silver chain. She dropped it on the desk. He reached over and picked it up. The price tag was still on it.

"I bought it on my relief period this morning," she explained. "I was on my way out for coffee, and I saw these silver pendants on a rack. So I bought one."

"But when did you make up the package?" he asked.

"Well," she continued, "between one and two o'clock, the department manager is out to lunch, so that's when I got this bag and put the stuff in it. Then I stapled it shut with the 53 cents register stub on the outside."

She went on to tell him how she had successfully carried out this procedure two and three times a week for several months. Later, when an investigator was dispatched to her home, he found over $800 worth of merchandise stolen from the store.

Why is sealing employee packages an invitation to steal? Why is the cash register receipt an unsatisfactory control? How do dishonest employees beat the system?

Employees who steal often start with small "impulse" items—a comb or a bottle of cologne, which they find relatively easy to palm and slip into their pocket. They find it so easy, in fact, that once they overcome their normal fears and feelings of guilt, they soon begin to feel that it's silly to pay for anything.

As their luck holds out, their greed grows. But suddenly the employee has a problem. What he wants to steal is a small appliance, and it won't fit into his pocket. Obviously, the only way to get such an item out of the store is to pretend that it has been purchased. At this point, the "petty" thief begins a careful examination of the stores' package control systems. It doesn't take long for him to discover a loophole.

Package sealing is the chief means used by stores to control employee packages. Some stores staple packages closed. Others use numbered package seals or seals signed by the store manager. Still others use specially colored sealing tape. All of these approaches are based on the assumption that once a package is sealed, it is difficult to add stolen merchandise to it. Nothing could be further from the truth.

The potential thief sees the sealed package as an automatic pass to get stolen goods past the door guard. Even when a store does a responsible job of protecting the package seals, management should never underestimate the cleverness of dishonest employees. They have steamed off seals, printed their own, and forged them with pen and ink so they could not be distinguished from the printed originals.

Some stores still rely on the method of stapling packages shut with the register tape folded over the top of the bag. Confidence in this control is based on the assumption that employees will not help each other steal. A store in Palo Alto, California, was typical of those operating under this theory. Increasing shortage figures, however, prompted management to call in a security consultant. The agent discovered that employees were making small purchases almost each day—a 10 cent comb, a 25 cent hair net, and so on. But when the clerk bagged the item, she would add other merchandise—hosiery, makeup, and, in one case, a hair dryer. A few weeks of investigation proved that every employee in the store was stealing or helping other employees to steal.

Even when employees do not steal in collusion, the use of a cash register tape on the bag is an unsatisfactory control. Tapes are too easily obtained. A clerk can withhold them from customers or can pick up discarded tapes from the floor. These tapes become convenient passes to remove stolen merchandise from the store.

Although every store package system contains some worthwhile control elements, seldom are they all combined into an ideal control technique. An effective employee package control should provide these characteristics:

1) *The guard must know what the package contains.* If the person checking out the packages knows exactly what each package is supposed to contain, he can verify its contents if he wishes. The simplest, most effective way of doing this is to leave every employee purchase package open and unsealed. By leaving the bag open, the store gains two advantages. First, it eliminates the false confidence management has in its controls. Knowing that merchandise can be added to an open bag puts management on its guard. Second, anxiety is created in the potential thief. He knows that an open bag can easily be examined, and this acts as a psychological deterrent.

2) *There must be a package inspection at the door.* In some stores, a few packages are selected for inspection each night. One night, it might be one package in 10 that has its contents compared with the sales receipt. On another night, it may be one package in 20, or one in 15, and so on. The person having his package checked is asked to step out of line for a moment to a side counter. Then the contents are removed from the employee's bag and carefully checked against the sales receipt. But the person being checked knows that his selection is completely impersonal, because employees have become accustomed to a random check each night.

A detailed sales receipt and a package inspection can also be used when a store employs a central package room control system. The packages are left in a central package room, the store manager's office, or are retrieved from the selling counters near the end of the day by a stockboy and brought to one of these locations. Then, before closing time, the manager or a designated assistant spot-checks the packages against the sales receipts. Under this system, it's important that employees *know* that packages will be in-spected. It's equally important that, after inspection, packages are brought to the exit door to be distributed as the employees leave the building, giving them no chance to include other merchandise.

Also, pay attention to night watchmen who go off duty before the store opens in the morning and be sure that their packages are checked. Actually, there is little reason for people working the night shift to take packages of any type out of the building. Any packages taken to work by night employees should be held at the entrance and then returned when the employee leaves the building.

3) *There must be only one employee entrance and exit.* Failure to use the authorized door when entering and leaving should be cause for dismissal. This will prevent employees from slipping merchandise into their cars by exiting across the back receiving dock or out an unauth-orized exit during selling hours.

Dishonest employees attempting to steal merchandise often use an unauthorized customer door to leave the building. Periodic surveillance should be made of these unauthorized exits to see if employees are using them to take out packages of stolen merchandise. They may do this on a lunch or relief period, or shortly before closing time at the end of the day. By placing people who know the staff on these doors, the dishonest employee can often be spotted and stopped. His packages should then be opened and checked.

Part-time employees who leave the store early on late-night openings present an additional problem. They should be required to use the authorized employee exit, and a spot check should be made of customer doors during the work-ing day to see if dishonest employees are going out these unauthorized exits.

By pinpointing what's inside a package, having regular inspections, and controlling the entrance and exit routes of employees, managers can stop most package thefts. Then, when you watch your workers leave at the end of the day, you'll know they're leaving your inventory behind.

Trash Removal Precautions

It has been said that successful management depends on the ability to realize the opportunities, while avoiding the hazards. Nowhere is this truer than in the control procedures used to prevent thefts in trash removal. Too often, store merchandise is hidden in trash removal vehicles or in bales of outgoing refuse. When these reach their destination, the thieves are waiting to retrieve them.

If your store does not have an incinerator on the premises, then you should take special precautions to have strong controls over your trash removal. This means having a supervisor or security person present when trash or bales are loaded onto an outgoing truck. Some stores make it a practice not to allow any truck or load of trash to be removed from the premises without someone carefully inspecting it for new merchandise.

The best answer, of course, is to burn all trash in your own store incinerator. But the incinerator room itself should be checked from time to time as a precaution against dishonesty. One technique used by some stores is to throw a piece of good merchandise in with the trash to see if the man in the incinerator room reports finding it. If he does not, then he should be interviewed and cautioned to be more careful in his work. In larger stores, where total trash inspection is often impractical, at least a spot check of the trash should be made at frequent intervals by a supervisor or security person.

Night Employee Security

A typical night porter theft operation occurred in a large St. Louis department store. Monk was indeed a clever man. The night porters at Ross's Store all agreed on that, even though he had served time for stealing. But tonight Greg wasn't so sure. For five years, Monk had been the leader of the cleaning crew and had organized the Thursday night store thefts. But their luck couldn't hold out forever. What troubled Greg was one member of the gang, Skinny-Roe, who was a heavy drinker. Tonight he looked drunk.

It was 2:15 A.M. when Greg and the other porters gathered in the alteration room to eat their sandwiches. In the center of the group, Monk took over. He explained what he had planned for the night's sweep-up. "Tonight, it is H-brand of suits and topcoats," Monk told the men. "We'll select 14 suits and 12 topcoats." He paused to eye the group thoughtfully, then he went on, "Now, for God's sake, watch out about the sizes! Remember, it's 42 longs and regulars that Rocco wants." Rocco Terrone was the "fence" where Monk sold the goods the men stole.

Skinny-Roe would be told a certain time to throw the stuff out the third floor window that overlooked the alley. Rocco himself would be in the alley at the exact minute they had agreed on for the throw. He would then gather up the bundles of garments, put them into his car, and drive off to his place. When the porters left work at 6:00 A.M., they would be "clean." Later on in the morning, Monk would go to Rocco and get the money to pay the men the next evening. Sometimes each man would get $20.00, sometimes $10.00, but each man got the same amount. For Greg it had the pleasurable thrill of "found" money.

Everyone had finished eating by 2:40 A.M., when Monk said, "Let's get with it." Silently, the men fanned out into the clothing department, checking labels and sizes, and putting their bundles of goods into the center of the floor. It was exactly 3:00 A.M. when Greg tied the last knot on the second heap of clothes and turned the bundles over to Skinny-Roe.

Monk looked over the bundles and pulled at the ropes to be sure they were firm. "Fine," he said. Then Monk turned to Skinny and announced, "Okay, Skinny, the time for the throw tonight is 12 minutes past 4:00. Have you got that?"

"Twelve minutes past 4:00 on the nose, Monk," said Skinny, his voice slurred somewhat with whiskey. "I won't miss," he added, as though to reassure himself.

Skinny dragged the bundles of suits and topcoats over to the freight elevator. He stored them in the stockroom next to the windows, so he could make his "throw" at the scheduled time. Work proceeded in routine fashion. Greg was just thinking it was a calm and uneventful night when suddenly, right before 5:00 A.M., the night call bell sounded three short rings. Greg had been throwing trash down the incinerator chute when he heard Monk's warning signal. Something had gone wrong. All of the men ran to the alteration room as fast as possible.

Greg started to perspire heavily. He bolted past the trash and headed for the meeting place. He was sure his worst fears were about to be realized. The other porters half ran, half tumbled into the room about the same time as Greg arrived. Monk was already standing there, glaring at the men in anger. Greg could see that Skinny was sort of huddled up in the corner, flushed with fear and shaking like a leaf.

"Get this," roared Monk, "and get it fast! We have trouble! Skinny missed the time for the throw. He threw the stuff too late." Monk paused to let the facts sink in, then went on, "Now, Skinny isn't positive, but he thinks that just after he threw the bundle, a police prowl car pulled into the alley."

Greg kept his eyes glued on Monk in horror. "Now, perhaps Rocco was still down there, and he may have been able to pull the stuff out of sight before the cops checked on it. But don't count on it." Monk paced to the other side of the room and glared down at Skinny. Then he wheeled around to face the men. "Chances are the cops will be in on us at any minute, so listen carefully. Let it stick in your mind like nothing ever stuck there before." Monk stopped for a moment so his next words would have impact. "Remember—no matter what questions the cops ask, no matter what things they say to you—you don't know nothin'!" Monk's voice was low and intense; he fairly growled the words as he repeated them, "You don't know nothin'!"

The men silently nodded. Greg was too frightened to speak. Far off on the lower floor Greg suddenly heard someone banging at one of the doors. "We'll let 'em in, in a moment," said Monk. "But be sure you got the story straight. Stick to it, and the worst thing that can happen is we get canned. Start to talk, and we're all dead pigeons. So, in plain words, keep your mouths shut!" No one answered him, but everyone understood.

When it was all over, Greg was astounded at how easy it had been. The cops had taken all the porters to the police station for questioning. For two hours, they questioned and cajoled, and questioned some more, but to no avail. None of the crew talked. Greg kept telling the two men interrogating him that he didn't know what they were talking about.

"I was emptying trash down the incinerator. I never heard nothin' about any stolen suits or anything like that." Finally, they let him go home.

Greg headed for the bar and grill where the men always hung out in their off hours. Monk was already there with the others when Greg arrived. At first, the men were grim and silent. They were plenty worried. But as time went by and nothing else happened, their spirits began to lift. Of course, Greg and the other men in the crew were severely reprimanded by the store manager when he fired them. But the store paid all the men their severance and vacation pay. Greg was glad to get a week's vacation after the ordeal.

Three days after the gang had been fired, Monk phoned Greg at his home and told him to meet him and the other men at the bar. When Greg got there, Monk was obviously in high spirits. The men asked him what was up, and he told them the good news. "It's like this," said Monk, "a department store across town happens to be in need of a crew for night cleaning. So when I found out about it, I hotfooted it over there and told them I had some men available—friends of mine. And would you believe it, they let me bring in my own crew! We won't be out of work even a week. Two weeks from tonight (I've arranged it with Rocco), we can have our sweep-up night again!"

It cannot be emphasized too strongly that where stores can, they should eliminate night workers of all kinds. Studies have shown that day cleaning is less expensive because it is better supervised and therefore more efficient. It also eliminates an important element of risk from the store operation. But if you must continue night cleaning, at least hire a reliable man at a good salary as supervisor for the crew. Be sure that night porters are locked into the building and cannot leave without breaking the perimeter alarm circuit. It is also good to have internal trip alarms to keep porters from moving into restricted areas.

Be sure any windows or doors opening onto back alleys are wired with your perimeter alarm system so night workers cannot throw merchandise out of the store windows. Have your supervisors or your security department regularly visit the store during night operations to be sure it is properly run and to keep workers aware of management's interest in them. The store manager and his assistant should also pay occasional visits to the store in the early morning hours. Make the visits unexpected, and make them reasonably frequent. Don't let the night workers feel that nobody is interested in what happens at the store during the nighttime hours.

The people working at night—night stockers, porters, and others—have special opportunities for theft. Because of the nature of night work, these people should be reminded to keep their conduct above reproach at all times. They should be requested to carry identification and should not enter any areas other than those in which they have been assigned to work, especially unlighted areas. Nor should they be permitted to lift cloth covers which are over goods on store counters.

Night people can cause major losses, especially when they work in collusion. Because of the potential dangers, your security program for night employees should emphasize store rules and the penalties for theft, and you should also test the night operation frequently with undercover observers.

Nighttime Garment Counts

Here is a simple method of checking high-loss departments to see if garments are being stolen at night. It can also be used to verify complaints by departments reporting items missing in the morning. Assign someone to work with the department head. Have him select several racks of goods and make a unit count at store closing time. This count is held until the next morning when the racks are rechecked shortly before store opening. If shortages start to appear in the counts, then you may want to make one or two unit counts of the same racks at different periods of time during the night. This will narrow down the time of the loss and help to pinpoint the thief.

Early and Late Shift Supervision

Every store should have a pass system for checking in employees who work early and late shifts. In one store, failure to have a door control resulted in two ex-employees getting into the store unnoticed at 7:30 in the morning. These two former stockboys stole over $2,000 worth of men's clothing during this one early morning visit. They put the loot into suitcases and shopping bags and took them out of the store shortly after the customer doors were opened for business.

No one should enter your store during nonselling hours without a door pass. Any employee leaving your store more than 30 minutes after closing time should also have a pass. If a person leaving the building after hours has no pass, then he should be required to show identification. A report should be made to the department manager concerning any employee staying late without permission.

The first hour after store closing in the evening and the last hour before store opening in the morning are the most critical times for security in terms of possible employee thefts of merchandise. During these early and late hours, attention should be given to employees loitering in both selling and nonselling areas. To do this, stagger the work hours of your supervisors. Have one group come in an hour early and the other stay a half hour after closing. The late group should make a complete patrol of fitting rooms and other vulnerable areas during the first hour after store closing. The early morning group should make the same kind of check the hour prior to the store opening. When first initiated, patrols of this type often detect dishonest employee activity.

Layaway Systems

A discount store manager recently expressed his dissatisfaction with his present layaway system. "Last week," he said, "the friend of a clerk who works in layaway came into the store and purchased a $150 television set on a layaway plan. He paid $10.00 down on the set. The next day he came into the store a second time, and the clerk put a 'security tape' on the television set so he could get it out of the store. Fortunately, the department manager saw the young man leave with the set and decided to check his layaway account. He found that no account had been opened for a television set and none had been closed out on that date. A glance at the waste basket told the story. The dishonest clerk had torn up the account card and thrown it away. But with the layaway sales check and security tape, she had set up an efficient way for her friend to buy a $150 television set for $10.00."

In many stores, this particular story hits an open nerve, because the layaway system is an unhappy situation. Cases like this one are often discovered too late to stop serious losses. The reasons for layaway being a soft spot for theft are easily explained. First, the store manager fails to recognize that layaways *are* vulnerable to theft attack. Management's reasoning is that there are much easier ways to steal than manipulating a layaway transaction, so it overlooks the fact that thieves often prefer to steal in a complicated fashion. They do not realize that a complicated system, such as layaway, offers enough red tape to help conceal their thefts. Juggling the records provides a possible alibi if caught, and the thieves feel they can confuse the situation by claiming error, negligence, or carelessness, so that the store cannot positively put the finger on them.

Second, there is the problem of leased departments. Lessees like to handle their own layaways, and management often finds it impractical or difficult to set up a centralized layaway procedure.

Third, since management is primarily a landlord in some cases and may not want to get into a centralized layaway operation, the control is often centered at the lessee's department, and there is no accounting cross-check to prevent fraud. The lack of proper controls plays into the hands of the thief. The clerk who makes out the layaway card can also destroy the records relating to it and pocket the money, or she can arrange to pass out stolen merchandise under the guise of a layaway purchase. Often a dishonest clerk will steal the last payment on a layaway made by a customer and then destroy the entire layaway record.

The solution to this problem usually has to be tailored to the situation in a given store. If it is possible to do so, setting up a centralized layaway operation for all departments is the most desirable answer. But if this cannot be accomplished, then at least a central storage room, properly protected, is needed to store all layaway merchandise.

The basic element of control is to have two or more copies of the original layaway ledger card on which the account is set up. These cards should be numerically controlled, and any missing numbers should be vigorously tracked down. The clerk who sets up the original ledger on a customer should send a copy of that account to a central control office or to the controller. At that point, the controller, or other central control person, should open a file on the new account. The clerk retains one card; the other is kept in a central location. These act as a cross-check on the layaway.

As payments are made on the account, they are validated on the register by inserting the account card. When final payment is made, the account is closed out and sent to the controller or to a central control office where it is matched with the open card in the files. The open card is pulled, and the two are examined to be sure the transaction was properly handled. They are then cancelled, either by perforation or by a rubber stamp, and filed in a dead-file. Any cards left open by the due date are investigated to see what has happened on the account, and any numbers not accounted for on the control cards are traced to discover the void or the reason the number is open and unused.

Tied into this cross-check control should be monthly or periodic audits of the layaway transactions. Such audits mean matching the open file numbers in the control office with the open file numbers at the counter and inventorying the actual merchandise being held in layaway with the open and partially paid layaway accounts.

If the merchandise for a layaway is lost, the clerk should *not* be allowed to help himself to a substitute item, but should be required to file a missing-merchandise report explaining the circumstances surrounding the loss. This form should then be used to authorize the removal of an item from stock to substitute for the missing goods. Whenever an inventory of the department is taken, the merchandise in layaway should be included in that inventory.

Another basic element of control involves the use of security tape. Many stores provide a narrow, colored tape at various locations so that layaway purchases, or bulk items paid for at the back of the premises, can be taken out of the store. These rolls of tape left carelessly about the store soon become a "pass" for employee theft. A dishonest employee, working in collusion with an accomplice, quickly learns that he can steal a piece of merchandise, attach a security tape, and use that to help his friend get the merchandise out of the store. Even large items, such as picnic tables, television sets, and tape recorders, are frequently stolen using the security tape.

A store would be wise to keep security tape only at the service desk. Every customer who makes a layaway purchase would then be required to take the goods and the proof of sale to this counter. There, the clerk can verify the sale and provide a security exit pass. This should be voided by black crayon as the customer leaves the store.

Improvement of security controls on purchases made in layaway departments may require a reexamination of the entrance and exit fixtures in the facility. The customer, of course, should not be able to exit by the same door through which he enters. The entrance door needs a turnstile to force the customer's exit through a controlled exit door. Where theft is high and customer traffic is heavy, the customer who is leaving the store should be forced to walk past either a guard or a cashier-checker. Do not provide the thief with any "escape" routes, or he will soon learn to use them.

Granting that layaway is a headache to many merchants, particularly where each lessee handles his own layaways, there are three possible solutions to the problem:

1) Set up a single centralized layaway department for the entire store. This will require cooperation from tenants. In this system, the customer may make payments to the lessee's department, but he will then present his receipt for payment to the central layaway desk. A better method would be to gain agreement to allow your company to set up and control all layaway purchases and to transfer such payments to the lessee's account. With a centralized layaway desk for the entire store, you can initiate an effective control. The layaway merchandise and payments should be balanced weekly. A complete audit of the layaway operation should be made monthly. This will prevent any large-scale theft losses from getting a foothold.

2) If the central desk system is not possible, then you should consider a monthly audit of layaway transactions in each leased department. Shoppers can also be used to test various suspect departments by making layaway purchases and checking to see if the test purchase is properly recorded and rung up on the cash register.

3) You might investigate having a local bank take over the handling of layaway deposits and payments. In some cities, banks have been contracted to handle store layaway transactions. They set up a loan account, make collections, and credit the store. This guarantees payment in full to the store and avoids the dangers of internal manipulation and theft. Check with your bank and see what type of service they might be prepared to offer along these lines.

If your store does not use a centralized layaway system, then you should move in and analyze the present methods of control to insure that merchandise cannot be stolen and layaway records destroyed. Layaway controls are important because failure to implement them properly

Deposits will be accepted on purchases amounting to $5.00 or more.
The deposit will be equal to 10 percent of the value of the merchandise with a minimum of $1.00.

The salesperson will:
1) Make out deposit tag
2) Attach top stub to merchandise
3) Fill in amount of payment on deposit card and on customer's receipt
4) Give customer her receipt
5) Certify in register amount of deposit on deposit card
6) File deposit card in department
7) Place merchandise in authorized hold area

When customer wishes to make another deposit, the salesperson will:
1) Enter payment on original deposit card and customer's receipt
2) Certify deposit card in register with amount paid

When customer wishes to pay balance and take merchandise, the salesperson will:
1) Write sales in send sales book, noting,
   a) Merchandise and amount
   b) Amount of deposit (total)
   c) Balance due
   (Carry only balance due out to amount column)
2) Certify balance due in register
3) Obtain blue pencil signature on sales check and notation "closed" and blue pencil signature on deposit card
4) Attach deposit card, merchandise tag, customer's deposit receipt, and original copy of sales check together and place in tally box.
5) If customer does not bring her deposit receipt with her when she picks up the merchandise, ask her to sign the deposit card verifying merchandise has been received.

When customer wishes refund of deposit, the salesperson will:
1) Return merchandise to stock
2) Attach deposit card, merchandise tag, and customer's deposit receipt together and take to service desk
3) Service desk will,
   a) Write cash refund for amount of deposit
   b) Attach deposit card and customer's deposit receipt to proper copy of credit

To follow up on held merchandise, the salesperson will:
1) Check held merchandise weekly
2) Telephone or send postcard to customer who has not paid an additional deposit within two weeks to ask her to make another deposit if she wishes to have the merchandise held
3) If the customer does not come in within seven days of notification,
   a) Return merchandise to stock
   b) Take tag from merchandise and deposit card to service desk
4) Service desk will,
   a) Write mail check refund for amount of deposit
   b) Attach deposit card and customer's deposit receipt to proper copy of credit

Figure 6. System for handling layaway deposits

will surely lead to employee theft. Figure 6 provides a useful outline for handling layaway deposits.

C.O.M. Sales Check Safeguards

Would you like to have a blank check signed by another store? Your customer's-own-merchandise sales check is just such a blank check to the dishonest employee. What is easier for the dishonest employee than to send out stolen merchandise to himself?

Unfortunately, this type of sales check does not lend itself to any realistic controls, but some measures may be suggested. Do not keep C.O.M. books at packing stations or in the warehouse. Use the C.O.M. sparingly. Send merchandise on this check only when there is no other way of handling the transaction. You should require at least two signatures to authorize every C.O.M. transaction. It is also wise to have the C.O.M. sales check printed in a bright color. The color will make the check stand out like a flag on any package sent this way, and the package will get special attention along its route of movement. Obviously, the C.O.M. book should be tightly controlled and should never be out of the hands authorized to sign it. The book should be kept locked away at night and should be audited frequently.

Checking C.O.M. slips is a time-consuming task, but it is necessary. Look through them to see if there is any duplication of names and addresses, then compare this with a list of your store personnel to see if any C.O.M's are being sent to the homes of employees. Be sure that each C.O.M. not only has a detailed description of the merchandise being sent out and its retail value, but that it also states the reason for sending it on a C.O.M. sales check. In reviewing the checks, be sure that the merchandise is properly recorded along with an adequate reason for sending it to the customer. A group of employees in one store stole more than $100,000 worth of merchandise on C.O.M.'s which called for "one gift box, value 5¢, left out of customer's purchase by mistake". Another store suffered substantial losses when its packers discovered the simple expedient of pasting C.O.M. address labels over the regular send labels on customer purchases. By so doing, they redirected the packages to their own homes and to the addresses of accomplices outside the store.

Another way to check on the legitimacy of customer's-own-merchandise sales checks is to make phone contact with the customer to be sure that she did receive such a package. Do this on a "service" basis, just as you would handle the tests on refunds. At present, there is really no safe control system for C.O.M. sales checks except to keep them under the supervision of a responsible executive at all times. Carelessness in this area can be costly indeed.

C.O.D. Merchandise Controls

In addition to instructing drivers in how to collect and record C.O.D. payments, the store should have a system of internal controls to protect the C.O.D. operation from theft. C.O.D.'s should be balanced out on a daily basis, and the driver should either turn in the merchandise or the money. If you allow C.O.D. accounts to remain open for as long as three or six months, you will be inviting drivers to pocket money collected from C.O.D. transactions.

Loaned Merchandise Procedures

A store manager confided recently: "We just caught two of our window display people, early in the morning, taking store merchandise out of the store to their car. When I questioned them, they admitted thefts of over $4,000, but from the looks of their homes, I think it is much more than that. From time to time, we considered having a loaned merchandise system, but we never seemed to get around to it. Now I realize that our negligence in failing to control this display merchandise is costly."

It is not unusual for stores to neglect the obvious, and the obvious is often loaned merchandise. Somehow the amount of goods loaned by departments seems too insignificant to merit the control work necessary to have a system or procedure. The problem is that we think of losses from loaned goods as being small because we consider only the material used in displays. Actually, however, display people are in the position where they can steal a wide variety of goods, in additon to the merchandise used in display work, without arousing suspicion.

Repeatedly, stores have uncovered large thefts by display staff. The reasons are obvious. First, they often have little or no supervision. If they do have a supervisor, he is often a display person who is only given the title of supervisor. Second, they generally work unattended in various parts of the store and often at a time of day when few department heads or other employees are on the premises. Since supervision is minimal, display personnel can wander about the store before or after hours, unattended and unwatched, digging into drawers, and removing handfuls of items without anyone heeding their activities.

Even when stores have put in so-called "loan systems," the enforcement of the loan procedure has left much to be desired. Often the design of the system is unrealistic. Some stores put a loan book in each department, but the display person frequently cannot locate it. As a result, he becomes impatient as time is consumed ferreting out the slips, and ends up taking the merchandise without signing for it.

The system also fails because all of the emphasis rests on recording the original loan, but nothing is done in terms of follow-up on the return of merchandise to stock. Without a control on the merchandise returns, the initial recording of the loan serves little purpose.

With the loan books made into a game of hide and seek, with the failure to follow up on return of the goods, and with the general neglect of the system that is typical in most stores, the end result is dusty loan books stuck in the backs of drawers—a meaningless control procedure.

A workable, practical control system has several benefits. First, it can keep track of the loaned merchandise, which is important to avoid both theft and carelessness. It eliminates the unpleasant discovery after six months that the topselling swimsuits are lying moldy and filthy in some corner of a display hideaway or that the 26 ties taken for a Father's Day window have mysteriously shrunk to 7 ties when brought back to the selling department.

Its second advantage is that it adds an invisible but valuable psychological control that can prevent display thefts in any store. The fact that display people can be held accountable, that there is a loan record that can be checked later, forestalls their personal appropriation of miscellaneous merchandise. A proper loan system also places accountability on the display person when goods are not returned in proper condition or in the correct quantity.

A workable loan system requires several steps.

1) To make the system flexible, the display person should carry a loan book with him. When he takes merchandise from a selling department, he should be required to fill out the loan book form and have the removal of the goods checked and authorized by someone in the selling department.

2) No loan should be allowed before or after regular store hours. Display people need to be disciplined to accumulate the merchandise they need during normal working hours. If an emergency requires after-hours loans, they should be made only if a security or management person is in attendance to approve the loan slip and the removal of merchandise from the selling area.

3) The loan slip should be designed to include the purpose of the loan and the promised return date, as well as the department and the person removing the goods. It should be made out in three copies. The display person keeps one copy with the merchandise as his record of the transaction. Another copy should be sent by house mail either to the security department, to shortage control, or to the store manager's office. The third copy should remain in the selling department as a record of the loan.

4) The control office manager should put his copy of the loan slip into a *promised date file*. Each day, this file should be checked; and if a closed-out copy of the loan has not been received, then an immediate investigation should be made to locate the merchandise. The closed-out copy should be the original copy signed by the person who checks the merchandise back into the selling department.

5) If the buyer finds that the merchandise is soiled or damaged, he should charge the markdown to the display department; and a record of the person's name who signed

out the merchandise, along with an explanation of the markdown, should be sent to management for disciplinary action.

Setting up and enforcing a loan control system may not seem important, but experiences of hundreds of stores prove that the display department is a vulnerable, high-risk operation; and without proper controls and proper enforcement, a store can unknowingly lose thousands of dollars in stolen and damaged goods in the simple process of loaning them.

Sales Book and Price Ticket Controls

Sales books can mean money to your store, and they should be treated with care and consideration. If a dishonest person has more than one sales book, he can defraud the store of cash by writing out sales in his "dummy" book, or he can use the uncontrolled sales checks to send stolen goods to his home. You can prevent this by not issuing a new book until the stub or the cardboard backing of the original book has been turned in.

The distribution of sales books should be recorded on an accounting control form. They should be signed for by the employee, and sales checks should be audited so that missing checks will be immediately apparent. When missing checks are noted, the situation should be promptly investigated.

Just as some stores are lax in controlling sales books, others are lax in their control of blank price tags. Price tickets should be treated with the same respect as money. Not only will dishonest employees misuse them to price merchandise far below retail for their friends, but a dishonest buyer may use them to cover up inventory shortages. If he is stealing either cash or merchandise on a large scale from his department, he may offset these high-loss figures by putting markdowns through twice on the same goods. Or he may mark up his merchandise, but not make any official markup record of the increased prices.

Furniture Sale Cross-Checks

In some stores, dishonest salesmen are able to steal furniture with ease. First, the salesman sells a chair to an accomplice. After the sales check is written and stamped "paid," he then changes the warehouse copy of the sales check by adding a list of additional furniture through the carbon. The chair and this "extra" furniture is subsequently delivered without question by the store to the accomplice.

To avoid this type of theft situation, always be sure that your furniture controls require the original sales check to be reconciled with the warehouse copies of the furniture sales checks. If they do not match, chances are that you have discovered a prime theft suspect.

Accounts Payable Procedures

When a store takes action to control employee thefts, but sees no change in its shortage figures, the reason is often that the major losses are occurring in the check disbursement or accounting areas of the store. It is important to protect disbursement checks. One good rule is to send payments to suppliers by mail. Do not pay a supplier's check directly to a salesman or deliveryman.

Other clues to weaknesses in check disbursement are the fact that there is only one signature on the disbursement checks and that the checks are not numbered. In addition, perhaps the disbursement checks, when voided, are not being retained. The manager may also be signing a blank check, which is a most dangerous practice.

Other safeguards for check disbursement include being sure that the name of the resource and the endorser on the check are the same as those that appear on the invoice or voucher used in making up the check. The store should, of course, use a check-writing machine, and the person handling the payment should be sure that the amount on the check reads exactly as it does on the invoice or voucher.

The checks paid and returned by the bank should be routed to a clerk other than the person who issues the checks. If a store discovers that a duplicate payment has been made to a supplier, this indicates a serious flaw in the control of check disbursements. A complete analysis is needed. Be sure you know what happened to the original check before you sign a duplicate. Investigate any old checks that are still outstanding, avoid signing any check made out for cash, and have the checks signed by a person who is careful about comparing the invoice with the check.

Payroll Fraud Protection

Payroll frauds are another source of loss to management. The paymaster of one large discount operation stole more than $200,000 from the payroll in a period of almost 15 years before his activities were detected. Two signatures were required on all paychecks: the paymaster's and the controller's. But the controller's name was imprinted from a plate in the custody of the paymaster. The thief's technique was simplicity itself; he merely marked "vacation" falsely on a time card, placed the two signatures on a vacation check for the employee, and cashed the check by forging the endorsement.

To be sure that fraud cannot exist without your knowledge in your payroll operation, do not allow the person preparing the payroll to handle cash, to maintain attendance records, or to sign checks. In addition, see that the endorsements of cancelled checks are carefully compared with the signatures in employment records. If you find that any of the above conditions exist in your payroll procedure, take immediate corrective action.

Petty Cash Records

Abusing the petty cash fund has become almost traditional in American business. Many employees who think of themselves as upright, honest citizens see nothing wrong in "padding" petty cash vouchers. And yet, these acts of "minor" theft can grow to staggering proportions without the knowledge of management. One store manager, recently apprehended in Illinois, admitted he had robbed the store's petty cash fund of more than $12,000 during his seven years of work. He made out fraudulent vouchers for supposed "gifts" to the Boy Scouts, Y.M.C.A., and similar charities. He also made out phony vouchers for small advertisements in high school program booklets, and so on. In addition, he overstated his car mileage when on company business, claimed false purchases of office and maintenance supplies, and put in phony vouchers for stamps for office use.

One of the reasons he was able to get away with stealing large amounts of money for so many years was the laxity of management in checking the petty cash fund. It was almost never audited, and there was no requirement that sales receipts should accompany any expenditure slips put into the fund.

Most important, however, was the fact that when money in the fund got low, cash from store sales was put directly into it before being properly audited and recorded by the store bookkeeper. This meant that there was no record of the excessive amount of money being drained from the business through petty cash disbursements.

Any store can reduce petty cash losses by taking a few simple precautions:

1) Require a "paid" receipt to be stapled to every cash payment voucher. This one rule can do a lot to cut down on petty cash losses. Periodic examination of vouchers will still be required to ascertain that receipts are being attached and that the receipt items and receipt amounts tally with the information on the cash voucher.

2) Schedule periodic audits of the petty cash fund. These audits should be carried out by a person other than the one responsible for authorizing vouchers. It is best to have an outside auditor do this, but the cashier or store manager can handle it, providing he is not involved in the use or authorization of the petty cash fund. The auditor should balance the expenditures with the vouchers. I.O.U.'s should not be accepted in the audit. Small loans to personnel who need $5.00 to $10.00 to hold them over until payday should be furnished by other means, such as through the manager or through the personnel office. These periodic audits should be conducted monthly in most stores. They should be "surprise" audits, so that people handling the petty cash fund cannot cover their shortages with phony vouchers, fraudulent I.O.U.'s or postdated bank checks.

3) Keep complete records on the amount of money put into the petty cash fund. This money should not be taken from

the day's sales receipts, but should be obtained by cashing a payment check from accounts payable. Management should keep careful and complete records on the amount of money paid into the fund each month as well as on the amount spent for the same period. These figures should be constantly reviewed by comparing them with the previous month and with records of the same period a year ago to see if there is any marked change. If a sudden increase in petty cash payments occurs, it is wise to investigate carefully in order to satisfy yourself that it is a legitimate and justified increase.

4) Restrict authorizing signatures for petty cash expenditures. The petty cash vouchers should show three signatures: the person *receiving* the money, the person *authorizing* the expenditure, and the cashier or person *making the payment* from the fund. In some stores, petty cash expenditures can only be approved by the store manager or his assistant. It is certainly wise to restrict approval signatures as much as possible. Also, see to it that the person authorizing the voucher is *not* the person receiving the payment.

5) In addition to using numbers on the petty cash voucher, write out the amount in full as you would on a bank check. A woman in charge of a petty cash account in a Western regional store office dipped into the till for as much as $100 at a time by a stroke of her pen. When an executive gave her a slip made out for $75.00 to be used for travel or entertainment funds, she turned it into $175. She then handed the executive his $75.00 and put the $100 into her own purse. Later, she even began to insert 2's instead of 1's, increasing her take to $200 on each slip. Finally, the alterations became more obvious and led to her ultimate exposure. In the meantime, however, the company had lost many thousands of dollars that could not be recovered. Be sure that vouchers are written in ink, not pencil, and that all vouchers are cancelled at the time they are paid to prevent their reuse.

6) Consider setting up a petty cash bank account for the store manager and having him draw checks against that account for each expenditure. Also, limit the fund to minor items. Don't buy stamps from this fund; use a store stamp machine. Don't buy advertising through this fund or make gifts to charities; use regular store purchase channels for such disbursements.

Stealing from petty cash can be made rather difficult if the above simple precautions are taken. Keep in mind that lax controls frequently make petty cash thefts too easy. So put tight controls on your petty cash funds.

Store Key Controls

The control of store keys seems an obvious matter, yet many stores do not keep keys under central supervision. All keys, whether to stock areas, display cases, receiving departments, and so on, should be turned in at a control key box each evening. Usually the key board can be set up at the employee exit door, so the store can account for all its keys daily.

It's important to issue as few keys as possible and to keep a record of the keys you issue. Exercise the same care with each key as you would if it were a $1,000 bill. Here are some suggestions:

1) Avoid the danger of key duplication. Caution managers not to leave store keys with parking lot attendants, in a topcoat hanging in the office, or lying about the office or stockroom.

2) Keep your records on key distribution up to date so that you know how many keys have been issued and to whom.

3) Whenever a key is lost or an employee leaves the firm without turning in his key, re-key your store.

4) Take special care to protect the master key used to remove cylinders from locks.

5) Have one key and lock for outside doors and a different key and lock for your office. Don't use a master-key approach, because this weakens your total security.

6) Have a code for each key so that it is not labeled with a visible tag. Tell only authorized personnel how the code system works. Never use a key chain with a tag carrying the store's address on it.

7) Take a periodic inventory of all keys. In taking inventory, be sure to have department supervisors or other employees show you each key, so you will know it has not been lost, mislaid, or loaned.

The objectives of adequate key controls are well known. Therefore, a well-designed key control system should be enforced in your company as part of your total security program.

Alteration Room Records

Do you check your alteration room? Alteration procedures should be watched closely, because this is an easy way for a dishonest employee to get merchandise out of the store. Careless operation of controls may allow an employee in the selling department to send a garment to the alteration room and then have it sent to an outside address on a customer's-own-merchandise sales check. Be sure your system protects the store against this type of theft. Cross-reference all sales checks with the alteration cards. Also, check to see if your employees are altering personal garments without any alteration card or other record.

If your store does cleaning and pressing on the premises, there should be a control to insure that all garments are sent back to the selling department after processing. When a department manager sends dresses with lipstick stains on them to the cleaning department for rehabilitation, does he know whether all of these garments come back to his selling area? A checkback procedure is important. Failure to have adequate controls here opens the way to theft by people in the cleaning and pressing workrooms.

'Hold' Area Investigations

Supervisors should make periodic investigation of ''hold'' areas in each selling department. There should be a supporting document on every piece of ''hold'' merchandise. Be sure that all ''hold'' goods are legitimate. The supervisor or the store manager should also occasionally go through an entire department, pulling out all packages and merchandise which seem misplaced or questionable or which have no supporting documents. Such checking not only uncovers leads on dishonest employees, but it results in better housekeeping and has a favorable psychological effect on employees.

Locker Room Theft Prevention

One store provided its employees with a small locker room because management felt that it would prevent some thefts if their employees kept their coats and purses in the lockers rather than in the sales and stockrooms areas. The procedure seemed to be working; but, after several months, employees complained of thefts of personal belongings from the locker room. The situation finally became so serious that the employees insisted on taking their coats and handbags to the departments where they worked.

This type of situation indicates a problem that needs to be solved for several reasons. First, the policy of not taking coats and handbags to these areas is a valuable way of preventing employees from being tempted to steal, and it should not have to be abandoned. Second, it means there are one or more thieves at large who should be located and removed from the store. Last, there is the possibility of undermining the staff's confidence in management's ability to run its own business. If management cannot control a ''simple'' problem like locker room thefts, then it obviously will not be able to control thefts of merchandise from stockrooms or thefts of cash from registers. So there is more at stake here than just the problem of employee losses in the locker room.

What can be done about the problem? An important step is to keep the entrance door to the locker room locked at all times except when employees are going on or off their shifts. If anyone needs entrance to the room during the day, he should be required to contact the locker room supervisor who has a key and who will escort him in and out of the area. This will prevent any thefts during working hours. There is little chance of theft during the shift change, because the workers act as a check on each other. Most locker room thefts occur when the room is deserted.

Although this approach will take some time and effort, the results are worth it. You will not only put a stop to the thefts, but you will also be showing a firm and decisive approach that employees respect. Once management demonstrates its ability to control thefts in the locker room, this definite action will undoubtedly prevent thefts in other parts of the store.

If you cannot close off the room, have a locker room supervisor or security person make frequent inspections of the area. Question any suspicious actions by any employee found in the room alone. Do not allow lounging in the locker room, and don't let it be used as a place for smoking or eating during relief periods.

If the situation is serious, put a two-way dressing mirror in the room on a wall that backs onto a stockroom. You will then have to build an observation closet on the stockroom side of the two-way mirror, but the trouble and expense may well be worth it. If you have any hard-hitting employee thieves, they will steal far more from your store than the cost of the mirror and closet.

Try not to let any employees know about the observation closet or the two-way mirror. This means building the closet on a weekend or at night. Care will also be needed by the person using the room as an observation post when entering or leaving it. Needless to say, if women change their clothes in the locker room, you will need a female observer.

In addition, check on the lighting in the locker room. The area should be brightly lit at all times, and you should put a clip on the light panel for the locker room lights so they cannot be switched off without a key.

Another precaution is to encourage your employees *not* to leave valuables in their lockers. You can supply small, transparent change purses for them to take their money onto the floor; and, until the theft problem is resolved, you can provide space in the manager's office for their handbags or any other valuables that they have brought with them to work. Last, warn your employees to keep their lockers *locked* at all times.

Dealing with lockers from another perspective, spot checks should be made of employee lockers periodically during nighttime hours to see if any stolen merchandise is being stored in them. If the store has public lockers, a regular inspection should be made by the locker attendant for "left" merchandise with a view to seeing if any of it appears to be stolen. Also, check your store's public lockers at closing time to determine which lockers are in use. Check again early in the morning before the store is open to see if any additional locker keys have been removed. If so, such a locker should be inspected. It has been found that dishonest night employees, on occasion, conceal stolen goods in public lockers, then remove them the next day during normal store hours.

Employee Sales Check Audits

With cycle billing, the control of employee charge account sales checks can be a problem. In one store, for example, there were more than 100 employees working in the audit department. All these people had access to the cycle-billing files. In order to overcome the danger of one of these people destroying his own sales check, this store made a periodic audit of employee purchases. Without the knowledge of the employees working in the cycle-billing area, the auditing department periodically took all of the store's sales checks at the close of a day's business, removed the charge purchases of employees who worked in the cycle-billing area, and photographed these sales checks on microfilm. After being recorded, the checks were put back into the regular flow of the sales check operation. At a later date, an audit was made against each employee's account to see if the photographed sales check had been properly posted.

Stores often learn too late that cycle billing is wide open to employee dishonesty. If you think about the availability of these sales checks, you can begin to recognize the problem. An employee who works in the cycle-billing area can go to the selling floor and make charge purchases of several items, then return to the cycle-billing department and wait for her sales checks to come through to her for filing.

By lingering for a moment at lunchtime or by coming in a few minutes early in the morning, this employee can take her sales checks out of the cycle-billing file and destroy them. As most stores do not balance their cycles within $50.00, these checks and the records of the purchases will be lost. Such thefts have been known to continue undetected for several years. Stores that have cycle billing and do not have a control on the sales checks of the employees working in that department are gambling heavily on human nature.

Employee Car Surveillance

The checking of parked cars, especially those parked around the store during nighttime hours when the store is closed, will often reveal large-scale employee thefts. To make such a check, you must first learn the identity of cars belonging to store personnel working at night. This can be done by observation or by a check of license plate numbers with state police. Particular attention should be given to cars belonging to night watchmen.

Control Suggestions for Smaller Stores

Here are some suggestions for small stores where only one office clerk is employed. This one person often combines the functions of bookkeeping with the collection and disbursement of funds. Good internal controls require work to be divided so that there is little opportunity for inside theft without collusion. In smaller stores, the most practical method calls for the store manager or owner to assume some of the duties of an internal auditor. This includes the checking of transactions, confirmation of items, and investigation of original documents.

The secret of good internal controls is a cross-check for every key procedure. One person should order the merchandise; a different person should approve payment of the invoice; one person should keep a record of the hours worked; another person should make out the payroll checks; and so on. Nevertheless, where a store owner has a limited staff, it is still possible to have a program of internal audit to compensate for the lack of internal controls. Such a program would require the following steps:

1) Deposit all cash receipts intact daily.

2) Make all disbursements by bank check and counter-sign them.

3) Personally reconcile the bank accounts each month.

4) On occasion, verify outgoing customer statements yourself, checking them against the accounts receivable ledger, and then mail them.

5) During the first few days of each month, receive and open all incoming mail yourself.

6) Compare all cash receipts with the store books and with the deposits shown on the bank statement.

7) Assign someone other than the bookkeeper to do all the receiving and shipping of merchandise.

8) Approve general entries, especially if they have to do with sales allowances or bad debts.

9) Bond the bookkeeper for a suitable amount.

10) Be sure your mail is opened by a trusted employee other than the cashier or cash receivables bookkeeper.

11) Have the person who opens the mail prepare a list of all mail received. Have it classified as to bank checks, money orders, stamps, and so forth. Compare this list regularly with the cash receipt book ledger.

12) Lock your cash registers so that the salesperson cannot

read the totals and later check his cash against the register total.

13) Prenumber all refunds and sales checks.

14) Keep a control on all sales books and credit books.

15) Record interest payments, rents, and other periodic non-sales income, so that failure to get a receipt would be noticed and investigated.

16) Have someone other than the cashier or accounts receivable bookkeeper directly receive bank debit advices.

17) Be sure that the duties of a cashier, accounts receivable bookkeeper, and general bookkeeper are performed by different people. They are intended to act as a cross-check against each other.

18) See to it that your cash is physically safeguarded.

19) Have your general bookkeeper maintain a detailed record of negotiable notes and securities, and have the actual documents held by another person so that comparisons can be made periodically.

20) Be careful about petty cash disbursements.

21) Also, be careful about check distribution. Are all of your bank checks on safety paper, serially prenumbered, and accounted for? Are all of your checks written in permanent ink or by a check-writing machine? Are you sure at the time of signing that your checks are completed except for the signature and are accompanied by supporting documents on which the check number and payment date appear in ink? Do you always prohibit the drawing of checks for cash, and do you also forbid the signing of any checks in advance?

22) Have totals of cash disbursement journals periodically verified and compared with general books by people other than the cashier, accounts receivable bookkeeper, or person keeping the general books.

23) Pay your payrolls by bank check.

24) Make an occasional audit of your pay rates and time-worked calculations.

25) Occasionally, distribute pay envelopes to employees yourself.

26) Employ special care in the handling of merchandise. See that all purchases are authorized by a responsible individual and that all purchase invoices are approved for payment only upon evidence of receipt of the merchandise. The receipt of merchandise should be in written form and numerically controlled. Your purchasing and receiving and storeroom functions should all be performed by different people who are held responsible for shortages and overages in their areas.

27) Have purchases and sales invoices checked for the following: quantity received or shipped, prices, terms, shipping charges, additions and extensions, and dates on purchase invoices to prevent reuse or alterations.

28) See that all accommodation purchases for employees are properly billed.

29) Base returns to manufacturers on written authorization only, and have them properly accounted for.

30) Clearly set selling prices. Any exceptions to the standard pricing formula should require special authorization.

31) Have all credits and return goods approved by a responsible person.

32) In addition to perpetual inventories, have periodic, unannounced counts made by employees other than the people operating in the department being checked.

33) Be sure to place responsibility for shortages or overages of inventory. See to it that all adjustments for inventory differences are approved by responsible people.

34) Have people other than those who keep the cash records reconcile monthly bank statements and cancelled checks with your general books.

35) Examine cancelled checks, signatures, and endorsements, and return the checks to the bank where necessary. Note deposit dates as shown on the bank statements compared to deposit dates as shown by your records of cash receipts.

36) Check discount allowances to see if they are contrary to terms of sale as approved by responsible officials.

37) Be sure that all credits to accounts other than those arising out of cash remittances and cash discounts are approved by an authority other than the cashier or accounts receivable bookkeeper.

38) See that the writing off of bad debts is authorized by a responsible executive.

39) Keep careful control of your records of bad debts which are less than three years old.

40) At least once each year, do a mailing of customer statements which is checked to see that it agrees with the accounts receivable records. This mailing should be under the control of some person other than the cashier or accounts receivable bookkeeper.

41) Be sure that all employees who handle securities or other valuables are bonded.

42) Require all employees to take vacations, and have their duties performed by other employees.

43) Be sure all accounting methods, routines, and systems are detailed in manuals.

44) Have physical safeguards for all important records.

45) Periodically change the combination of your safe.

Created Systems Tests

While all these control systems and procedures are highly recommended to curb theft, a manager can't watch every single transaction. There is, however, an excellent general way of testing store procedures. It's called *created systems testing*. This method has been used effectively by many stores from coast to coast. In Washington, D.C., for example, one store uses it as a central technique for controlling the entire operation. The store undertakes 200 separate tests of systems and procedures each month to insure that its controls are working as planned.

Created systems checks serve two purposes:

1) They determine whether your system is being operated as intended.

2) If the system is not being operated properly, they act as a dramatic lesson for educating the people responsible for the error.

Here's how the testing worked in one problem department in a New York chain store. The company was having trouble getting the receiving department to use more care during the early morning hours. The crew was leaving the dock doors open and unguarded from 7:00 A.M. on. As soon as the bread man and delivery drivers came to stock the store's restaurant operation, the dock doors were open and remained open for the rest of the day—even though the receiving room workers did not start work until after 8:30 A.M. There was no one to guard this vital entrance into the store. With this setup, the store was inviting major theft.

The company's divisional manager repeatedly warned against the practice, but he could gain no compliance. Finally, he decided to take action. He rented a truck and hired two men dressed as ordinary deliverymen. Early one morning they ''delivered'' a large carton of old telephone books to the store. Their instructions were to see how much merchandise they could ''steal'' from the receiving room.

The men arrived at 7:00 A.M. and found the receiving room wide open—as usual. Within a few minutes they ransacked the area of $4,000 worth of slacks. At 9:00, they phoned the store manager from a nearby diner. ''Are you missing anything from your receiving department?'' the truck driver asked the store manager.

''No, not that I know of,'' was the manager's cheerful response.

''Well, look again. We have $4,000 worth of your slacks on our pickup truck,'' replied the driver.

A gasp echoed on the phone. Did this created systems test have an impact on the store manager and his receiving staff? You bet it did! During the four years that followed, frequent spot checks were made of that store's receiving door early in the morning, and it was *always* closed and locked; or, if it was open, an employee was clearly visible on the dock guarding the store entrance.

Created systems tests can be used to gauge the effectiveness of every company procedure and rule. For example, do you want to know if your buyers are following the store rules on checking the purchase journals? Plant a ''created'' figure error in this journal, and see if they catch it. How about your store transfer controls? Short a shipment going between stores. Take off four blouses from a transfer and see if the receiving store reports the shipment as being short. Do you have personnel inspecting employee purchases and comparing bag contents with the sales checks as employees leave in the evening? Test their effectiveness by planting ''extra'' merchandise in a bag going out, and see if the inspector catches the ''overage.''

One store had a sealing system for purchases made by employees outside the store and brought back during lunch hour or relief. Such outside purchases were supposed to be checked at a service desk against the sales receipt and then sealed by the service desk attendant. To test the thoroughness of the service desk attendant, the manager added three pieces of jewelry to just such a package, placing them underneath the slacks that were called for by the sales receipt. The service desk checker made a superficial investigation of the bag and did not catch the "stolen" jewelry items concealed under the slacks. She approved and sealed the package. Later, when the service desk attendant was called to the manager's office, she was horrified to see the jewelry tumble out of the bag. From that day onward, she checked every employee purchase carefully.

Created systems checks are one of the best investigative tools you have available. They can be applied to any area of the store and can be used to check on the efficiency and accuracy of people at all levels of your organization. Since all areas of the store lend themselves to created systems tests, you can reassure yourself that your store is operating well by having a year-round program of this type. The number of ways in which this investigative tool can be applied is only limited by your imagination.

General Control Principles

Here are some of the general elements of internal control:

1) A plan of organization that clearly establishes lines of authority and responsibility and keeps the accounting functions as separate as possible from the operational functions.

2) A chart of accounts for the classification of data in a way that will help to produce consistent and meaningful reports.

3) Records and forms designed to be easily understood and to show clearly whether control procedures have been followed.

4) Sound practices, such as a division of duties, so that no one person will handle a transaction from beginning to end.

5) Personnel selection and training which will tend to eliminate applicants of poor character and to encourage observance of established procedures.

6) Supervision and enforcement of the control systems and procedures.

7) A program of created systems tests.

Finally, it must be realized that the control systems and procedures can make theft difficult for the employee but not impossible. Although good controls will discourage many potential thieves and often expose fraud and thefts in their early stages, you are still in danger of loss due to collusion or a steal-and-run type of theft.

Some people steal—they always have; they always will. There is no absolute deterrent that operates against human craving to get something for nothing. Therefore, in the final analysis, we must see to it that we have protected our assets to the best of our ability. We need more and better internal controls and more and better supervisory coverage to meet the ever-increasing problem of internal theft.

10

FRONT-END CONTROLS

Twenty-five years ago, when the supermarket concept was created, the checkout operation was little more than a cash register on a table. Today it is the heart of the entire operation. To protect this vital point from the cash and merchandise thefts to which it is susceptible, management must give the front end primary security emphasis. This will include four main elements: 1) accountability, 2) cashier rules, 3) audits, and 4) supervision.

Establishing Accountability

Front-end controls must begin with the principle of accountability. To your staff, accountability means being responsible, answerable, and liable. To management, it means being able to identify the source of a violation when checking back on any transaction. Therefore, control systems must establish lines between bookkeeping, the head cashier, the cash register, and the specific cashier at the register. Accountability is effective only when it is a complete and unbroken line from the customer to the store's bank deposit.

At the checkstand, accountability begins with providing each checker, including the relief checker, with her own separate cash drawer or cash tray. A store that allows more than one cashier to work out of the same cash drawer has no way of proving who took the money when shortages occur. Today, most of the registers used in supermarkets provide for the identification of the checker on the detail tape through a special code. The checker simply inserts a key into the register, turns it to a position that identifies her, and her code is then printed on the detail tape. If the register is not so equipped, then the store can establish accountability by having the cashier sign her name and the time on the detail tape when going onto or coming off a register.

Every checker should also count and sign for her cash bank when she receives it at the start of her shift. At the end of her workday, she should again count her cash and turn in a tally sheet showing her cash total. She should neither have access to the total sales figure when that reading is taken by the manager, nor should she be given any clues as to how much money she should have taken in during her shift.

Keep in mind that having control records is an important part of accountability, but these records must be used effectively to protect store assets. If they are not used, they are meaningless. Managers need to recognize that store records are vital tools for improving performance and that they are not merely historical documents.

Finally, accountability also requires the store manager or his assistant to firmly but tactfully notify each cashier of any violation of store policy or of any shortages or overages in her previous day's work. In addition, the manager should have a schedule of reviewing overages and shortages periodically with each cashier.

Instituting Cashier Rules

Another major consideration in developing front-end controls is to establish control rules that are simple, clear, specific, and understood by every checker before she is assigned to a cash register. A good procedure when hiring a cashier is to supply her with a written copy of the rules and to have her sign and date a second copy. This will prove that the rules have been reviewed with her, that she understands them, and that she agrees to operate by them.

While most checkers are honest, the few who are not can easily drain the store of its profits when rules are either nonexistent or not enforced. The stringency or leniency of the rules shoud obviously reflect the store's experience with front-end losses, and a happy balance should be struck concerning the effects on customer service, productivity, and employee morale, as against the amount of the loss that can be recovered through instituting each type of control.

The following is a list and discussion of suggested rules that can be tailored to fit your store's cash-handling equipment and its particular operating philosophy:

1) *Every sale should be rung up in proper sequence and in the correct amount.* This rule eliminates one of the most common alibis offered by the employee caught stealing by an honesty shopper. Without such a rule, the thief can claim that the shopper's test purchase did not appear in the correct amount or at the right location on the detail tape because she recorded two or three items as a single ring on the register.

2) *A cash register receipt should be issued with each and every purchase. Except for the purpose of making change, money should not be allowed to remain on the slab of the register.* If the cashier must give a register receipt to the customer on every sale, she cannot underring and pocket the difference without undue risk. She knows that the customer might later realize that her sales receipt is less than the amount she paid and then complain about this to the manager.

Requiring a sales receipt to be given to every customer also tends to minimize the danger of a dishonest cashier stealing on an even-money sale. Because she must ring up the sale to provide a receipt, this eliminates the pretense that she has left the money on the register slab to ring up later. Nor can she accept an exact amount from a customer for a single item while she is ringing up another order. Without this rule, the cashier could leave the money on the slab until she has completed the second order, and then pocket the cash when the customer leaves. The rule requires her to put the money into the register at the conclusion of each sale when she hands the customer the sales receipt.

3) *The price of each item should be called aloud as it is recorded on the register.* This rule reassures the customer that she is not being overcharged. It also prevents serious losses caused by careless ringing of sales. Most important, it makes underringing more difficult to achieve without observation.

4) *Each transaction must be completed and the cash drawer closed before waiting on another customer. Never work from an open cash drawer.* Normally, it is difficult for the supermarket cashier to steal except on even-money sales. However, if she is allowed to work from an open drawer, this introduces a new avenue of theft. Requiring the register drawer to be completely closed after each sales transaction prevents the cashier from selling merchandise and making change out of the register without recording the sale. If management allows cashiers to work from an open drawer, this is the same as offering an engraved invitation to the cashier to steal. In fact, it makes stealing so easy that sooner or later every potentially dishonest cashier will be helping herself to company funds.

5) *No pens or pencils should be kept at the checkstand.* Many stores have operating policies that require the use of a writing implement at the checkout counter to record departmental errors, overrings, etc. However, a pen or pencil can be put to clever use by the dishonest cashier. Any store suffering high cash shortages should evaluate the higher labor costs it would incur by having supervisory personnel fill out such forms for the checker, as against the losses that could be prevented.

If writing implements must be made available at the checkstand, then their use to add on an item to an original receipt should be forbidden. If the order has already been totaled and the customer asks for an additional item, the separate item should be handled to completion as a new purchase.

This rule helps to eliminate a common theft device in which dishonest checkers ring up a large order of merchandise but "forget" to ring up one of the most expensive items. As she bags the groceries, the cashier pretends to discover her so-called "error," explains her mistake to the customer, and receives the additional money. The clerk then adds the amount in pen to the cash register receipt, and the customer leaves assuming she has a correct receipt. The dishonest cashier later slips the money into her handbag.

6) *All voids and overrings over a specified amount should be immediately approved by the signature of the manager or someone assigned by him to handle this responsibility. Overrings should not be corrected by undercharging on other items in the customer's order.* Most security men agree that probably the easiest method of theft by cashiers is to write out phony overring error slips, put them into the register, and remove an equal amount of cash. In stores where controls on overring transactions are lax or nonexistent, this method of stealing is so easy that the dishonest person latches onto it at once.

Ideally, all overrings should be approved. However, the number of items that comprise an average supermarket order make it impractical to follow such a procedure without seriously slowing down productivity at the checkstand. Therefore, many companies have a policy that all overrings above 25 cents require approval. While this figure will vary from one company to another, any overring that requires approval should be verified by the manager at the time that it is committed. In addition to the manager's signature, the cashier should be required to write out the amount of the overring in longhand on the error slip so that it cannot later be altered.

Every cashier will sooner or later make an overring error and will be tempted to undercharge on another item of the customer's order to correct her mistake. This should not be allowed. It further distorts the figures on the customer's sales receipt and opens the door to the practice of deliberately ringing incorrect prices and manipulating the records of sales transactions. This defeats the efforts of honesty shoppers to prove thefts of cash when shopping tests are made.

If the register has a refund key, it should be used to correct the overring. If the register does not have a refund key, then the overring should be corrected after the entire order has been rung up and totaled. The overring should be deducted from the "before-tax" total and then the correct tax should be computed. In addition, all overrings, in any amount, should be entered on the overring sheet and charged to the proper department.

7) *The release lever located inside the register must never be used to open the cash drawer. If a customer requests change, ring a "no sale" or a "no change" key to open the drawer.* The right-hand door or back panel which houses the release "trigger" for opening the register drawer should be kept locked at all times, and only the store manager should have the key in case the register jams shut. In many stores, unfortunately, this door is either not kept locked, or the cashier on the register has the key. This allows the cashier to open the drawer without recording the opening on the detail tape. For this reason, the key should be "off-limits" to the cashier.

8) *Receipt and detail tapes must be replaced if they run out. Be sure that the date key is set correctly before starting*

the day's business. It is nearly impossible to catch a thief if there is no printed record of the sales transaction. Therefore, one gimmick used by the checker-thief is to let the detail tape run out. In this way, there is a period of time in which the store has no printed record of the sales transactions to uncover theft manipulations. This is also true of failing to set the date key properly.

Customer receipt rolls and detail tapes should be checked at the beginning of the day and replaced if the supply is low. The detail tape should have enough paper to last the entire day. Any checker who frequently lets the detail tape run out or who forgets to set her date key should be shopped by honesty shoppers and should be carefully observed by front-end supervisors. She should also be interviewed by the store manager and cautioned about her carelessness.

9) *If you are assigned to a "change computation" register, always use the "amount tendered" key. This important register key should not be bypassed.* Obviously, if the change computation key is used at all times, it is extremely difficult for the cashier to manipulate the register sales figures to her advantage. It is particularly useful in preventing her from short-changing the customer since the customer can "audit the sale" by watching the register window to see the amount of money she has paid and the exact amount of change she should receive. It also prevents the cashier from claiming to have made a "mathematical" mistake if she deliberately counts out an incorrect amount of change to the customer.

10) *Cash registers must be kept locked when not in use.* If a cashier leaves her register unattended and unlocked while she goes to check a price or to take her relief period, this invites till-tapping by an outside thief. It also invites a dishonest cashier in the next aisle to steal money from the unlocked register under the pretense that she is "getting change."

11) *Product refunds and checks should be approved by the manager or his designated assistant.* Cashiers have enough work to do without handling product refunds. These should be issued at the store office, not at the register. By doing so, you insure that the customer is treated with courtesy, and you cut off another possible road to dishonesty.

A manager should not only authorize product refunds but should also approve checks. It's difficult enough to train one or two supervisory people to spot fraudulent checks without having to train each cashier to do so. In addition, if a dishonest checker is allowed to accept checks without supervisory approval, she may work out a deal with an accomplice outside the store to accept worthless checks from her partner and to split the proceeds from the purchase.

12) *Change may not be bought from another cashier. When change is needed, it should be obtained from the office or from the front-end supervisor.* Some stores allow checkers to buy small amounts of change from each other, say a roll of pennies. This is a practice that should be carefully watched as it creates theft opportunities for the dishonest employee. It allows for an excessive number of undetected "no sale" rings on the register and can lead to collusive thefts.

When the cashier needs change, it should be brought to her by a supervisor. She should not be allowed to take bills out of the register and leave her checkstand unattended while she goes to the office to get change. If she forgets to lock the register, the funds might be stolen by a till-tapper. Also, if allowed the freedom to walk around the store with cash register money, the checker will be given an opportunity to go to the ladies' room on her way to the office and pocket any money she has stolen during the day on sales.

Remember that the register thief is always faced with one critical problem—how to get the money she wants to steal *out* of the cash register. When you allow cashiers to buy change from each other or to take bills out of the register and walk across the store to get change, you set up situations that help the thief, because they conceal her activities by making them appear routine.

13) *Trading stamps, like cash, should be inventoried at the time the register is opened and closed for the day. This inventory should be reported on a cash register tally sheet. All rejected trading stamps remain the property of the store.* If a store is heavily involved in trading stamps and its stamp shrinkage figures are excessive, tight controls are recommended. Obviously, it is unrealistic to spend $50.00 to control a $5.00 loss; but, in any stamp store, trading stamps should be treated with the same respect as money. The cashier should be held accountable for her stamps and should be required to inventory them, just as she inventories her cash both at the start and conclusion of the day.

14) *Purses and personal packages should be kept in the office or in a place designated by the manager. They should not be kept at the checkstand.* Stores that allow checkers to keep their handbags and personal packages at the checkstand are asking for trouble. Handbags are particularly dangerous. Dishonest cashiers frequently use their handbags as a storage place for stolen cash, and they have even been known, on occasion, to use their handbags as a private change drawer, making change for customers directly out of their own leather cash tray.

You may well ask, "Why don't customers report such a situation to the store manager?" Perhaps they would have a few years ago, but today most customers are unlikely to do so. They often resent the higher prices they are paying for items because of inflation and tend to blame the store and its management for these increases. Thus, their sympathies are often with the checker rather than with management. But the main reason customers don't report such shameless stealing is simply because they do not want to get involved.

15) *All purchases by employees must be rung up and checked out by an employee designated by the manager. Checkers should not check out any member of their own family.* One of the most common methods of cashier dishonesty in supermarkets is the practice of giving special "discount" prices to friends and family, and particularly to other employees. The only sure way to stop such dishonesty is to have a firm rule that all employee purchases *must* be handled by an authorized employee designated by the store manager. In some companies, the authorized employee is rotated on a daily and random basis so that no employee knows beforehand who will have that responsibility on any particular evening.

Checking out a member of one's own family should also be controlled by turning relatives over to another checker. In a recent case, for example, a cashier was giving special prices to 27 employees and relatives each week. She was selling $20.00 and $30.00 worth of groceries to her "customer following" for as little as $2.00. By the time she was caught, her discount policy had robbed the store of more than $57,000 worth of merchandise.

These are 15 simple, but important cashier rules. If followed and enforced, these rules can eliminate or control most methods of front-end theft. But to see that they are being followed entails careful auditing by the manager.

Applying Audit Techniques

The word "auditing" is usually interpreted as a bookkeeping term meaning "a formal or official examination of the books of account." But auditing, as it pertains to controlling front-end operations, means "a methodical examination and review of all records of sales transactions and procedures occurring as part of the front-end operations.'' This means that you don't just assume a transaction is legitimate; you check it out. Situations are not always what they seem on the surface, and you may often catch a thief.

For example, the newly hired manager of a large Detroit supermarket stayed late one night to scan the register detail tapes of the day's sales. Unlike most supermarkets, this company used itemized tapes. Examining them was a routine the manager had performed hundreds of times at his previous job, but this particular night was far from routine. One of the detail tapes practically spelled out ''theft'' to his experienced eyes. Every 15 transactions, ''no sale'' rings appeared. Odd prices cropped up consistently on other tapes he examined. Re-rings of errors represented by error slips could not be found on several of the tapes.

The manager spent most of the next day going over past detail tapes. They confirmed his suspicions. Within a week, four dishonest cashiers had been caught. The store had formerly been a ''problem store'' with inventory shortages of 2.7 percent, but losses on the next inventory dropped to 0.8 percent.

Many managers do not know how to ''read'' tapes. They don't know what to look for in terms of ''clues'' to dishonesty. Yet the itemized detail tape is one of the most important theft-control tools available.

Reviewing Detail Tapes

Register detail tapes should be carefully inspected every day. Here are some points to look for:

1) *Continuity of transaction numbers.* A break in the continuity of transaction numbers can mean a dishonest employee is at work. The thief closes her register out early in the evening after the manager has gone home, then immediately reopens it with a fresh tape and a fresh bank. She rings up all sales from that time until closing, but she pockets the money and destroys the detail tape. This type of theft can occur where supermarket managers do not make a practice of checking each day's tapes to be sure there is a continuity in transaction numbers between

the previous day's tape and the new one. It also occurs when they fail to check the locked-in group total (the Z reading) to be sure that the closing and opening figures agree.

2) *An excessive number of "no sale" transactions.* If store policy prohibits cashiers from filling customer's requests for change, detail tapes should show a "no sale" ring only at the time the person goes on the register, when she leaves for her relief and lunch period, at the time she comes back and her tray is replaced in the register, and at the end of the day when she closes out the register. With the exception of these "no sales," which are related to putting in the cash drawer and removing it as part of the normal business procedure, any other "no sales" are questionable. When the manager, in reviewing a detail tape, finds a "no sale" ring every 10 transactions or so, this is a definite clue to possible thefts.

3) *Odd prices.* Sometimes a thief gives herself away because she rings up prices which are not common to the store merchandise. If your store has standard prices, be sure the detail tape shows only prices that correspond with your store's usual pricing pattern. If, for example, your store has no merchandise priced at 64 cents or at 91 cents, and these prices appear on an itemized detail tape, this can indicate sloppy procedures and careless ringing by the cashier. It can also suggest that the cashier is dishonest and is under-ringing on some of her sales.

4) *The number of voids or overrings.* Many thieves use the void or the overring slip as a method of concealing cash thefts. Once the slip is in the register, they can remove an equal amount of money, and yet their cash and sales will balance at the end of the day. Therefore, all voids and overrings over 25 cents should be authorized by the store manager or his designated assistant when they occur. In reviewing the itemized tape, be alert to any unauthorized overrings or voids. In addition, look for an exces-

sive number of overring errors even though they are authorized. Sometimes the supervisor is too near to the forest to see the trees and approves fraudulent overring errors without realizing that the number being presented for his approval is excessive in terms of the number of sales handled.

5) *Patterns of overages and shortages.* A series of small overages can in some cases be more dangerous than an occasional shortage. Shortages are often caused by errors, and they may indicate that the person is not properly trained or does not have the accuracy necessary to be a good cashier. But overages, on the other hand, are likely to indicate price manipulation and possibly dishonesty by the cashier. Particularly dangerous is a series of almost daily small-amount overages with an occasional large-amount overage. Such a pattern suggests that the cashier may have been underringing and was unable to remove the accumulated money on one particular day. Thus, the money remained in the register as a substantial overage.

When a cashier is underringing and stealing the accumulated amount of money from the underrings, she is often careful not to take the full amount of her unrecorded sales for fear that it will leave a shortage in her register which may draw management's attention to her operation. Therefore, she is apt to leave a small amount of extra money in the register, feeling that an overage is much safer. This is why overages must be examined as carefully as shortages.

6) *Blank spots on the detail tape.* Places where there should be a sales ring, but where no figures appear, may be caused by a skipping of the mechanism in the cash register, or it may indicate that the register has been opened without allowing the record of that opening to be printed onto the detail tape.

For example, during a slow period in the evening when the sole cashier went on her relief period, the assistant night manager of one supermarket would go to the unguarded checkstand and purchase a pack of cigarettes. He would also carry in his pocket an already prepared refund for $10.00 or more. While he was at the checkstand, he would ring up the refund and pocket the money. But to avoid detection, he would take a business card and insert it over the detail tape. When he rang the refund into the register, there was no imprint on the tape; it appeared instead on his business card. The thief was finally discovered when management became concerned at finding, through a routine audit, that the refunds in this store were out of proportion to those in other stores of the chain. They put the night assistant under surveillance, and he was soon caught when he was observed manipulating the tape with his card.

As we can see, the store manager who knows how to "read" his cash register detail tapes often finds that the dishonest cashier has written the word "thief" on them just as plainly as though she had written out a confession and signed her name.

Examining Department Key Errors

Some store managers are not too concerned if a checker rings the wrong department key for an item of merchandise. They reason that this type of mistake has little or no relationship to thefts by cashiers. "It may cause a bookkeeping error," explains one manager, "but you don't lose anything by it. It doesn't affect your store shortages." Doesn't it?

Recently a shopping service on the West Coast was running routine shopping tests in a client's store. Part of its testing program involved shopping cashiers to see if they were ringing departmental keys correctly. Interestingly enough, shoppers seldom come across this type of error; so when they do, they investigate it carefully.

In this particular store, they did find one checker who was making an unusually large number of departmental errors. The shoppers kept testing her and soon found that the cashier was deliberately ringing grocery items on the produce key. Further investigation disclosed that her boyfriend was the produce manager.

This suspicious connection led to the discovery that the produce manager was hiding boxes of high-priced merchandise in the trash container outside the back receiving dock. Late at night, he would drive back to the store, recover the stolen goods, and put them into the trunk of his car. He would then sell them to a friend who owned a restaurant.

The checker was helping him to conceal his thefts by ringing grocery items on the produce key. The two thieves were shrewd enough to realize that high shortages, or a low sales figure for produce, would focus management's attention on the produce operation and its manager. By deliberately ringing groceries on the produce key, they made sure the gross profits for the produce department were average or above.

Obviously, it pays to audit the cash register operation occasionally and to spot check purchases in order to determine the percent-to-total of departmental sales. Variations may indicate that sales are being recorded on the wrong department key.

Checking Bottle Refunds

While most bottled beverages are sold in nonreturnable containers, the growing concern over ecology may reverse that trend and make bottle refunds a more significant factor again. Even at present, however, the matter cannot be dismissed simply because individual thefts amount to "nickels and dimes." Though each theft may be individually small, when multiplied by 7 to 15 cashiers over a period of a year, they can amount to a staggering loss.

It is, at times, surprising to see how unconcerned many managers are over the potential losses that can come from inadequate controls in this area. Some stores let the cashier write bottle refunds and cash them in her register, giving the customer credit or money for the returns. To believe that such a lax policy won't result in cashier thefts through the creation of phony bottle refunds is naive. Even the most honest cashier, put into such a lax operation, will be severely tempted to steal. What is worse, once the cashier dips into the till to take even a small amount of change, she soon gets to like the taste of this "extra" money and begins to devise bigger and better schemes for robbing the register.

To prevent this type of small-time stealing from getting started and growing into big-time losses, it is important that bottle refunds be written at a service desk or at the office, not at the cash register. Most important of all, periodic audits need to be made by cross-checking the returned bottle inventory with the bottle refunds.

Keeping Track of Discount Coupons

"Gang-clipping" is a new addition to the special language of stores with checkout counters. It is a term used to describe the dishonest employee who steals and conceals her thefts by using promotional discount coupons. For example, a supermarket runs a full-page newspaper ad with several discount coupons in it. One advertises 20 cents off on a certain brand of laundry detergent; another gives the customer 10 cents off on a certain brand of coffee; and another gives a 15 cent discount on a large jar of peanut butter, and so on. The dishonest employee buys 150 or more copies of the newspaper, removing the page in each issue that contains the discount coupons. She then stacks these pages in groups of 10 and uses a razor blade to cut out the 10 coupons at a single stroke. This is "gang-clipping."

But the clipping does not end with cutting out the coupons. Later, the dishonest cashier sticks the gang-clipped coupons into her cash tray and removes and pockets the equivalent amount of cash. This practice is so common, and is obviously such an easy method of stealing, that the store needs to be constantly on its guard or it will be victimized by the gang-clipper.

Auditing of coupons is an important part of your front-end controls. Careful training of cashiers and proper supervision should insure that the customer purchases the item for which the coupon is intended. Compare the amount of products sold with the number of coupons redeemed.

Some cash registers are equipped with refund keys. Make it an inviolate rule that no cash is to be paid out of such registers for coupon refunds. Instead see that the refund key is used. This will avoid the risk of an eager-beaver cashier philanthropically redeeming promotional coupons for cash.

On all other registers, the cashier should give the customer the cash equivalent to the value of the coupon, after the order has been totaled. She should not mentally subtract the value of the coupon from the order total. This invariably leads to error.

It is clear that special attention needs to be given to promotional offers and merchandise coupons. Housewives who come into the supermarket each day loaded with coupons testify to the effectiveness of this form of promotion. The use of these coupons is on the increase. This fact means the store has no choice but to see that cashiers handle them properly.

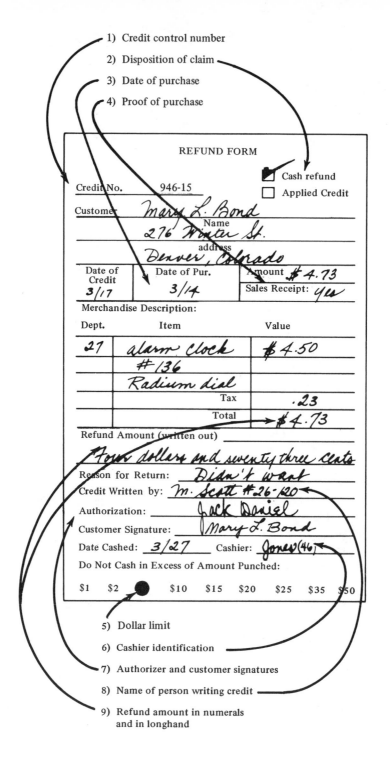

1) Credit control number
2) Disposition of claim
3) Date of purchase
4) Proof of purchase

REFUND FORM

☑ Cash refund
☐ Applied Credit

Credit No.   946-15

Customer   Mary L. Bond
                    Name
            276 Winter St.
                    address
            Denver, Colorado

| Date of Credit | Date of Pur. | Amount $4.73 |
| 3/17 | 3/14 | Sales Receipt: yes |

Merchandise Description:

Dept.	Item	Value
27	alarm clock	$4.50
	# 136	
	Radium dial	
	Tax	.23
	Total	$4.73

Refund Amount (written out)

Four dollars and seventy three cents

Reason for Return: Didn't want
Credit Written by: M. Scott #26-120
Authorization: Jack Daniel
Customer Signature: Mary L. Bond
Date Cashed: 3/27   Cashier: Jones (46)
Do Not Cash in Excess of Amount Punched:

$1 $2   ● $10 $15 $20 $25 $35 $50

5) Dollar limit
6) Cashier identification
7) Authorizer and customer signatures
8) Name of person writing credit
9) Refund amount in numerals and in longhand

Figure 7. Nine control factors in credit slip design

Regulating Refund Procedures

To stay competitive, you have to give customers refunds. Whatever the reason—damaged goods, spoiled perishables, faded soft goods—the customer has a right to demand her money back. In most cases, she is entitled to it. But the *kind* of refund you write out and the *procedure* you use in returning the money can make all the difference in the security of your credit operation.

A poor credit procedure is dangerous. It not only attracts shoplifters who prefer money to merchandise, but it makes it easy for the dishonest employee to steal from the store. In fact, a poorly controlled system attracts dishonesty. To insure a sound refund procedure, three elements are required: 1) a well-designed refund form (see Figure 7), 2) a sound refund procedure, and 3) a program of credit testing.*

A sound credit form can incorporate many factual and psychological barriers which will make it difficult for dishonest employees to embezzle from the store. All credits should be consecutively numbered, with a first number to indicate the credit book, the second to indicate the number of the individual credit.

Copies of the credit should be in triplicate. The original should be given to the customer for cashing; the duplicate should be held by the head cashier in the office; and the triplicate, a tissue copy, should remain in the credit book. The credit should have a place for the date the credit is written, the date of purchase, and an indication as to whether or not the customer presented a sales receipt. The amount of the credit should be written out in two places, once in numerals and once in long-hand. In some stores, the credit has a series of dollar amounts at the bottom of the credit slip, and the highest amount nearest to that of the credit is punched out. Thus, the credit cannot be cashed for any higher amount.

Naturally, the credit should be signed by the manager or, in his absence, the assistant manager. Although the design of the credit is important, the procedure can only be effective if the credit is used in a sound, enforced control system. This means protecting the credit book from theft. When not in use during selling hours, it should be out of sight. After hours, it should be locked in the store safe. Finally, as a matter of practical control, it is important to match the duplicate credit

* (In *Security Control: External Theft,* the author discusses credit testing techniques.)

copies with the original credits turned in by the cashiers each day to be sure that all parts are identical.

In auditing daily credits, look for erasures, write-overs, or any irregularities on the original copy that is handled by the cashier. If any questionable situation arises, investigate immediately. Credits can be an area of considerable theft vulnerability in the average store.

Controlling Trading Stamps

Employee thefts take a variety of forms. One newly married super-market cashier persuaded another cashier to help her furnish a new home by jointly stealing trading stamps each day or by confiscating the stamps rejected by customers. She was able to furnish much of her house before management finally lowered the boom. When questioned about their activities, neither cashier really looked on the scheme as stealing. "After all," said one, "trading stamps don't cost the store anything, and taking them isn't the same as if you took money." This remark, of course, shows a deplorable lack of communication between management and its staff concerning the value and cost of trading stamps to the company.

While a number of companies have discontinued trading stamps, others still promote them heavily. In such companies, these stamps often represent a substantial investment by the store, and they need to be given the same procedural and auditing controls as those provided for money. This means having the cashier inventory her stamps at the start of her day, just as she does for her daily cash bank. She should then inventory the trading stamps again at the end of the day, just as she does for her cash receipts. A record of the opening and closing inventory of her trading stamps should be entered on her daily tally slip that is turned in with her cash drawer when she finishes work.

In most stamp stores, trading stamps are issued from a mechanical or electrically operated dispenser. In stores where stamps are issued from stapled books with cardboard covers, it's a good practice to require the cashier to turn in her empty cardboard cover before she is given a new book of stamps. In addition, cashiers should be told that all stamps rejected by the customer remain the property of the store. To emphasize this point, furnish each cashier with a brightly colored envelope to turn in these rejected stamps with her cash when closing out her register.

Making Baskart Checks

The risk of cashiers giving special prices to friends and relatives can be greatly reduced if the manager does frequent shopping-cart checks. To do this, select a customer with a large order for the test. After she has passed through the checkstand, approach her and ask if she would mind your checking her basket of merchandise. Give the customer a gift coupon, such as a slip entitling her to a half-gallon of ice cream, as compensation for her trouble.

Check the items against the sales receipt the cashier gave the customer. If this baskart-check technique is done frequently on a random basis, it will not only uncover certain checkers who are prone to make frequent and costly errors, but it will also act as a psychological restraint on cashiers who might otherwise sell items at reduced prices to their friends. The cashier will become concerned about giving special prices because she doesn't know when you may check a customer's transaction that she has handled.

Conducting Surprise Register Audits

Another test that management should set up to reduce the danger of cashier thefts or manipulation of credits is the surprise register audit. This technique is especially useful when employee cash register thefts are suspected. On different days of the week, and at random times of the day, have your head cashier select a checker who is processing a customer. After she has finished with the customer, have the front-end supervisor move in and chain off the checkout lane temporarily. The supervisor should then remove the cash tray and register detail tape, replace the detail tape, and replace the tray with a new bank. This allows the checker to continue waiting on customers immediately after she has counted her new cash bank, while the head cashier takes the detail tape and cash drawer to the office for balancing.

If serious overages or shortages appear, the manager should undertake an investigation to determine whether the cashier is making errors or is stealing from the store. If the investigation reveals she is stealing, then the manager should have her tested by shoppers; and the extent of her thefts should be established before she is pulled from the floor for interrogation.

Providing Supervision

The store manager, assistant manager, head checker, or some other responsible individual designated by him should police the front end. The checkstand is such a vital element in store profits that a supervisor should be on hand most of the time, especially during peak business hours. The front-end supervisor should enforce the store rule that no merchandise is allowed to leave the store without going through the checkstand and unless accompanied by a cash register receipt. He should also be alert to any checker who repeatedly has customers waiting in line, while other checkstands are open and free. She may be popular because she's giving special prices to her friends. The supervisor should watch for checkers who make unrecorded sales, who work out of an open cash drawer, or who violate any of the "cashier rules" previously listed.

The front-end supervisor needs to be a person who is thoroughly trained and who is able to direct people. He must accept responsibility for the operation and control of the front end of the store. This includes seeing that register price sheets are checked daily to insure correct prices, being alert to keep the gates closed on unused checkout lanes, and making sure that cash registers are locked when not in use. His job also involves handling product refunds and approving overrings, voids, no sales, and all credits.

The front-end supervisor should see that the window on each cash register is kept free of papers and litter so that the customer can audit her own sales. It's his job to make sure that displays of "impulse" merchandise around the registers do not conceal the cashier's hand or the register drawers from distant observation. He should also be certain that no handbags or personal packages are kept at the checkstands by the cashiers.

The front-end supervisor will often meet friends and relatives of employees at company or other social functions. He should speak to these friends or relatives whenever they come into the store, this is an excellent way of letting the checker know he recognizes these people.

Whenever a supervisor sees a cashier violate store policy, he should call that employee into the office and let her know that such conduct won't be tolerated. If he feels it is necessary, he can write the person up; but the important thing is to call the violation to the employee's attention. The checkout supervisor is responsible for letting his employees know that he is aware of what is going on at the front end of the store and that he cares about both the store and its people. He doesn't ignore any violation of store rules and hope that it won't happen again.

If you are managing the front end, it's important that you remember to give each cashier a lot of personal attention. As the manager, keep in mind how much attention you paid the new checker during her training period. In contrast, after you assigned her a register, she may have soon felt out of touch with you. All of a sudden, she is on her own, standing each day in a narrow cubicle facing a giant money box. This bright, alert person, who showed so much promise during her training period, is now handling more money than she ever dreamed of. Then, one day, it happens. While she is checking out customers, with all the money running through her hands, the thought suddenly comes to her: "With so much money, who would miss a few dollars? After all, management doesn't really care about me or the money anyhow."

Keep one point always in mind: a cashier often begins to steal money from her register for only one reason—because it is so easy to do. It's up to you to convince each cashier that you are aware of what she is doing at the front end of the store and that you really *do* care!

11

CONTROL THROUGH CASE ANALYSIS

Harry Childs, the manager of a supermarket in Oakland, California, caught a checker giving special prices to another employee. The employee was buying $21.00 worth of groceries, and the checker sold them to her for only $5.00. Naturally, Harry fired both employees. But what makes the case interesting is that it was the seventh theft of this kind that Harry had discovered in the past nine months.

Roger Mapes, a store operator in Pasadena, California, was having similar problems. About three months earlier, he had discovered that four night cleaners were looting the store of merchandise, particularly cartons of cigarettes. Of course, Roger fired them. Then he hired a whole new crew. But just the other night Roger received an unpleasant shock. The Pasadena Police Department telephoned him at home at 3:00 A.M. to report that his entire new crew had just been apprehended in the act of theft. Now Roger has to fire these workers and start all over again.

As managers, Harry and Roger were certainly on top of the theft situation in their stores. They had gotten rid of a large number of dishonest employees in under a year, and they were really making inroads into their theft problem. Right? Wrong! Because neither manager had taken the time to find out *why* these thefts were occurring, and more importantly why they were being *repeated*, they hadn't solved anything at all.

Harry and Roger's mistake was in approaching the theft situation in their stores as if the individual incidents were the problem. Instead, they should have regarded them as a warning signal indicating the presence of certain unidentified and more basic problems in their operation, problems which were helping this dishonesty to flourish. The approach Harry and Roger had chosen made it impossible to take intelligent corrective action.

For example, if you go out to your garage and find that your car won't start, you have a problem. But is the problem the fact that your car won't start, or is it the fact that you are out of gas or that your battery has gone dead? Once you correct the condition by filling the tank or recharging the battery, the problem is solved. You must treat the *cause*, not the *effect*.

What is the answer, then, for Harry and Roger and for all store managers faced with incidents of theft. Obviously, it is to analyze each and every dishonest employee case to try to uncover the underlying causes of the situation and to develop more effective counter-measures to prevent similar thefts from occurring in the future. Analysis can reveal loopholes in control systems and can show unsatisfactory supervisory performance. It can reveal other weaknesses, such as the lack of physical barriers and inadequate locks. Analysis can discover what controls are ineffective or are missing entirely and what management practices or employee attitudes need changing. The greatest value from a dishonest employee apprehension, therefore, may not be the removal of the thief, but the lesson you learn regarding the proper management of your business.

Where to Begin

Discovering the causes of the problem through case analysis often involves an investigative process, and, in some cases, this means "trial and error.'' There are usually several possible causes for any given theft situation. At first glance, the numerous possibilities look like a giant pile of jackstraws, a tangled mess; but by taking the situation step by step in a systematic fashion, you will frequently discover that the number of possible causes can be reduced to less than a dozen *primary* possibilities. These, in turn, can be examined and tested, usually with a limited amount of time and effort.

The main approach is to separate the whole into its component parts. It is like taking a clock apart to see what makes it tick. You separate each spring and gear, laying them out on the table. Then, using a magnifying glass, you can examine each part for weaknesses. You look for missing units, cogs that are bent, or wheels that are warped. Are any of the cogs or wheels missing? Is the mainspring broken? Are the parts fouled with grease and dirt from misuse? Is the unit suffering from neglect? Similarly, by analyzing an actual theft situation, you can bring the problem down to a workable size.

The question often asked is how analysis may be undertaken without a theft apprehension. If you have a situation in which high shortages exist but no suspect has been identified, your first step is to review each element in the procedural control system. When this is completed, check on the adequacy of the department manager's enforcement of these procedures. Then study the physical layout of the department, the locations of the cash registers, and so on. You may also try some created systems tests to see if the procedures are being operated as intended. A systematic analysis may bring fruitful results, but investigation without a suspect will be difficult.

If, on the other hand, you have caught a dishonest employee stealing in a high-shortage department, or if you have discovered a dishonest employee in a problem store that is showing excessive shortages, you at least have a starting point for digging out the underlying causes of your losses. The dishonest employee case helps bring the situation down to a workable size.

For example, let us return to the situation confronting Harry Childs. When Harry studied the case of the checker who gave special prices to other employees, he found that his policies on controlling employee purchases were weak. Because he allowed his cashiers to check out each other's purchases and the purchases of their families, he provided them with the opportunity to give price favors to each other and to their friends.

Once Harry recognized that his lack of controls was the cause of the dishonesty, he installed new rules requiring all employee purchases, or those made by their family and friends, to be checked out by someone authorized by him. In addition, he established a policy that restricted employee purchases to the end of the workday. Harry further improved his controls by using honesty shoppers to test the accuracy of his checkers, and he occasionally did audits of his regular customer purchases.

When Roger Mapes reviewed his problem concerning night porter thefts, he came to the conclusion that night cleaning in his store was too much of a risk. The store could not be properly protected, and night cleaners could not be properly supervised and checked. So he changed his procedures. Now the porters start to work at 8:00 A.M., and all cleaning is done during the day when the store manager is on the premises to supervise their work.

Set Up a Systematic Program

Every store should have a program which requires the systematic review of a dishonest employee case within a reasonable length of time after the employee is apprehended. This review should be undertaken while the facts of the entire incident are still fresh in the minds of the people who investigated it, who did the interrogation, or who were in any way involved. Internal control weaknesses should be corrected as rapidly as possible. A dishonest employee case is like a crack in the dam of the store's security; the sooner it is repaired, the less the possibility that employee thefts will spill over in major proportions.

There are many ways to analyze a theft situation. A company might consider a systematic program of this type:

1) Initiate a program to gain full benefit from every dishonest employee apprehension by organizing a case analysis committee. Its role should be to analyze every case to locate the causes of the employee theft and to identify the operating weaknesses which allowed the dishonesty to occur. Plan to include two or three top management people as permanent members of this committee. These may be the store manager, controller, personnel director, and, if you have one, the security director.

2) Set up a specific day and time for each monthly review of your dishonest employee cases. Give the committee the known facts about the case in advance so they are prepared to discuss causes and possible counter-measures.

3) Start the monthly meeting by having the committee chairman read a summary of the case to refresh the minds of the members and to provide any additional details that are needed. Be sure that all committee members are clear on the facts related to the incident. Encourage members to ask questions to insure that they have a full understanding of the case. All members should be familiar with the following specifics:

   a) The method of theft.

   b) The length of time the thefts covered and the frequency of thefts.

   c) The types of merchandise stolen.

   d) The extent of admitted thefts.

   e) Whether or not there were accomplices.

   f) Any other available details. (What might have triggered the thefts? Was more than one person involved? And so on.)

4) Next, throw the case open for discussion. The members of the committee should hit hard at one key question: "How can such thefts be prevented in the future?" In other words, who was the dishonest employee? How carefully was he screened at the point of employment? Were his references checked? If so, were there any derogatory factors that should have made the store more cautious in hiring him? Was the thief reviewed recently by his supervisor concerning his job performance? What were his find-

ings? How did the supervisor of this employee feel about him as a worker and as a person? Did he ever have any doubts about his honesty? Had he reported his suspicions to anyone? What went wrong in the control systems and procedures? Or what went wrong in the supervision and enforcement of the controls? Why, exactly, did this case occur? What can management learn from it?

5) Finally, if the committee has successfully explored the problem in a logical and systematic fashion, it will arrive at some important decisions for improving store operations, supervision, security, or control systems and procedures. Once the committee decides what action should be taken, corrective steps should be assigned to those responsible for implementing the changes. In some cases, if the problem is complex and requires an approach from several angles, it may be necessary to set up a timetable for action. It is also advisable to have intermediate reports on the progress being made in correcting the underlying causes of the theft problem. Then follow up to see that your plan or corrective action is being carried out as intended.

Every dishonest employee case, if properly analyzed, reveals important information to management, facts that can help improve internal controls and supervision, management's relationships with its employees, and the problems of employee attitudes and morale. For the small amount of time and effort involved in the analysis of dishonest employee cases, the payoff is handsome indeed.

PART **SIX**

Encouraging Honesty
Among Employees

12

BUILDING EMPLOYEE MORALE

Emotional security and a sense of personal value and importance are essential human needs. If such needs are not fulfilled in the retail setting or, what is worse, are undermined, aggression and frustration—the characteristic emotions that trigger theft—will begin to grow. In a short time, management will find that instead of encouraging honesty among its employees, it is, in fact, provoking dishonesty.

Fortunately, only a few simple steps are needed to avoid such potentially damaging situations. Through such measures as supervision, motivation, communication, and cooperation, management can establish an atmosphere of positive attitudes that will benefit the store not only in terms of increased honesty, but in terms of increased productivity as well. To accomplish this, however, managers must apply the principles of employee discipline and impelling leadership.

Employee Discipline

If you were asked today to name the most critical problem faced by management in most stores, what would your answer be? High wages? Absenteeism? Inflation? These guesses are logical because each is a critical problem. But there is one hidden element more important than the rest. It is a factor that has the greatest influence on the effectiveness of a retail operation, and yet it is seldom in the spotlight. If your answer is "employee discipline," you are right.

As we learned earlier, an aggressive and frustrated employee will often steal when he encounters a situation in which his theft is unlikely to be detected. Employee discipline is directly related to this problem. It reduces employee frustration and helps to establish an environment of control. In a disciplined work situation, the tempted employee is less apt to take a chance on theft, because he believes he will probably be caught if he does so.

This fact is vaguely recognized by some retail executives. One controller recently wrote saying, "I must tell you that our shortage experiences are worsening steadily." His letter went on to discuss in great length the steady increase in losses suffered by his store over the past five years. Almost as an afterthought, he added: "My opinion is that we are suffering from an overall lack of management discipline of our people. I see this constantly in my own department. Reports that are required from managers are never turned in or they come in late. Many times, they are inaccurate—just loaded with errors. There seems to be a continual disregard for all procedures, rules, policies, and controls relating to the protection of the assets of our company." His letter ended: "I begin to think that we are never going to lick our shortage problems until we solve the problem of employee discipline. Wouldn't it be a better operating situation if we could find a way to police and enforce our basic operating controls and procedures? But the question is 'How can we do it?' "

Obviously, the controller has zeroed in on the key factor—the critical control switch—that turns internal thefts on or off. With notably few exceptions, American retailing has never mastered the art of getting the most from its people. If the problem is traced to its source, we find that retail leaders have either ignored or overlooked the overriding importance of satisfying the fundamental need of store employees for "emotional job security."

And what have been the results of this tragic failure? First, there is the loss of millions of dollars in productive labor which can never be recaptured. Second, because retailers have failed to do the job voluntarily, unions have often forced them to do it with a staggering loss in capital as well as in terms of prestige. Third, it has resulted in skyrocketing internal thefts because of weak internal controls and employee frustration.

The retailer first became aware of the problem in the late 1930's when large-scale union organization began. Management initially fought hard to retain control of its stores, but, in many cases, it was unsuccessful. What it did not understand was that unions were offering to fill the employees' need for *emotional job security,* which management had not.

Then someone came along with an answer which looked like a sure-fire approach. The result was a new school of management called "Let's be nice to our people." This approach took root and grew rapidly. Thus, we entered a new era of "human relations" management, with extended coffee breaks, soft music, soft lights, and soft, pleasant, permissive management and supervision. Store managers and other supervisory personnel sat back and waited hopefully for the "grateful employees" to begin to perform with a new sense of responsibility and improved efficiency. Alas, the expected miracle never materialized.

The so-called "friendly" management approach ended in overpermissiveness and resulted in more indifferent, even hostile, employee attitudes. Work methods became sloppier than before. Carelessness, negligence, and shoddy work performance was more common. And along with these undesirable work habits came an increasing number of burdensome theft losses. Each attempt by management to improve "human relations" by becoming more and more permissive was accompanied by more and more shortages. Finally, they reached staggering proportions.

The "treat-them-with-kindness" philosophy of management, like so many panaceas, just didn't work. Hindsight shows us that the approach was akin to trying to put out a fire by pouring gasoline on the flames. It did nothing but increase the blaze. Employees sought emotional security, and overpermissiveness only exaggerated their feelings of insecurity.

The lesson many stores still have not learned—even though the loyalty of workers to their unions should have been the handwriting on the wall—is that to fully understand the importance of satisfying the employee's basic need for emotional job security, four fundamental factors are brought into play.

First, the primary job of any manager is to motivate his workers properly. This is vital to the success of the store operation because there is not a single problem from sales to shortages that does not involve people.

Second, everyone, no matter what his level of work in the store—porter, stockboy, salesperson, cashier, warehouse man, supervisor, assistant manager, manager—has a basic, emotional need for job security which can be met only by direct, personal, face-to-face communication with his superior.

Third, when a boss fails to satisfy the basic emotional needs of his employees through direct, personal, face-to-face communication, he creates a feeling of job insecurity in his workers; and this results in a dangerous emotional vacuum.

Fourth, because every person fights an emotional vacuum, something or someone must rush in to fill this void. The result can be increased internal theft.

If we know these factors, then why can't the problem be easily solved? There are several reasons. In the first place, many managers avoid facing up to the need to deal directly with people on problems which are emotionally charged. They look upon these unpleasant situations as messy and slippery, and they prefer to get their hands on less gritty, factual things.

In addition, many bosses are poor communicators. They think they are communicating with their people, but they are not really doing so at all. Communication cannot take place when the employee is not allowed either to ask questions or to respond with his own ideas and suggestions.

Most important of all, many store and department managers simply don't know how to do an effective job in terms of satisfying the emotional job security needs of their employees.

Research has pinpointed four major areas in which employees require reassurance. These are as follows:

1) What does my boss expect of me in the way of performance and conduct on the job?

2) How do I stand? Am I carrying out my job to the boss's satisfaction?

3) Am I being treated fairly and impartially? Are all the employees being treated the same way I am?

4) Does my boss make his judgments of me on the basis of facts, rather than on the basis of his opinions and his assumptions?

One way to check out the accuracy of these findings is to ask yourself the same questions. Even though you are a boss, you are also an employee, right? Now ask yourself if you have the same four needs listed above. Of course you do, and you depend upon your superiors to satisfy them. But what about the people under you? Don't they, in turn, also have these same four needs? And don't they depend upon you to satisfy them?

If you want to test the premise further, ask your employees to make a list of the qualities that describe the best boss they ever worked for. When you look over their responses, you will find that their lists tie right into these same four basic employee needs.

The president of the Standard Oil Company of California, H. G. Vesper, put it this way: "In my experience, people reporting to managers tend to reflect our emotional needs as human beings. It is interesting to discover how readily we place the obligation for satisfying our personal human needs on those to whom we report, but at the same time how easily we can overlook or fail to recognize the identical obligation which is placed on us by those who report to us."

The fact is, the outstanding characteristic of the relationship between the subordinate and his superiors is his *dependence* upon them for satisfaction of his needs. Psychologically, this dependence is quite significant, in part because of its emotional similarity to the dependency relationship of an earlier relationship—namely, between the child and his parents. The similarity in relationship is seldom recognized by supervisors.

Granted the four basic emotional needs are valid, what then? What *is* the best way to satisfy these job security needs?

Experience has shown the answer to be a well-organized and consistent program of store discipline. When we use the term "employee discipline," we do not mean regimentation. We mean a method of "teaching employees to follow and adhere to reasonable and practical rules of conduct, with punishment to be used only as a last resort when all other corrective methods have failed." One vice-president in charge of personnel in a large retail establishment put it well: "In our company, discipline does not mean strict observance of rigid rules and regulations. What it does mean is employees working, cooperating, and behaving in a normal way as anyone would expect an employee to conduct himself. It means such things as reporting on time, doing a fair day's work, respecting the authority of the supervisor. It also means cooperating with others and, in general, conducting oneself in a reasonable and orderly manner. And that includes obeying reasonable orders and carrying out job assignments."

The maintenance of discipline in a store is management's responsibility. The company establishes rules, and it disciplines for violations. In a unionized store, the union is, of course, free to challenge the application of any rule in a given situation; but only after the fact. Management sets up the rules and determines the penalty for abuses.

To create a disciplined work environment in your store, consider some of these basic principles governing the application of store rules:

1) The employee is entitled to know the rules. To facilitate this, copies of company regulations should be posted throughout the store on employee bulletin boards. They should also be included in the employee handbook. The rules should be written in simple language which can be readily understood by every member of the staff. A look at the "cashier's rules" presented in a previous chapter provides a good example of the type of rules we are talking about. In addition to publishing the regulations, the store should also publish the minimum and maximum penalties for violating each rule.

2) Managers must accept full responsibility for assessing discipline. It is the manager's job to maintain discipline in his store or department. Since he is held accountable for this responsibility, it is also his job to assess the penalties

for infractions of the rules. He may, and should on most occasions, consult his superior for advice, but the final responsibility is still his. It is his choice whether to suspend an employee pending a complete investigation or to discharge him on the spot for a serious rule infraction.

3) The manager should have all the facts before deciding on the penalty and should assess the penalty on the basis of the penalty spread—the minimum and maximum posted penalty—within which penalties are set. To determine the extent of the penalty, four factors should be reviewed in each case, namely:

—the seriousness of the offense

—the past record of the worker

—the situation surrounding the particular incident

—store practice in the past in similar cases.

Discharging an employee is usually reserved for only two types of situations:1) where the offense is so serious as to make any other discipline inadvisable, as in the case of employee theft or an assault upon a supervisor, and 2) where repeated violations have occurred and all other correction methods have failed. Management, of course, should be willing at all times to have any disciplinary actions reviewed by an impartial umpire to determine if the action was justified in view of the facts.

Are good employees bothered by store rules? The answer is *no*! Naturally, employees will be upset when a store changes its working climate from that of being overpermissive to that of being properly disciplined. But experience shows that good workers will say that the establishment of rules and management discipline are measures that were "long overdue."

Many managers are surprised to learn that people really want them to run a tight ship. They needn't be surprised, however, because psychologists have proven in recent years that enforcing the disciplinary aspects of supervision gives workers a needed feeling of security. It also is an effective measure in curing shortages caused by dishonest employees.

Since there are so many benefits to be gained from employee discipline and since it can do so much and cost so little, every store should make extensive use of it. It is a most valuable commodity to have on hand at all times.

Impelling Leadership

In addition to employee discipline, a major factor in reducing frustration is the nature of leadership provided by managers. There are two basic types: impelling and compelling. The impelling type of leadership tends to reduce employee dishonesty because it reduces employee frustrations. The impelling manager leads his staff, making use of forces within the employee himself. He gets them to want to do an efficient and capable job, instead of directing or commanding them to do so.

Compelling leadership, on the other hand, relies on authority, power, and rules to direct employee behavior. These forces come from outside the employee and are imposed upon him by the compelling supervisor. This individual uses the power of his position or the symbol of his authority, he uses real or implied threats and direct orders and commands, and he gives little attention to his employees' personal desires and goals. This approach quite frequently leads to frustration.

As you review some of the results of these contrasting methods, you may be surprised to learn how much more productive impelling leadership can be. In spite of its superior results, however, many managers continue to rely on compelling methods as their management strategy.

We hear many executives today complain that workers lack initiative, are careless, indifferent, and lazy. They do not realize, however, that leadership methods are often the cause of such complaints. Workers' initiative, in many cases, has been destroyed by efficiency engineers, by time studies, by authoritarian managers, by written orders, and by assumptions that the workers will cheerfully fall in line with these types of procedures. Top management is often puzzled as to why its orders are not carried out.

Leadership sometimes fails because it arouses the employees' destructive emotions: feelings of fear, hatred, jealousy, despair, anger, rage, and hostility. Usually, these destructive emotions remain latent, but they can be stimulated, even unintentionally. Untrained but well-intentioned managers sometimes touch off such reactions.

The fastest checker, for example, is set up as a model for other checkers because the manager thinks that competition will act as an incentive to increase productivity. But this motivational attempt invariably backfires. The slower checkers become even slower, feeling a sense of defeat and a loss of self-esteem. Even the better checkers do not improve. Instead, they join with the slower checkers to make life miserable for the model checker. They look upon her as the boss's pet. Rather than showing teamwork, the group become a shambles of feuding, angry employees.

In contrast to these destructive feelings, we are also endowed with constructive emotions, such as laughter, love, compassion, sympathy, cheerfulness, affection, and hope. These constructive emotions can likewise be stimulated, and they lead to improved production, closer teamwork, and higher efficiency.

To contrast the effectiveness of the two leadership approaches, an experiment was conducted in a food distribution warehouse. Management was disturbed that production in picking merchandise to be shipped to its affiliated stores was lower than seemed reasonable. The equipment could not be changed, and the only solution was to attempt to motivate the warehouse stockmen to increase their productivity. The employees were on a piece-rate commission basis and normally should have had a personal interest in turning out all the work they could.

Experts were called in to see what steps might be taken. As there was a day shift and a night shift, it was decided to try a different approach with each. On the day shift, the boss held a meeting and told the group that a time study showed that they should be picking far more merchandise than they were. He pointed out that increased production would mean more money for them.

In the months that followed the meeting, the boss put more and more pressure on his men to make them work faster. But his pleading and nagging brought no improvement. In fact, during the next few months, this group's average output actually dropped. Some workers became physically ill as a result of the strain. Three men said they couldn't take the pressure and quit their jobs.

The night crew, on the other hand, was brought together in small groups to talk over what might be wrong with present production. The workers did the talking, not the boss. In this case, an expert discussion leader ran each meeting and acted as the stimulator. He kept the men talking and kept them to the point, but he didn't tell them how to turn out more work. He left that up to the employees to decide. The night crew first explored where improvements might be possible, and then how these could be carried out.

After a series of discussion meetings, these groups decided that an increase in production was possible, and they set new goals for themselves. The first week after the new goals were established, their production output jumped to a new high; and during the next few months, it averaged 18 percent higher than it had been before the impelling leadership method was used. No one had to tell the staff to "move faster" or to "waste less time." The decision to work harder and faster was their own, and therefore they had no motivation to slump on the job in order to prove that their boss's approach was wrong.

Impelling leadership is important to your store. Few companies operate at an efficiency rate as high as 85 percent. Most are probably closer to 50 percent, despite continual efforts to improve their effectiveness. The harder management drives to increase production, the lower production generally becomes. This occurs because most store bosses use compelling methods.

Keep in mind that whenever any change is contemplated in the company that directly affects the workers' jobs, the strategy of impelling leadership is essential before making such a change. Employees don't resist new policies if they are allowed to take a hand in developing them. Decisions on company finances, expansion, and similar top-level decisions can be made autocratically by management without harm. But if changes directly affect the everyday working lives of employees, the people doing the job should be given a chance to participate in helping to make these decisions.

Impelling leadership is a vital part of any program to reduce internal theft, not only because it reduces employee frustrations that trigger thefts, but for another good reason. When employees have a chance to share in shaping the decisions affecting their work, they come to feel as though they are partly managing the company, that this is their own firm; and people do not steal from themselves.

Impelling leadership cannot be handled by just anyone. The peppery manager who wants things done as of yesterday may lack the patience to lead employees by allowing them to take part in the decision-making process. Impelling leadership requires a manager who is willing to be a team worker with his associates. Some managers are too vain to handle this technique. They have to dominate every meeting; they have to make all the decisions; and they have to run the show. Sad to say, it would be more effective if they merely presented their problems to the employees involved, gave them any technical information they might need, and left them alone to solve the problem.

As Philip D. Armour summed up, "Most of my success has been due to keeping my mouth shut." The manager who knows when and how to keep his mouth shut has mastered the secret of being an impelling leader. He may know the answer, but he keeps quiet and waits for the others to discover it. Forcing subordinates to admit that your idea is the right one doesn't make for impelling leadership.

As it has been outlined here, impelling leadership skills may seem easy to acquire, but they are not easy to carry out in practice. It takes real managerial ability and supervisory skill. It also takes self-discipline and patience and a willingness to respect the ideas of others. The impelling leader has to accept the fact that there are many different ways to solve a problem, and several of the solutions may be equally effective.

He must keep in mind that merely talking things over is not impelling leadership. The talking over must lead to a decision by the employees, and it must be *their* decision. This means that he must arouse constructive emotions, have patience, and be willing to stay in the background at times. He must plant ideas and watch them grow, stimulate discussions on problems among his employees, and encourage employees to solve the problems affecting their own work.

A manager may take a while before he can learn the knack of leading workers to make their own decisions. But the impelling leader will gain recognition and promotions because impelling leaders invariably outproduce compelling leaders. And the impelling leader will have far fewer shortages from internal theft than the compelling leader, because compelling leadership generates the kind of hostility and frustration that is a primary cause of employee thefts.

13

NONDIRECTIONAL COUNSELING

One of the situations that often misleads management into believing it is having operating problems is employee complaints. Interestingly, however, an analysis of employee complaints often reveals that rather than involving problems on the job, they actually involve the personal fears and frustrations of the employee. For example, in a large East Coast store, five different employees went to their bosses on the same day to complain about their jobs. When these complaints were analyzed, it was discovered that only one of the five truly concerned working conditions. The others involved such situations as these:

1) A cashier-checker was severely upset because her fiancé had been postponing their wedding date. The fear that she would lose him was enough to bring on physical illness.

2) A stockman had become ill with guilt because he thought that he was the cause of his wife's state of mental depression, a state which had resulted in her threatening to kill herself and their two children.

3) A young man working in the receiving dock was torn by feelings of frustration because he was unable to decide which of two girls to marry. He believed himself to be in love with both.

4) A middle-aged man who worked in the meat department had become preoccupied with a nightmarish fear that he had inherited a heart disease similar to the one that had killed his father.

Such cases are by no means unusual; they are found in the best-managed companies and among the best-managed personnel. The important point to recognize is that although these employees are airing anxieties and complaints about their job, many are really using this as a substitute form for expressing their fears and frustrations concerning their personal lives. They are apt to keep these worries to themselves until they explode over ''working conditions'' or until they react in an antisocial manner by stealing. Likely as not, what causes this emotional explosion is not the ''rational'' reason they describe when they run to their manager with a long list of complaints about the job. It is a deeper, more emotional problem that has been building up to a state of increased tension and frustration, usually for weeks and months, and, in some cases, for years.

Naturally, the manager feels sympathy for troubled people and wants to help them. But even if he didn't, the stern realities of what we know today about the causes of internal theft make it imperative for him to do what he can for his troubled employees. The key question is, ''How does he go about doing it?''

Whether he realizes it or not, employee counseling is one of the manager's major responsibilities. Today, a number of firms have assigned trained professional counselors to their personnel department whose full-time job is to help employees with private and on-the-job problems. But most companies have no professional counselors available. Therefore, the manager or department head must assume this role.

Counseling with his employees whenever the occasion warrants, listening to their problems, and helping them to reach a solution that will reduce their frustrations is not merely humanitarian, it is good, hard, business sense. The person who is frustrated or frightened is not only likely to steal as a response to his feelings of depression or misplaced hostility, but he is also unable to concentrate properly on his job.

For these reasons, counseling is a skill that needs to be developed by every manager. You may say that the manager already counsels in some manner or form each day, particularly if he is people-oriented and is concerned about the well-being of his staff. But it is important for him to learn additional counseling skills so he can do an even better job of listening to and helping his employees.

Two Counseling Approaches

There are two basic types of counseling: 1) directional counseling and 2) nondirectional counseling. Most of us are familiar with directional counseling, which might also be termed "giving advice." Using this approach, the manager listens to an employee's problem, decides what he thinks the employee should do about it, and then recommends a course of action. The manager, therefore, plays the dominant role.

This approach is not usually desirable. Some personnel directors, and rightly so, object strenuously to having managers attempt any direct counseling of employees. Their objections are well-taken. A person should not play the role of psychologist and advise an emotionally upset employee. The advice may be given in a well-intentioned manner, but it may actually be the wrong advice and may further complicate the person's situation and increase his emotional disturbance.

In addition, even if the manager's advice is sound, people rarely follow direct advice unless it happens to agree with their own particular viewpoint. Therefore, direct counseling, except when a problem is posed that only the manager himself can solve, seldom achieves the success that the nondirectional type of counseling does.

Nondirectional counseling, on the other hand, does not carry the dangers or problems inherent in the method of giving advice. The manager does not directly advise, criticize, or try to help the person being counseled. His primary role is that of being a good listener; and to do this, he has to learn certain listening strategies. He must also learn techniques for encouraging the employee to discuss his problems and to bring them out into the open. He listens, asks questions, and stimulates conversation.

Although this type of counseling is somewhat time-consuming, it is extremely effective. Dramatic results are often achieved because it places responsibility on the person who has the problem. We all have within us a tremendous capacity to solve our own difficulties if we can identify the true source and meaning of these problems and gain the insight to face them squarely.

In a nondirectional approach, the manager encourages the employee to think through and to talk out his difficulties so he can gain a better understanding of them and discover their underlying causes, implications, and possible solutions. The manager becomes a listener. He does not offer the employee suggestions or advice, but he does encourage him to examine his problem from all angles and persuades him to plan his own course of action. It is an approach that works.

Responding to Emotional Distress

Every manager is confronted almost daily or most certainly once or twice a week with an emotionally disturbed employee. How he handles this particular situation can have a far-reaching effect on that employee's job performance, on his relationship to the company in the future, and often on the employee's honesty. Recently, one manager described the case of an employee who stomped into his office, slammed the door shut, and angrily declared: "I hear you gave that promotion to Jerry Doyle. Well, I should have gotten the job! I have been working here three years, and I've never once taken a day off sick! I come in every day on time, and I work hard! I earned the right to that job, and you had no right giving it to Jerry!"

As we can see, this emotionally overburdened employee had dumped his anger into the lap of his manager. Does this seem familiar? Perhaps it's just another case of an employee with ruffled feathers that need to be smoothed down. And it's true that you may be able to handle it from that point of view by reassuring him that he'll be considered for the next opening or by offering him some other generalization. But, if you are wise, you won't dismiss this incident quite that quickly. Perhaps this situation is not so simple or so obvious as it appears on the surface. Think about it! Is this just another brush fire to be snuffed out with a few well-chosen words? No, indeed!

Actually, this situation contains hidden dynamite. If the possible consequences of this employee's anger are not evaluated properly, if you don't recognize the element of frustration and provide needed counseling, the end result can be costly for the individual and for the store. The manager should acknowledge this fact and deal with it; otherwise, the frustrated employee may, in the next few weeks, start to steal cash from the register or begin to smuggle store merchandise out under his jacket when he leaves in the evening.

A frustrated worker usually wants to react aggressively against the person who he feels is responsible for his frustration. But openly aggressive action against an individual, particularly one in a supervisory position, can be risky, because it may bring reprisals in the form of punishment. So the employee seeks a substitute satisfaction. He "gets even" by stealing from the company. Psychologists say that aggression builds up inside until relief from inner pressures becomes imperative. This expression, when it occurs, acts as a "catharsis" or temporary release of the person's tensions.

Although the Yale scientists came to the conclusion in their 1939 study that frustration almost always results in some aggressive reaction, it is reassuring to know that the aggressive reaction need not be physical in nature. The person can gain relief and be purged of his aggressive response by allowing it to come out in *words*. He can verbalize his aggression. This is one important reason for using nondirectional counseling. It helps the employee cleanse himself of these feelings.

If there is no immediate catharsis, the employee may react by temporarily restraining his drive toward an aggressive reaction. One of the first lessons we learn is that if we are to be accepted socially, it is safer for us to suppress our overt aggressive reactions to frustration. If we strike back outwardly, we may be hit with painful reprisals.

But suppressing this emotion does not eliminate it. The employee may temporarily delay, disguise, displace, or otherwise sidestep the desire to react aggressively, but this does not lessen his need to retaliate. Instead, it may come out later in destructive behavior against the person he blames for causing his frustration or against the company because it is a safer target. These later aggressive reactions may be unconscious retaliations. Consciously, he may not in any way tie the act of stealing to the fact that it is an aggressive way of trying to hurt the company because of frustration which he was unable to handle.

By using nondirectional counseling with his emotionally disturbed workers, the manager can relieve them of their frustrations and thus prevent their aggressive acts against the company. He can use his counseling skills to prevent theft problems from developing. Anything that a manager does to make conditions in the store better or to reduce the amount of frustration among his workers represents a substantial gain for the individual and for the company. Studies made in some of the best-managed stores in the country have revealed that as many as 85 percent of their employees at various times would have welcomed a chance to speak their minds to management about some personal, managemement, or operational problem. However, only a scattered few did so, and an even smaller number reported that they actually felt free to speak up or to criticize at all.

Therefore, unless management works at the counseling process and knows how to apply listening and interview techniques so that employees are encouraged to express themselves freely, there will remain this underlying obstacle to efficient management and this underlying motivation for employee theft.

Developing Listening Skills

The first skill the manager must learn is the ability to listen, because listening, in this context, involves far more than just refraining from talking. A good listener must, by his behavior, *show that he is trying to understand the employee and that he accepts the person, as well as what the person says.*

One reason why some managers lack this ability is that they are not always able to concentrate because of the numerous responsibilities and constant distractions they face. As a result, they often miss a substantial amount of what the speaker is saying. Worse yet, they may assume information which is not true and fail to "read" the speaker's feelings accurately.

To listen well, therefore, you have to learn *to concentrate on what the person is saying.* This is not easy. In fact, listening is one of the hardest jobs that a person can do. One psychologist said that an hour

of listening is more tiring than playing a set of tennis. Certainly, concentrating on what a person is saying and making the mental effort
needed to grasp the information and the feelings behind the facts does
take physical effort. It should, therefore, merit the manager's full con-
centration.

This means, particularly, that he should not destroy his own listening ability by trying to do some other little job on his desk while he's
attempting to listen to the person speaking. He should not start signing
invoices and say, "Go right ahead now; I'm listening." Famous last
words! Seldom can we do two jobs at once and do either of them well.
Certainly this is true when listening, because this requires a person's
complete and undivided attention. When an employee is trying to talk
to a manager, it is a display of ignorance and bad manners for him
to work on his calendar or dash off a quick note to his associate or
indulge himself in any other desk work. In fact, it is even unwise for
him to take notes on what the speaker is saying, because note-taking
can be distracting and can block communication.

Another reason why some managers lack listening ability is that
their mind sometimes blocks out what they hear because they dislike
the employee who is speaking. This can be a very real problem. A
person often cannot hear what an employee is saying to him simply
because he doesn't like the person who is speaking. Perhaps it's a minor
thing he dislikes: the style of his clothes, his sideburns, his posture,
or some mannerism. Then, too, the speaker may be a person with whom
the manager has had some unpleasant experience in the past. Perhaps
there was a conflict of ideas. Any of these factors or others can cause
him to tune out the speaker's words. To be a good listener, the manager
must overcome his own personal prejudices.

These are some of the problems encountered in being a good listener. But what are the desirable traits that he must have? First, he
must learn to give the employee his undivided attention. He must not
only pay attention to what is being said, but he must also let the speaker
know that he is concentrating on his words by looking directly at him
in a friendly and interested fashion. He should sit reasonably upright
in his chair and may even lean slightly toward the speaker to show
that he has an interest in what he is saying.

Some managers say they listen best while they are relaxed. This
may be true, but it is a poor practice to stretch out in a relaxed pose
with your hands clasped behind your head and your feet on the desk,

or to curl up comfortably in your chair like a tired cocker spaniel. The appearance of being half asleep makes the employee feel that his words are falling on deaf ears. Even though the counselor may actually feel that he can listen better in this position, he conveys the wrong impression to the employee. Such listening habits usually appear rude, and certainly they are not productive to good communication.

A second trait of the good listener is to learn to hear what is behind the words and to understand what the employee's *feelings* are. What he says is not as important as how he *feels* about what he is saying. For example, it is not important that the employee says: "I should have gotten that job. I have been working here three years, and I've never once taken a day off sick. I come in everyday on time, and I work hard," etc. These comments may be true, but they aren't the important point. What the employee may be really saying is that he feels a loss of self-esteem or feels he is not liked or appreciated.

In order to dig out what an employee *feels* in a given situation, the manager must relate the employee's statements to his personal background. He must consider the words in a proper frame of reference, keeping in mind that the worker's background, his job, his salary level, his aspirations, his personal life, and his prejudices are all tied in with what he is saying.

The counselor also has to listen to the employee's nonverbal statements, which are often quite different from his spoken words. Sometimes his posture, his facial expression, and what he does with his body and his hands are important. Is the employee nervously drumming his fingers on the desk, even though his voice sounds calm? What about his facial expressions? How does he sit? Is he leaning forward on the edge of his chair?

Let's suppose the employee comes in, sits down across the desk from you, and says, "This is a minor problem of no real importance, but I did want to bring it to your attention." Now, as he is saying this, you notice he is sitting ramrod straight in the chair. He is smiling, but with a grin that shows clenched teeth. You glance at his hands and see that they are tightly shut and that his knuckles are white. Obviously, you would be unwise to believe that the problem he is going to discuss is really of "minor importance" to him. It must be of considerable importance. You can "read" this in the statements of his body language.

The manager wants to make every listening situation productive.

He can help to achieve this by making the interview a permissive situation, treating the employee just as he would a friend in his living room at home. The employee should feel that he can speak freely, without danger of reprisal, criticism, or fear that what he says in confidence will later be repeated or used against him. Only if the employee believes that you have an attitude of reassurance and interest can he feel personally secure when he is with you. This freedom to be himself and to say what is on his mind without any fear of unpleasant consequences is vital if he is going to be able to talk out his problem freely and work out a solution.

It goes without saying that the manager must keep everything that is said in a counseling interview *confidential*. The restriction is seldom a handicap, as this method rarely turns up derogatory information about other employees. The fact that the manager is an authority figure is a limiting factor in this respect. If an employee does say something to his supervisor that he later regrets or worries about (such as having criticized the interviewer or a co-worker), it is helpful for the manager to show by his manner that he has not been angered by the criticism and that the information will go no further. When the interview reveals a problem that can only be solved by making certain changes involving other people, this should be worked out in advance with the employee being counseled to avoid any feeling that his confidences have been betrayed.

Of all the listening skills the manager needs, then, the most important is learning to listen in a *neutral manner*. This is not an easy skill to master. Most of us feel obligated to respond to what others say with expressions of approval or disapproval. As Norman Maier explains in *Psychology and Industry,* this neutral attitude is important. "If a counselor or listener indicates doubt, surprise, disagreement, or criticism, this at once places him in the role of a judge or a critic. If he expresses agreement, pity, or even sympathy, this puts the listener in the role of a supporter. Neither role is desirable because as a judge he stimulates defensive behavior by the employee and as a supporter he stimulates dependent behavior by the supervisor."

Although the good listener keeps his expressions or judgment out of his responses, this doesn't mean he has to remain neutral in terms of wanting to understand what the employee feels and what he is experiencing inside himself. It also does not mean the counselor must be silent. He can and should respond so long as his comments are suitable, but usually they should be noncommittal phrases such as these:

"I see."
"I understand."
"That's interesting."
"Do you want to tell me more about it?"
"Mmmmmmmmmm."
"Uh huh."

Noncommittal replies are not difficult to utilize unless the employee asks the manager point blank for his opinion or for his advice. If this should happen, then the manager should avoid a direct response by turning the question back to the speaker. For example, he might say:

"Would you like to tell me how you feel about that?"
"What is your opinion about it?"
"I think it's best for you to tell me about it."
"I'd be interested to learn just what you think could be done."

In any emotionally charged situation, the manager would be wise to avoid answering any request for advice. It is better to try to turn the question back to the speaker and suggest that he may be able to provide an answer. If the employee is successful in finding an answer for himself, this will be a far more meaningful counseling session than if the manager gives a direct answer.

Disturbed people often find an outsider's advice confusing. No matter how you identify with another person, you never completely understand his feelings or how he looks at things. Even though he appears to be sincerely seeking your advice, he may instead resent it because he feels that it is not suitable. He may even turn it against you later, claiming that you really don't understand his problem. In some instances, the employee will expend some considerable effort in proving that the advice you provided so gratuitously is inadequate, and he actually does prefer to have an insoluble problem.

These precautions, of course, are limited only to those situations involving a disturbed employee or a request for advice relating to emotional problems of a personal nature. In any general learning situation or job appraisal, or where an unemotional problem-solving discussion occurs, the questions are not emotionally loaded. Therefore, these safeguards do not have to be observed by the manager.

The average store manager spends a lot of time listening to people. Studies reveal that, on the average, he spends three hours and 12 minutes of each day listening either to employees, customers, or salesmen. Since listening is one of the manager's primary functions, it makes a lot of sense for him to develop his listening skills to their fullest ability.

Applying Reflective Techniques

Many of the principles and skills essential to success in dealing with people involve techniques related to nondirectional counseling, sometimes also referred to as "reflected intervieweing." As mentioned previously, nondirectional counseling is an approach which stimulates the employee to discover his real problems for himself. It also helps the employee to decide on his own course of action regarding how to solve them. A person is more likely to act on a solution that he works out for himself, and this solution is also more likely to be compatible with his particular needs. The nondirectional approach is employee-centered, because the employee, not the counselor, decides what will be discussed and because the entire interview centers around the employee's feelings rather than on a diagnosis or a judgment by the manager.

Usually, when we associate with people, it is a give-and-take relationship, each person alternating between talking and listening. In nondirectional counseling, the manager must learn a new type of verbal reaction. Rather than responding by giving advice, the nondirectional counselor must respond to the employee's statements by restating or reflecting his feelings. For example, in the case of the angry employee who stomped into the manager's office, slammed the door shut, and declared: "I hear you gave that promotion to Jerry Doyle. Well, I should have gotten the job!" the manager should respond by saying something to the effect, "You feel that you were not treated fairly with regard to Jerry Doyle's promotion?"

This remark is in the form of a summary statement of the employee's feelings. It is a rhetorical question that requires no answer.

The question or the flat summary statement is spoken fairly slowly and quietly and pretty much in a monotone. It does not contain emphasis or emotion. In addition, while the response summarizes the employee's feelings, it is not phrased in the employee's own words. If the manager uses the employee's words, it may sound as though he is mimicking the employee. This can be detrimental to the counseling relationship.

The manager should also be careful not to make assumptions and should feed back only the feelings actually expressed by the employee. He should not look for hidden thoughts or search out his own interpretations of what the employee may be feeling. The purpose, again, is not to diagnose the speaker's emotional reactions, but rather to listen and to hear the feelings he actually states and then to reflect these back to him. A cardinal rule is to reflect only those feelings he *actually expresses*; in other words, *don't try to read anything between the lines*. At first, you may feel awkward in trying to reflect the other person's feelings, but listening carefully and selectively will help.

There are several phrases that may be used as a preface to feeding back the employee's feelings. It is best to make the first few feedbacks by prefacing them with words such as:

"You feel that . . ."
"You think that . . ."
"It seems to you that . . ."
"It sometimes appears to you that . . ."

But later as the interview continues, you can drop such prefacing remarks and just feed back the reflected feeling in this manner:

"Bill's attitude makes the work unpleasant?"
"You have to be out on top no matter what you do to others?"
"The group doesn't accept you?"

Let's suppose the employee makes a long speech in which he indicates several *different* feelings. Now the problem is: which one should you reflect back to him? For example, the employee might say: "I hate Walter Jones; he's always acting superior about everything. Sometimes I'm afraid of him, too. Yesterday, when I was by his locker, he grabbed me by the shirt and said I'd better stay away or he'd let me have it. He's sneaky. You can't trust him, and he's underhanded. Just last week, for instance, he went home two hours before quitting time, and he made Bill punch out his timecard.''

This employee has expressed several feelings: first, that he feels Walter Jones takes a superior attitude; next, that he, at times, feels afraid of Jones; and, finally, that he feels that Jones is not to be trusted. Which would you reflect? The answer is to reflect the *last feeling he expressed*. In this case, the last feeling expressed was that Walter Jones is sneaky. So the manager says, "You feel Jones is not to be trusted?"

Once this reflective interviewing method has helped to remove the tensions of frustration through verbal release, the employee then begins to gain some new insight into his problem. It is surprising to find that he will usually see himself and his problem in a more mature and rational perspective. From this point, it's not difficult for him to develop an effective solution.

To help him do so, the manager reflects only the speaker's feelings. He ignores factual material such as rationalizations, justifications, and details about who did what, and so on. They are all "accepted" by the manager, but allowed to fall into the background without comment.

To encourage the continuing free expression of feelings by the employee, the manager does not challenge any statements made by the speaker, does not ask any probing questions, does not argue with him, and does not attempt to explain anything. All inconsistencies and contradictions are completely ignored. Such contradictions usually mean that he is gaining fresh insight into his problem and that the situation is coming more clearly into perspective for him. The counselor should listen to the feelings and not merely to the words used.

Problem-solving behavior is characterized by a desire to explore the existing realities, to look at various approaches to the person's goals. General possible steps must be examined and evaluated before the final decision is reached. This means reflecting proposed solutions back to the employee. The restatement of his solution in different words as you reflect it back to him enriches it. You also encourage him to re-examine it, to seek new meanings, and perhaps to find a better solution to his problem.

For example, the head of a department complains to a supermarket manager: "I think we have been too lax with our employees. If the men persist in violating store regulations, we should fire them. We've got to get tough with stronger penalties."

The store manager replies by saying, "You feel the way to solve our operating problems is to discharge anyone who doesn't follow the rules?"

The department head responds to this by saying, "Yes, I do! I can't do this job alone, the other department heads have to do a better job. They're all soft and namby-pamby. They won't fire anyone. Once they let a guy get away with something, it's easy for them to ignore the others. The other department managers have got to stop making exceptions." (There is a long pause.) "Of course, maybe the trouble is that the penalties we've prescribed are too severe in some cases. They're too tough for a particular rule violation. It's easy to make a tough rule, but it's harder to lay a guy off."

Here, as we can see, the reflected interview has allowed the department head to re-examine his original proposal that all rule violators be fired. He has been forced to look again at his problem and has discovered that perhaps his first proposal isn't so sound after all. He has gained sufficient insight now to approach his problem from a different point of view, and he'll undoubtedly find a more workable solution. Probably, he'll suggest a review of the excessive penalties now prescribed for minor rule infractions. He sees that the firing rules are impractical.

Using Questions Effectively

Questions in the early part of the interview should be kept to a minimum because they tend to lead and direct the conversation. This is not desirable. They also channel the employee's thinking along the lines of the manager's thoughts, and this changes the situation into a directional interview. Questions often subtly indicate the answers that will please the manager, and they can block candid comments and emotional expression. They can also put the emotionally upset individual at a disadvantage, because he often doesn't know the answers.

Any questions the manager does use should be noncommittal and general in nature. They should be questions used to encourage further expression of feelings rather than to dig out any additional factual information. The manager can say, for example:

"Would you like to tell me about it?"
"Did that bother you a lot?"
"Was anyone there at the time?"

Questions such as these are acceptable because they tend to encourage further expression of the employee's feelings. Of course, questions that can be answered "yes" or "no" should be avoided. It's better to provide an open-ended question which requires a comment from the employee. The counselor should take care, however, to avoid unnecessary questions. Whenever you ask a question, it interrupts the employee's flow of thought. You won't get the entire story from the employee if you interrupt him.

Also use silence. Silence is often a powerful communication tool. You may think that the employee has stopped communicating, but actually he remains silent because he is thinking. If you have the self-discipline to remain quiet, you will often find that he will start to talk again shortly on his own initiative. He will pick up the threads of his story where he left off. He has only taken a few moments of silence to review the situation mentally and perhaps to clarify his own thoughts.

Problem-solving behavior is also helped by the effective use of questions. Once you get to the problem-solving stage, you can increase the range of the employee's thinking by asking good questions. A question can take a person out of his mental rut and encourage him to explore the various possible consequences of his proposed solutions. Some examples of questions useful at this stage are as follows:

"What do you think would happen if you did that?"
"How would that affect others?"
"Do you feel that you could eventually adjust to that?"

Such questions, related to the consequences of his proposal, help the employee to see any weaknesses in an unsatisfactory solution. They can help him find an even better answer that is sound and workable. The manager needs to appreciate the fact that every solution must be worked out within the framework of the person's own sense of values and that each person knows his own sense of values and his own aspirations best. Here, again, questions are valuable to assist the employee in directing his thoughts to meaningful areas.

Scheduling and Setting Up Sessions

When the purpose of the counseling interview is to assist a disturbed employee seeking emotional adjustment, it's likely that more than one interview may be required. Nevertheless, if the employee asks, "Do you want me to come for another discussion?" the manager should reply: "That is up to you. If you feel that you would like to come again, the time is yours." Even here, the person must assume responsibility for deciding whether he will return or not. It is interesting to note that employees who have been requested to visit a supervisor and who show resentment on their first visit usually do return voluntarily for further counseling. Nothing creates a sense of responsibility better than having responsibility.

All interviews should have a time limit which is stated at the start of the session, and the employee should be made to feel that the alloted time is all his if he wishes to use it. If you have a prearranged time for ending the interview, then it will not be necessary for the manager to find an excuse for breaking off a long and sometimes uncomfortable session. The employee will also never have to feel guilty about possibly overstaying and taking up too much of the manager's time. The spacing of these interviews, a week apart, will allow the employee to consolidate his gains and achieve adjustments and growth between visits.

The actual number of visits will vary with the seriousness of the problem, but improvements usually occur even after only one counseling session. Problems that don't extend into a person's past require fewer visits, because it is relatively easy for the employee to locate the factors disturbing him. A manager should not, however, assume that the true character of the problem has been located just because the problem points to a difficulty on the job. Incidents on the job trigger an emotional reaction, but they may not be the underlying cause of the trouble.

Counseling should, of course, be done in private. This is essential if the employee is to feel at ease in discussing his personal problems and innermost feelings. The employee should be put at his ease both physically and mentally before any serious discussions can begin.

Counseling across a desk, for example, presents a psychological barrier that stifles free discussion. It is better for the manager to sit on the same side of the desk as the employee to eliminate having the desk between them. Above all, there should be no interruptions or distractions. During the interview, shut off incoming telephone calls, and see that you are not interrupted.

Adopting Constructive Attitudes

The effectiveness of the interview depends on combining good attitudes with skillful techniques. Of the two, attitude is more important. The most successful users of nondirectional interviewing are those who like and respect people. Such individuals can do a better job of listening and reflecting feelings than the manager who secretly dislikes people and feels superior to his employees. Nondirectional counseling requires constructive, healthy attitudes that are consistent with and supportive of this method of behavior control and employee development. Fortunately, these beliefs are also consistent with leadership skills required of those who aim toward moving upward in their work as professional managers. Learning to use this counseling method also improves the manager's overall skills.

To be effective at employee counseling, you must subscribe to the following attitudes and values:

1) The manager must believe that each person is basically responsible for himself. He cannot share in that responsibility and must be willing to let each person keep that prerogative to himself.

2) He must believe that every person is capable of solving his own problems once he recognizes what they are. And he must believe that every person basically wants to do the right thing.

3) He must accept the fact that every solution is workable within the framework of the employee's own scale of values and beliefs and that only the person himself knows his own standards of value and his own aspirations.

4) He must develop a nonthreatening attitude, because only then can a person admit his true feelings. The employee must feel confident that he will not be judged. Often during the process of seeking out answers to his problems, the employee may need to express absurd, unconventional, contradictory, or even hateful feelings. He can do this only if the manager provides a nonthreatening interview situation which allows this type of self-expression.

5) The manager must accept the person who is emotionally disturbed as a worthy individual. He must also recognize that the employee's problems are important to him. He should keep in mind that a disturbed person often feels that he doesn't belong, that somehow he is alone and outside his peer group. He feels he is in some way abnormal or "different." Therefore, it's vital for the counselor to convey to this individual that he accepts him as a person of value. The thoughts and the feelings expressed by the employee must also be accepted by the manager if he is to stimulate the expression of even more deeply guarded and deeply hidden feelings needed to gain a true perspective of the problem.

6) The manager has to have a profound respect for the feelings of others if he is to help those around him to learn to live a satisfying and full life.

Employee counseling is probably one of the most important shields against internal theft. It can be truly effective in substantially reducing internal theft because it helps to eliminate the frustrations that trigger them and helps to improve employee morale and behavior.

INDEX

INDEX

355